The
Learning Process
Theory and Practice

Rosella Linskie
University of Nevada, Reno

D. Van Nostrand Company
New York   Cincinnati   Toronto   London   Melbourne

87267

To all my students everywhere who taught me most of what I know.

D. Van Nostrand Company Regional Offices:
New York   Cincinnati

D. Van Nostrand Company International Offices:
London   Toronto   Melbourne

Copyright © 1977 by Litton Educational Publishing, Inc.

Library of Congress Catalog Card Number: 76–62886
ISBN: 0–442–24801–6

Published by D. Van Nostrand Company
135 West 50th Street, New York, N.Y. 10020

10 9 8 7 6 5 4 3 2

Preface

It seems almost presumptuous to begin a book about the learning process when, in fact, so little is known about how the mind works. Fifty years ago as a young beginning teacher I could have tackled the job without a qualm. After all, I had a good liberal arts education. There were eighteen textbooks (all with teacher's manuals) for the nine subjects I taught in each of the two grades in my crowded little classroom. Besides, the state course of study outlined every detail except what one should eat for breakfast on the day of a specific lesson!

The psychology book I had studied at a small private liberal arts school had the chapter on prenatal care carefully snipped out before the books were issued to the students (it was a girls' college), and one passage on controlling children explained quite specifically, "The teacher should never allow children to speak to one another in the classroom because it is highly unlikely that children can learn anything from one another."

Armed with all that knowledge, I felt secure indeed and happily embarked on a career that has taken me around the world and back (literally), into outer space (vicariously), and, best of all, into inner space (personally).

Now, I approach this task with humility and with full awareness that what I have to offer, if not genius, is at least a vast store of experience. From it I have learned to question absolutes, to challenge formulas, and to enjoy divergent thinking. I even get a great deal of satisfaction and some real joy out of rocking the old boat of institutionalized education—never to be confused with learning.

The text will often refer to the term "learning process" with heavy emphasis on *process,* because I believe that learning is just that—a process. It is an on-going process, a life-long odyssey that continues until death—or who knows how long after that! Learning is not, in my view, a nice neatly packaged item that one can consider finished after twelve or sixteen or even twenty-four years of schooling then put carefully away on a shelf in the mind to be brought out as a display on proper occasions. It must continue to grow and expand and broaden and deepen to the fullest capacity of the learner. It's a beautiful universe; it's a *real* universe and its future belongs to those we teach. How they succeed or fail depends on how we prepare them.

The Learning Process is divided into four main parts. Part I, *The Learner,* and Part II, *The Teacher,* deal with the physical, emotional, social, and intellectual aspects of the learner and the teacher in the education process. Part III, *The Learning Process,* emphasizes the interactions of learners and teachers and some specific philosophies and methods employed, such as Gestalt, Piaget, and Montessori. Part IV, *The Never-Ending Odyssey,* expounds the main theme of the text, that learning is an on-going, life-long process.

The book is intended as a text in the course and as an in-service reference later. The special features, listed below, make it a valuable tool for anyone who works or will work with learners:

Case studies at the end of chapters are taken from my personal experiences. Questions are provided to encourage readers to react to the incidents. Space is provided to write other personal cases.

A self-rating scale for teachers is included in Chapter 8.

There is a model outline for developing an integrated unit of study, which is described in Chapter 10.

An extensive alphabetical list of readings related to all aspects of education, included at the end of the text, provides a broad reference source for prospective and current teachers.

The Learning Process is offered as one teacher's effort to share a lifetime of experience in the learning business. Take from it what you need; discard what you think is old-hat. In any case, use it to begin to develop your own patterns of thought, to guide and direct your own personal educational odyssey.

Acknowledgments

To my good friend Hyung W. Pak, who insisted that I begin; to my devoted colleagues Kathi and Warren d'Azevedo, Rosalie and Howard Rosenberg, Don Lynch, John Dodson, Carl McKinney, and Helen Ann Willey, who encouraged and supported me along the way; to Marian Abel and Martha Gould, of the Washoe County Library staff, who met my every request; to Norma Cowlishaw, who so beautifully typed the manuscript; to Jack Rittenhouse, who fought the battle of the computer search; and finally to my dear companion April, who supervised the writing of every word from her vantage point on the office sofa.

Contents

Part I THE LEARNER   1

1. Basic Needs: First Things First   3

What Is Basic?   3
How Students Survive in Our Classrooms   4
Physical Needs   4
Emotional Needs   5
Social Needs   7

    The Case of Margaret   10
    The Case of Henry   13
    Your Sample Case   17

2. The Self-Concept: Who Am I? Who Are You?   19

The Self-Image   19
The Reflected Personality   20
Self-Awareness and Self-Esteem   21
The Expanded Self   22
Self-Actualization   23

    The Case of Jimmy   25
    The Case of You—For You   28
    Your Sample Case   29

3. Self-Directedness, Self-Discipline, and Self-Control   31

Self-Directedness   31
Self-Discipline   32
Self-Control   33

    The Case of Mrs. Karl's Seventh Grade   36
    Your Sample Case   42

87267

4. **The Self-Fulfilling Prophecy**   44

The Theory of the Self-Fulfilling Prophecy   45
The Teacher as Prophet   45
The Permanent Label   46
Prophetic Counseling   46
Prophetic Discipline   47
Prophetic Dollars   47
The Prophetic Curriculum   48
The Teacher as the Key   48

   The Case of Ellen   50
   The Case of Timmy   54
   Your Sample Case   58

5. **The Learner as Curriculum Builder**   60

What Is the Curriculum?   61
Who Should Design the Curriculum?   62
Modalities of Learning   63
Imagery, Modalities, and Successful Teaching   64

   The Case of the Totem Pole   65
   The Case of Pauline   69
   Your Sample Case   72

Summary Part I   74

Part II THE TEACHER   75

6. **The Teacher in Focus**   77

Physical and Mental Health   79
Preparation   81
Enthusiasm   82

   The Case of Mrs. Colby   83
   The Case of Mrs. Evans   87
   Your Sample Case   91

7. **Role Modeling: The Self-Concept of the Teacher**   93

Role Perception   93
Self-Concept   93

Role Conflict 94
Role Modeling 95
Traditional Roles 96
Changing Roles 96

The Case of Mrs. Wills 98
The Case of Mr. McKinnon 102
Your Sample Case 106

8. The Ideal Teacher 108

Who Is the Ideal Teacher? 108
Rating Scale for Teachers 109
Becoming "Ideal" 111
A Letter to My Favorite Teacher 115

Summary Part II 119

Part III THE PROCESS 121

9. Experience, Experience, Experience 123

The Tabula Rasa 124
See, Hear, Feel, Touch, Taste 125
How Do Concepts Develop? 126
From Concepts to Generalizations 128
Vicarious Experience 128

The Case of Franklin 130
The Case of Cam and the Snow 132

10. Gestalt and the Integrated Curriculum 136

History 136
The Whole versus the Part 137
Analysis versus Synthesis 137
Experience and Perception 138
Learning, Thinking, and Problem Solving 139
The Integrated Curriculum 140
Cultural Universals 141
A Model Outline for Developing an Integrated
Unit of Study 143

11. **Piaget and Developmental Learning**   **148**

Piaget's Theory of Intellectual Processes   **149**
Periods of Cognitive Development   **151**
Implications for the Teaching–Learning Process   **153**

The Case of Kim and the Ice Cubes   **155**
The Case of Scotty and the Reading
    Readiness Test   **157**
Your Sample Case   **159**

12. **Montessori and the Orderly Mind**   **161**

The Method   **162**
The Technique   **162**
The Didactic Materials   **166**
Summary   **177**

The Case of Bruce   **179**
The Case of Sherri   **183**
Your Sample Case   **186**

13. **Motivation**   **188**

Definition   **188**
Motivation and Learning   **189**
Failure and Motivation   **190**
Motivation and I. Q.   **190**
Goal-Setting as Motivation   **191**
Competition as Motivation   **192**
Teacher Variables Related to Motivation   **193**
Student Variables Related to Motivation   **195**
The Curriculum as Motivation   **197**

The Case of George   **198**
The Case of Clara   **201**
Your Sample Case   **204**

14. **Operant Conditioning**   **206**

Conditioning and Human Learning   **207**
Programmed Instruction   **208**
Teaching Machines   **209**

Computer-Assisted Instruction   210
Learning Kits   211
Behavioral Objectives   212
Descriptive Objectives   213
Contingency Management   213
Token-Economy Programs   214
Sample of a Programmed Text   215

   The Case of Donnie   225
   The Case of the Telephone Operators   227
   Your Sample Case   229

15. **Open Schools**   231

Definition   231
Basic Assumptions Justifying the Open-Concept
   Philosophy   237
Operating Principles of the Open Classroom   240
The Role of the Administrator and the Teacher
   in the Open School   241
What the Community Expects of Its School
   System   243

   The Case of Richard   245
   The Case of Mrs. Woods   248
   Your Sample Case   250

16. **Evaluation**   252

What Is Evaluation?   253
Grading   255
Who Knows What the Teacher Has Taught?
   Who Knows What The Learner Has Learned?   256
Testing as Learning   258
What Is Accountability?   260
Samples of Rating Scales   263

   The Case of Burns   276
   The Case of "Hot Seat"   278
   Your Sample Case   281

Summary Part III **283**

Part IV THE NEVER-ENDING ODYSSEY **285**

    17. Learning for Living a Lifetime **287**

        Ending or Beginning? **288**

        Re-tooling and Re-education **289**

        Aging and Creativity **290**

        How Does One Begin? **291**

        Where Does One Begin? **292**

        What Has Our Educational System Done to

            Prepare Us for a Lifetime of Learning? **293**

        What Opportunities Are Open to Everyone? **295**

ADDITIONAL READINGS **298**

INDEX **307**

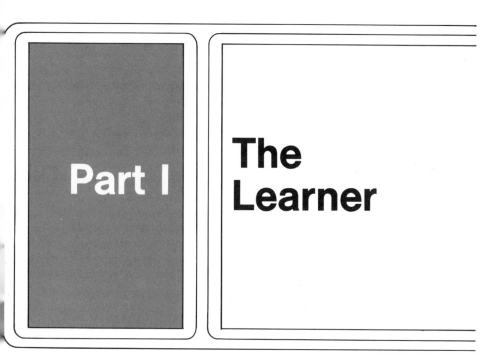

Part I

The Learner

Basic Needs: First Things First

*What educators ought to keep firmly in mind is the . . .
proposition . . . that the head has a body.*

JOAN D. GUSSOW[1]

What is Basic?

For many years, basic needs have been interpreted quite simply as food, clothing, and shelter. Today, this interpretation can be seen in the generous efforts most Americans put forth after a disaster to assist those in need. Almost invariably "in need" is taken to mean in need of food, in need of clothing, or in need of housing.

It is not hard to grasp the idea that anyone who is hungry or sick or miserable has difficulty thinking—particularly about abstract concepts or rational solutions to problems. Most behavior exhibited under such unfavorable conditions is almost reflexive in nature. Someone who is starving grabs at anything to eat. Someone caught in a sudden situation of danger intuitively reacts to survive or to save another, even taking personal risks to do so. Most of these actions, when analyzed later, are almost always explained by some remark like "I really don't know what made me do it."

There is little argument that survival is a primary motivating force and that, in threatening situations, those needs basic to survival become overwhelmingly important. As psychologists and sociologists have learned more about the human organism, however, it has become apparent that we need more than mere means for survival. People need, as Laswell points out, some sense of sharing in those intangible values which contribute to one's sense of worth—well-being, respect, affection, wealth, enlightenment, rectitude, skill, and power.[2]

True, changes in daily circumstances cause one's hierarchy of values to change or shift, even if only temporarily. A person who is seriously ill is more concerned about well-being than about wealth. But there does come a time in the recuperation period when medical costs occupy one's thoughts.

Thus arise the questions: What are basic needs? Do they vary with

3

time and place and human condition? What about the basic needs in that human condition known as formal schooling?[3]

How Students Survive in Our Classrooms

Many of the living experiences children have in our classrooms today come within the category of survival training. Picture the typical classroom in the United States: a square box within a larger square box; windows at a level no one can look out of; seats or desks all the same size; hot in spring and summer, stifling in winter; a bit shabby with no indication that anyone is concerned about beauty. Then there is the schedule. Toilet needs may be taken care of only at a specified time, and food needs are clearly the province of the noon hour.[4]

Order, silence, conformity, docility, regimentation—these are the major characteristics of the typical classroom. This kind of dehumanizing experience has been well described and, sadly, only too well documented in Silberman's *Crisis in the Classroom*.[5] No need to dwell further on it here. Rather, here we will emphasize the physical, emotional, and social needs of students—no matter what their age or grade level.

Physical Needs

To be mentally alert, one needs to be relatively comfortable. Not too comfortable. A classroom is not the beach, and a totally relaxed atmosphere does not provide the best setting for learning. However, one should be free of pain and should not be distracted by hunger or the excessive need for sleep. Students (and faculty, where possible) studiously avoid classes at 8 A.M. or 8 P.M. While the early hour may be good for some who are "morning people," the evening schedule usually finds most people with a low level of blood sugar and thus tired, easily distracted, and weary.

Furniture should be of suitable size and design and, above all, appropriate to the learning task. An entire class period (or the whole day, in the case of some elementary schools) spent in verbal receiving (with the teacher doing all the verbal sending) requires a different kind of seating–working arrangement than does an open activity–oriented classroom.

Heating and lighting should be adequate and appropriate. Some students, especially those who wear glasses or contact lenses, are utterly miserable in a room with fluorescent lighting. Ventilation and sound control should be arranged to provide maximum comfort. It is rather difficult to carry on a discussion, to read quietly, or to write creatively if the band is practicing in the next room or is marching up and down the campus. (There is a new school of thought, however, which supports the idea that one learns better in a relatively noisy environment.)

Regardless of the physical arrangements, even the most carefully planned environment becomes tiring if occupied for very long. Variety, movement, change of pace—all these provide relief from monotony.

Visually, too, we need variety and change. If the students can't look out the windows, then the teacher's responsibility for providing some beauty and interest becomes even more important. The cleanliness and order of the classroom, the appeal of attractive bulletin boards, the graciousness of fresh flowers or plants—even a bunch of wild flowers or dried grasses—all lend color and warmth to a room and soften the surgical–clinical atmosphere so often found in schools. The person of the teacher—dress, style, grooming—also become a part of a pleasant visual environment for students.

The concept of enlarging the students' "vision" through field trips and study tours is as old as the Middle Ages.[6] Yet even today, while educators talk and write glibly about the "school without walls," it is the rare administrator who enthusiastically supports field trips.

A certain amount of personal freedom is another requisite for physical well-being. Some students delay taking care of personal needs because they fear embarrassment or because they are afraid of being "challenged" in the hall. One vice-principal, meeting a student in the corridor of a large high school during a class period, barked, "What are you doing here?" To which the student replied, "Everybody has to be somewhere."

Emotional Needs

Even in the most ideal physical surroundings, it is possible to ignore the emotional needs of students or, worse still, to add to their emotional problems. Rare is the student or the teacher who comes to the class with a clear, happy, and uncluttered consciousness, ready to concentrate only on the topic at hand. In this increasingly complicated world everyone deals with personal and social conflicts which cannot always be turned off or set aside until after the class or until the end of the school day. A family squabble at breakfast, a flat tire on the way to school, an uncompleted assignment, a harsh word from a friend, a cold shoulder from someone special—all or any of these can create an inner turmoil which may block any real enthusiasm for learning.

In addition, a teacher's unsympathetic approach or bit of sarcasm or "drill instructor" attitude are all guaranteed to create the kind of tension in a classroom that no amount of brilliance or academic preparation can overcome. Sometimes, for their own protection, students tune you out and become expert at looking alert without hearing a word you say. In such cases, the teacher takes a solo flight into the curriculum while the students remain on the ground of their own distractions or hostilities. The key to a healthy emotional climate in the classroom is *respect.* Not fawning or apple-polishing or ass-kissing, but good, old, honest-to-goodness respect, not only for one another but for the job at hand. In this case, the teacher sets the tone by his or her attitude toward the work to be done, enthusiasm for learning, and courtesy and kindness, all tempered by fairness and firmness. If the students sense the attitude that the "stuff" they are being asked to assimilate is dumb and dull and uninteresting or if they sense in the teacher a lack of concern or preparation, then the whole learning process becomes a charade. With one eye on the clock and one foot out the door, everyone is impatient for the painful period to be over. In the self-contained classroom these attitudes can be devastating when one considers that they must be endured for a full five hours each day.

It is not necessary to love children or young people to be a good teacher, but it is absolutely essential to respect the person of each student and to respect yourself enough to give the job your very best efforts. Without these attitudes, all the love in the world is not going to culminate in a decent teaching–learning experience. The best indication of your love for your students is to teach them well and to expect from them the best of which they are capable. They may not love you for all that, but you will reap a much greater reward —lasting respect from them.

There are times when the teacher becomes aware that a student is emotionally troubled. The student is not just experiencing some passing aggravation, but a really traumatic experience: physical or sexual abuse, or both; deep disturbances about family disorganization; fears, real or imaginary. These are not simple everyday problems that can be solved by the classroom teacher. In such situations, an expert is needed to provide help for the student and reliable advice for the teacher. There was a time when the teacher was expected to handle every problem which arose. Not so today. It is part of your professional responsibility to become aware of the sources of help available. Don't wait until there is a problem; find out about these ahead of time. A good time for such questions is in the hiring interview. "What if . . . ?"

Social Needs

Whatever else we know or don't know about human beings, one thing is clear—we are essentially social beings. We need society as a fish needs water, as a bird needs air. Society is our natural habitat and there are few conditions more painful than loneliness. Prisoners of war can endure many kinds of hardships as long as these are shared. The pain of solitary confinement is almost unendurable even when there is no physical abuse such as torture or starvation. Aleksandr Solzhenitsyn describes the sub-culture of even the most miserable Soviet prison in his *Gulag Archipelago*. However, he always speaks with warmth and feeling of the ideas shared with other prisoners.[7]

A famous English physician imprisoned by the Nazis during World War II gives a graphic account of the extremely difficult effort she put forth to remain sane. One example is her regular physical exercise even in a five-by-seven-foot cell. She calculated how many times she needed to walk from wall to wall to complete a mile. However, walking a mile or two daily in the semidarkness could have become mind-stultifying. Therefore, each time she started out, she pictured the physical surroundings and the people she would meet were she actually taking her walk at home. Through these fantasies of social contact and conversations, she managed to remain sane for seven long years.

The first American general captured by the North Koreans in 1950 and kept in solitary confinement for three months spoke movingly of his experience trying to keep his mind alive by repeating all the poems he had ever memorized, all the songs he had ever known, and even the multiplication tables.[8]

This need to keep in touch with reality by simulating social intercourse runs through every prisoner-of-war story ever written.

Many of the problems in homes for old people are not really so much concerned with poor food, inadequate care, uncomfortable surroundings. It is the sense of aloneness that destroys. It is the loss of the feeling of worth inferred from physical neglect which gives pain. Much of what we call senility is simply loss of touch with society.

At the other end of the life cycle—early childhood—there are many examples of young children who have failed to thrive, regardless of diet, if they have not been loved or have been left unattended or have not experienced warm personal closeness with some adult. The medical profession is beginning to look at the imprinting which takes place even in the hours immediately following birth. Isolation, even for medical reasons, seems to foster a lack of a sense of security and self-worth. The anthropologists put it another way. They say that we are not born human but become human through social experience.

If one accepts all of the foregoing, then, logically, one asks the next question: How do we provide for social needs in the typical classroom? Sadly, after observing and listening and reading, we must conclude that many classrooms are not warm, accepting places, directed by warm, accepting adults. They are more like prisons or even asylums where many students have developed a sub-culture much like that which exists in prisons and in hospitals. This sub-culture is valid in every technical respect. It has a language all its own, a value system, and a set of behaviors different from the institution's "requirements."

In a survey taken among the students enrolled in the TV College of a large midwestern city, one question concerned itself with whether or not the students felt more comfortable with the TV teacher on the screen or with the real live teacher in a typical classroom. To everyone's amazement, the TV teacher was favored. The reasons: "there ain't no interruptions while she yells at kids"; "the TV teacher don't care how you smell"; "the TV teacher can't tell what you're doing while the lesson is going on." What happened to that long-cherished idea that every classroom needs the physical presence of a leader, a director, a teacher? What the students seem to be saying is that even a simulated teacher-pupil contact which does not put the student down is better than the hostile environment often created in the person-to-person relationship in many classrooms.

There is, of course, a flip side to this. Isn't it possible that much of the problem is a result of the passive character of the TV generation? Students seem to drag their bodies into the classroom, slouch down into their seats with the unspoken "here-I-am, I-dare-you-to-teach-me-anything" attitude. The TV tube has never expected or required that they respond or react or, for that matter, that they even pay very close attention. An enthusiastic teacher tries to excite students and gets shafted. The electronic age has taken its toll in the small percentage of truly interested learners, in the dearth of motivated scholars, and in the "dish-it-out, take-it-or-leave-it" attitude of some teachers, weary of competing with current favorite television programs.

In such mutually boring conditions, it is not surprising that many students just sit and stare or indulge in their favorite fantasies or fail to react at all. Worse still, many of them develop hostile attitudes when the teacher really does try to inject a little life into the classroom or does truly expect (or even demand) some results. On the other hand, many teachers for their own safety and protection (physical as well as emotional) have given up. They go into class each day armed with an air-tight lesson plan, a bundle of behavioral objectives, and a completely impersonal attitude toward the whole performance. The bell rings. "Thank God it's over for another day! What did you say your name is? Are you in one of my classes? Who's your advisor? See me during my posted office hours." Maybe the teacher, too, accustomed to watching the unreal, hesitates to react to dirty or inappropriate clothes, to kids stoned out of their minds, or to situations that cry out for some strong guidance and some real caring.

The inability to deal with social problems of any kind or degree seems to have grown out of the passivity and docility developed by the "boob tube." On the other hand, here is a magnificent resource for learning unlike anything the world has ever seen before. There must be a way to use it without destroying the social interaction and that bit of tension which, like the spring of a watch, is necessary to keep our minds and our world ticking.

Even if all this sounds a bit dismal, there is hope. Many students appreciate the efforts made by their teachers to help them, to teach them, to care for them in the deepest human sense. Many of us have ample proof that such appreciation lasts long after the diplomas have been mislaid and the class rings lost.

What can one say to the young, hopeful, idealistic teacher-to-be? *Be firm, be fair, be prepared, be strong, and, above all, be honest.* If you enjoy new ideas, you can expect to inspire enthusiasm for learning in others. If you are willing to try new ways of doing things, you may encourage creativity in students. If you come to class with a cheerful, friendly attitude, you will see this feeling spread to the students and thus create an atmosphere of "groupness" that will enhance motivation and make the learning task much easier for both you and the students. Take reasonable care of your own physical health, your own emotional balance, your own social well-being. Usually, the physically, emotionally, and socially competent person can become a happy and successful teacher. In rare cases, a teacher who has overcome serious personal problems is more sensitive to the problems of others. However, in general, the complexity of human relations and social role-demands made by the teaching profession allows one little time for personal therapy. Do not be attracted to teaching because you expect the "dear little children" to give you the affection and respect you should normally be getting from other adults. This is to put an unfair burden on the teacher–pupil relationship and to condemn yourself to failure from the outset. Many cruel jokes about the manner and character of the typical primary teacher found their source in just such a dependent attitude.

Be a person, be an adult, then be a teacher.

The Case of Margaret

Margaret was a junior high school student who was overweight, over-sexed, over-everything for her grade. She had been in the classroom approximately five weeks, during which time she did not participate in discussions or hand in assigned work. Margaret sat in the back of the room in something of a catatonic state. The teacher, a very sincere young woman without too many years of experience, was genuinely concerned about Margaret's apparent inability to learn and her unwillingness to participate or even to act and look alive in the classroom. However, she was reaching a point of not knowing what to do.

This was a small school in a rural west Texas area; the class was composed of about twenty students. There was no counselor, no guidance specialist, no one to whom the teacher could go for expert help. When she spoke to some of the older members of the staff about Margaret, they all threw up their hands and said, "We don't know what's come over that girl; she's been such a nice, quiet, good student and now, all of a sudden, she's beginning to act like a zombie." These typical teacher's-lounge comments didn't help Margaret's teacher very much.

One morning the teacher went into her classroom a little early to get ready for the day. To her very great surprise she found that Margaret was already in the room and had come up to stand beside the teacher's desk. Without preliminary comments, with no explanations, Margaret leaned over the desk, looked the teacher squarely in the face, and said, "Do you think it would be very bad if I killed my stepmother?"

At first the teacher was speechless. However, she regained her presence of mind and was able to sit down and get Margaret to talk with her. The talking was interspersed with sobs and crying, but there was not much explanation. The teacher suggested that Margaret go into the nurse's room and rest while she talked with the principal to see what should be done to give her some relief or some help—still without knowing the real basis for this explosion.

As soon as the teacher could get away from her classroom, she called Margaret's aunt who was an elderly spinster and who lived alone in the same town. She learned to her very great dismay that Margaret's mother had been killed in an automobile accident during the summer. (No one had mentioned it at school.) To make matters worse, Margaret's father had remarried almost immediately. The combination of the shock of her own mother's death and her father's sudden remarriage had been a traumatic experience for Margaret.

Possible Solutions

1. One solution to this problem would have been to report Margaret to the police or to the juvenile home and have her detained there while the juvenile officers looked into the details of her homicidal threat.

2. An alternative might have been that the teacher ignore the outburst and try not to disturb Margaret so that Margaret would not become a severe problem in the classroom.

3. A third solution might have been for the teacher to talk with the spinster aunt to see what the possibilities might be of moving Margaret from a hostile home environment to a more calm living situation, at least, for a while.

Would you choose any of these solutions? If so, you may write your explanation below. However, if you would not choose any of these, you may go on to the next page and write your solution to the problem.

Your Solution to Margaret's Problem

The Case of Henry

The fifth grade teacher had been coming to the principal's office daily for weeks complaining about Henry: "Henry has been late every day this year." "Henry comes to school a half hour after the opening bell. He promptly sits down and goes to sleep." The principal was becoming very weary of the problem. Henry got to be a permanent fixture in the principal's office—always tardy—no excuse—sound asleep by 10 o'clock in the morning.

The principal found little jobs for him to do but this couldn't go on forever. Finally, one day after the usual tardiness complaint, the principal sat down beside him and said, "Henry, I am not going to have you coming to the office again. We have to get this settled. I have written notes, and I have tried to reach your mother. I think that we will have to do is suspend you from school until you bring your mother for a conference." At the mention of bringing his mother for a conference, Henry acted as if he had been stabbed. He screamed and cried and knelt down on the floor. He put his arms around the principal's legs in a spirit of great penance and sobbed, "I will stay in everyday after school for the next ten years! I will do anything if you will not make me bring my mother!" "Aha," thought the principal, "now I have found the weak spot. Now, I have found some way to get at this kid and find out what is going on with him!"

"No," said the principal more sternly than before. The louder Henry yelled, the more stern the principal became. "No, Henry, you may not come back to school until you bring your mother. Go home now, but I want your mother here in the morning."

The next morning before 8 o'clock, the principal was in the office, the teachers were in their classrooms, there were no children around when all of a sudden the door burst open and the air was blue with cursing and swearing and drunkenly slurred screams. "I told you you don't have to go to this rotten school! You don't need no education! I don't care if they throw you out of the school!" All of this was coming from the mouth of a woman who looked as if she had never had a bath, had never had her hair combed, had never lived in a house or slept in a clean bed. She was dragging along behind Henry, cursing and swearing and telling him how stupid it was for him to try to go to school. Henry, meanwhile, was trying to hush her up and to drag her in the direction of the principal's office.

When they arrived at the principal's office, Henry stood there with big, sad eyes downcast and said, "Here's my mother." The principal was truly shocked, and, after handling the mother as gingerly as possible, she managed to get her out of the building and on her way back home. Then, she brought Henry in for a different kind of conference.

Henry told her the whole story. The mother was constantly drunk from morning till night. There were strange men coming and going in the shack all night. Henry and his little sister had to be responsible for getting themselves up and coming to school, usually after having had not too much sleep and always without breakfast.

Possible Solutions

1. One solution to this problem would have been immediately to report Henry and his little sister to the juvenile authorities as neglected children—which they certainly were.

2. The principal might have solved the problem by calling in the police, describing the woman's behavior, and taking legal action to have her parental rights suspended.

3. The principal could have ignored what was going on. She could have tried to provide breakfast for Henry and his little sister and, most of all, tried to help the teacher accept the fact that Henry was doing the very best he could.

Would you choose any of these solutions? If so, you may write your explanation below. However, if you would not choose any of these, you may go on to the next page and write your solution to the problem.

Your Solution to Henry's Problem

Your Sample Case

If you have witnessed or experienced a case in your own school life that you think indicates the very great importance of physical, emotional, and social needs and their satisfaction, describe the case and explain how you saw the case solved. Did you agree with the solution? Why?

Notes

1. Joan D. Gussow, "Bodies, Brains, and Poverty: Poor Children and the Schools. *IRCD Bulletin,* Vol. VI, No. 3, Sept. 1970, p. 6.

2. Harold Laswell, *The Social Process.* (Wilmette, Illinois: Encyclopedia Britannica Films, 1956).

3. As early as 1938 Daniel Prescott described in great detail his perception of basic needs. His book, *Emotion and the Educative Process* (American Council on Education, 1938, pp. 114–25) listed three large categories: Physiological, Social, and Ego (or Integrative) needs. His approach was much ahead of the current thinking in Educational Psychology and seems to be valid today.

4. Much research has been done on the relationship between nutrition and learning. Several of the representative studies on this topic are listed in the bibliography.

5. Charles E. Silberman, *Crisis in the Classroom.* (New York: Random House, 1970).

6. Rosella Linskie, "The Field Trip as an Educational Technique," *Texas Journal of Secondary Education* (Winter 1956).

7. Aleksandr Solzhenitsyn, *Gulag Archipelago.* (New York: Harper & Row, 1974).

8. General James Dean. An informal lecture before the PTA of the American School in Yokohama, Japan, September (1950).

The Self-Concept: Who Am I? Who Are You?

Is it really me,
This body outside,
This shelter, this cover?
Is it really me?
No.
My heart is me.

DAISI ORANTES[1]

How many times have you asked yourself questions like: Who am I anyway? What is my life all about? How did I get this way? Am I really worth much? Who cares what happens to me? And, on the other hand, Who are you? Do you like me? Do you understand me? What do you think of me? While these may appear to be just simple questions, they represent the complicated psychological concepts of the self-image, the reflected personality, self-awareness and self-esteem, the expanded self, self-actualization, and a host of other even more involved socio-psychological concepts.

The Self-Image

Chapter 1 introduced the idea that we are not born human, but rather we develop our humanity within the framework of social interactions with others. A very significant part of our humanity is the awareness of self and the ability to contemplate our own image as if looking at another person. This is extremely difficult to do. How do you feel when you look at the proofs of your own photograph? Do they really look like you? Do they look the way you'd like to look? It is a very strange feeling to see one's self in a photograph or on the TV screen, or horror of horrors, in a candid shot taken without your knowledge.

What is the self-image? Carl Rogers says that ". . . everyone has an image or concept of himself as a unique person or self, different from every other self. . . ."[2] This is true of the physical self as well as of the psychological self. These images are never complete, never exactly as one would like them to be. Change your hair color; buy a wig; choose a new shade of make-up; wear a padded bra; select clothes that emphasize your best features; grow a beard; wear a necklace or beads. Part of our dissatisfaction with our physical selves comes from television and magazine commercials' invasion of our most private secrets of self-image. Even our deeper psychological images of ourselves are affected by outside sources as well, always changing and adapting to the environment and to the response of others.

Although most people are stable enough to be somewhat predictable, we are all accustomed to wearing various "masks." Each person has a home self, a school or business self, a social self, an angry self, a happy self, a sad self, and many, many other selves. All these various "selfs" or masks change depending on the situation and on one's reaction to the situation. An angry motorist might scowl at the driver who nudges his rear bumper until he suddenly realizes that the driver is his boss's wife or an old friend. The scowl mask is instantly changed because the motorist wouldn't want this person to see him in his angry face.

Even during the sensitive and sad occasion of a funeral, persons most affected by the death usually shield their faces from the more casual mourners. Thus, we have the widow's veil or the recent device used in most funeral homes of screening the family from the main chapel.

Very young children already have developed certain attitudes about themselves and their abilities which greatly influence the way they behave in school and elsewhere. Let's look at some of the factors which contribute to these attitudes about the self.

The Reflected Personality

In the early 1950's there was a television commercial for a certain brand of face soap which went something like this:

I look into the mirror and there I see
Someone dearer than all the world to me—
Me!

Corny? Maybe. But that silly jingle encompasses the whole theory of the reflected personality or what Cooley and Mead called the "looking-glass self." This theory, developed by these two highly respected social psychologists at the University of Chicago in the early 1900's, holds that we each look into the eyes of others and see there the clues to our own behavior. Thus, our behavior is the reflection of what we imagine we appear to be to others, what we think the judgments of the others are regarding our appearance and the feelings about self which result, such as pride or humiliation or anger. This is what Cooley and Mead meant by the "looking-glass self."

> Each to each a looking-glass
> Reflects the other that doth pass.[3]

However, the thing that moves us to pride or shame is not the mere mechanical reflection of ourselves, but the imagined effect of this reflection upon another person's mind and attitude toward us. For example, we are ashamed to seem evasive in the presence of a straightforward man, cowardly in the presence of a brave man, or gross in the presence of a refined man. You might boast to one person about an action that you would be ashamed even to acknowledge to another. Therefore, the identity of the other plays a very large part in the construction of one's self-image.

What does the teacher think? What does the teacher want? How will my steady feel about me in this outfit? All of these are indications of our concern with the reflected self.

Cooley and Meade were not the first to develop this idea of the reflected personality.[4] The ancient Greeks and Romans suggested this concept in their languages. In Greek, the word *prospon* means literally "the face" or "countenance." Later, the same word was used to denote a character in a stage performance. The Latin *persona* is translated in German as *gesicht,* and in English as: What a sight you are! or I don't like his looks! In China and Japan a loss of face means a loss of prestige and is to be avoided at all costs—even by suicide if necessary. Thus, we see that there has always been a great concern about the judgment of others.

Self-Awareness and Self-Esteem

As a person becomes aware of self, this awareness is never neutral, unless one thinks of one's self as a blah person. Along with awareness (and an essential part of it) comes the positive or negative self-attitude that has been developed through the looking-glass technique.

Babies seek approval and reassurance for their self-esteem largely from the mother, who for the first few years of life is the source of all—good and bad, pleasure and pain, happiness and sadness. As the young child's sphere of experience enlarges, he or she begins to look to teachers as the significant others who approve or disapprove; confirm or negate a sense of personal worth. After about nine or ten years of age, the typical young person relies more and more on the reflected self as it is expressed by peers: friends, class-mates, teenagers in the group or neighborhood. This last stage of peer dependence lasts most of us a lifetime. We are never quite free of the concern with the opinion of others. What will the neighbors think? How will your father react to that report card? What will your best friend do when he finds out? What will my wife do if she hears about this?

However, if you mature as you grow older, you come to the ultimate in source of approval, namely, your own approval. This does not mean that you can fly in the face of society or family or friends. It simply means that your own sense of self-esteem becomes a more sure guide for your behavior. It means that the person whose approval you must have each day is YOU. This is really another way of describing integrity. Because each person instinctively tends toward some degree of self-direction, it becomes more and more important that one develop a positive sense of self, a realistic sense of one's own ability, and sufficient self-esteem to enable one to set worthwhile and achieveable goals.

Only to the degree that you accept and like yourself can you hope to accept and like others. Only to the degree that you recognize your strengths and weaknesses can you hope to choose realistic goals for yourself. Only to the degree that you are willing to accept responsibility for your own behavior can you hope to enjoy to the fullest a real sense of freedom and self-direction. There is nothing wrong with knowing you are really good at something and not so good at something else. Theologians, as well as psychologists, define true humility as recognizing the truth about oneself.

In a society like ours which emphasizes groupness and to some extent looks askance at the loner, it isn't always easy to be completely truthful about yourself—even to yourself. However, a deep and abiding sense of your own worth, your own integrity, and your own self-esteem will shine through all you do and will be reflected in the image others have of you.

The Expanded Self

The Self comes in a variety of sizes. Some are small and mean and cold and threadbare. Others are large and warm and open and rich. In between, there are various sizes and kinds. The classic example of the miser huddled alone in his frugal room, unwilling to share anything with anyone is probably the smallest size self there is. On the other hand, the generous, open person, willing to risk even being hurt by others, is the large economy size. Often the idea of the expanded self is derived from wealth and riches. However, it is used to mean that attitude of giving and sharing of one's time and talents and love that we often refer to when we say things like, he is a big person, or she would give you her right arm if you needed it. You can surely think of similar metaphors which refer to that concept which means giving one's self with one's gift, no matter how large or how small the gift. Giving of one's goods without giving of one's self is not giving at all.

Another aspect of the expanded self is derived from all that a person calls his or her own: *my* home, *my* family, *my* club, or *my* car, *my* wardrobe, *my* custom-made golf clubs. All those things (or persons) that can be considered extensions of yourself provide the others a fuller definition of YOU. Even when you hand a written assignment to your teacher or present a finished piece of work to your employer or serve a meal to your family, you are really saying: Here is a picture of me and my abilities. Here is my very best. If the product is not the very best of which you are capable, the others may develop a mistaken notion of what you really are. Nobody can get inside your skin. They can only judge you by those parts of your expanded and extended self that you present to them.

Self-Actualization

One of the outstanding psychologists of our time, Abraham Maslow, has developed what may be considered the crowning point of the theory of the self-concept. He calls this the theory of self-actualization. According to Maslow, all human beings have, to some degree, built into their personalities an inclination to strive for the greatest possible development of their own unique abilities and potential for creativity.[5]

Often one meets and deals with individuals whose attitude seems to contradict Maslow. Yet, even a failure complex or what appears to be a conscious effort to choose failure over success, can, in a negative way, be seen as supporting Maslow's theory. We each "actualize" or bring into being that self that we imagine ourselves to be. This concept will be met again later as we discuss the self-fulfilling prophecy. Iris Murdoch says it in another way when she writes: "Man is the only creature that makes pictures of himself and then strives to become like the picture."

The information presented in Chapters 1 and 2 now allows us to construct a pyramid of the self-concept using Maslow's theory as the apex.

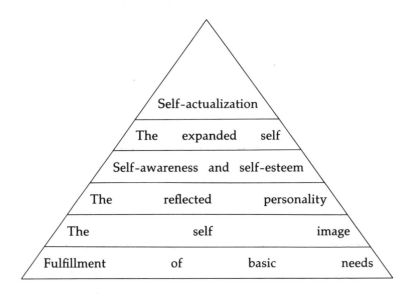

All of what has been said about the self is dependent on the fulfillment or lack of fulfillment of basic human needs. Christopher Jencks, in his classic work, *Inequality*, emphasizes the lack of opportunity as a major factor in individual differences and thus a large factor in the construct of the self-image.[6]

Now we can answer with some authority the question, Why do some students succeed while others fail? The causes are complex and different for each individual. However, one factor remains constant—the way in which each student views him or herself and his or her abilities. This view can be changed by any number of circumstances. Nevertheless, the end result is Mead's looking-glass self and each of us becomes what we imagine ourselves to be.

The Case of Jimmy

The teacher was young but well prepared for her new job—an eighth grade teacher in a small school in an oil-boom town in Oklahoma. She had arrived several days early to get a feel of the community. Then, after the official orientation, she was eager to get to her classroom to begin to prepare for the opening day of school.

As she was working alone in the room one morning before the first day of class, a tall, skinny boy came in. He was all arms and legs and a big broad smile. "Are you the new eighth grade teacher?" "Yes, I am." "Well, my name is Jimmy and I've been in this school ten years and I've flunked twice and my twin brother is already in high school. All the teachers have told me I can't learn very fast so I thought I'd better tell you before school starts. I don't want you to worry about me and I sure don't want you worrying me about eighth grade math and stuff. I know it's going to be hard and I'll probably flunk again anyway, so there is plenty of time."

All this came rushing out without a pause for breath. At the same time, Jimmy didn't seem the least bit upset or abashed. He seemed like a pleasant, happy, honest boy.

"Do you have a desk big enough for me? Can I help you around here? I always help with the little kids."

The teacher could hardly believe her eyes and ears. Here was a student—a young man, sixteen years old—who had failed twice and who had undoubtedly suffered by comparison with his twin brother John who was already a junior in high school. According to all the psychology books, Jimmy should have been dejected, depressed, and hostile. He was none of these. Instead, he was a very pleasant boy stating what he perceived as facts about himself.

The teacher invited Jimmy to sit down and they talked for a while. She pointed out that each new school year is a new beginning, a new page without any old history of failure, and that she would do all she could to help Jimmy if he would try. It was a pleasant visit and, as the teacher and the much taller pupil walked out of the building, the city garbage truck came by. Jimmy smiled and said, "That's the guy I'll probably replace when I get old enough to quit school."

One of the first parent conferences the teacher arranged was with Jimmy's mother. She turned out to be a handsomely groomed woman from an upper-class family. She had five children, and all were doing well in school except Jimmy. She pointed out that tutors hadn't helped and that while Jimmy didn't seem too upset, his father was very disturbed. Jimmy's father was an independent oil producer and money was no problem.

Possible Solutions

1. The financial well-being of the family might have suggested to the teacher that it might be a good idea to recommend they continue using a tutor.

2. A second solution might have been found in the available medical records of Jimmy. He was surely growing very fast and there was a real possibility that he was going through a period of physical growth and development that often interferes with mental development for a time.

3. A third solution might have been for the teacher to have more in-depth conferences with Jimmy to try to discover if he were really so well-adjusted to failure and what kind of self-image he had developed. Perhaps he had become used to wearing his happy mask to hide his real feelings.

4. A fourth solution might have been to have Jimmy tested for interest and aptitude as well as mental maturity.

Would you choose any of these solutions? If so, you may write your explanation below. However, if you would not choose any of these, you may go on to the next page and write your solution to the problem.

Your Solution to Jimmy's Problem

The Case of You—For You

1. How would you describe your own self-image? Try to step outside yourself and see yourself as another person. What do you see? Begin with the physical characteristics.

2. Who are the significant others who have influenced your view of yourself? Are you ready and willing to accept the image these others have projected?

3. What is your level of your own self-esteem? Do you really like yourself?

4. What size self do you think you have? Are you a small self? A large one? An in-between? What size self would you like to be?

5. Make a list of all the things that you usually put the word "my" in front of when you talk. Study the list. Are there some things you'd like to add? Some things you'd like to delete?

6. If you could change any one thing about yourself, what would that be?

7. Where are you on Maslow's pyramid? Do you feel that you are making progress toward self-actualization? Why? How?

8. Try to imagine how you will look and what you will be ten years from now.

All that you write on this page is for YOURSELF alone. You don't need to share it with anybody if you don't want to. Above all, don't let the teacher put a grade on it!

Your Sample Case

If you have witnessed or experienced a case in your own school life that you think emphasizes the great importance of the self-concept, describe the case and explain how you saw it handled. Did you agree with the solution? Why?

Notes

1. Daisi Orantes, "Is It Really?" *Just For Me, Please.* (Los Angeles: Los Angeles Unified School District Publication, 1974).

2. Carl Rogers, *On Becoming a Person.* (Boston: Houghton Mifflin, 1961), p. 91.

3. George Horton Cooley, *Human Nature and the Social Order.* (New York: Charles Scribner's Sons, 1927), p. 184.

4. George Mead, *Mind, Self and Society.* (Chicago: University of Chicago Press, 1940), p. 322.

5. C. W. Maslow, *Motivations and Personality,* 2nd ed. (New York: Harper and Row, 1970), p. 56.

6. Christopher Jencks, *Inequality.* (New York: Basic Books, 1972), p. 3.

Self-Directedness, Self-Discipline, and Self-Control

Let them pile the bricks in on me.
But let me build with them for myself.

ROBERT FROST[1]

Self-directedness, self-discipline, and self-control are really only three different facets of the concept of freedom. FREEDOM has no meaning of itself but rather derives meaning from the terms that define its limits. Are you free *from* something or free *to do* something? A man alone on a raft in the middle of the ocean is surely free; he is free *from* social pressure, cultural taboos, and group mores. But what is he free *to do?* Survive! That is about all.

Often we tend to confuse freedom with license: I can do anything I want. That is really not freedom; it is anarchy. Confusion about the definition of freedom is the root cause of many of the social ills we are confronting not only in schools but in all institutions. Fulton Sheen has defined freedom in three categories: there is the freedom to do only what you *want* to do; there is freedom to do only what you *must* do; there is freedom to do what you *ought* to do. The freedom to do only what you *want,* he calls anarchy; the freedom to do only what you *must,* he calls totalitarianism; the freedom to do what you *ought,* he calls democracy.[2] It is in this last context that we will equate freedom with self-direction, self-discipline, and self-control.

Self-Directedness

From early childhood each individual is dependent on some adult for basic needs. As children grow and develop, they begin to feel the urge to do things their own way. This urge is defined variously by the responsible adult as, he's getting too big for his britches or she's acting up or he's becoming something of a problem.

Many of the "symptoms" of a stirring sense of independence on the part of the child are seen by the adult as indications of rebellion, nonconformity, or truculence. If we plant a seedling, we often tie it to a stake so that it will be secure in its initial growth. However, as the small

31

tree grows and begins to take on its own direction, the ties that held it to the stake are no longer necessary. In some cultures, it is considered artistically desirable to stunt, change, or in some way to control the growth of plants. Thus we see espalierred plants decorating walls and bonzai trees in formal gardens and miniaturized plants growing in glass bowls. However, when adults attempt to raise children in a "dish garden" atmosphere, they are usually designing a disastrous situation.

Some young people are ready for self-direction and self-determination much earlier than are others. Nevertheless, some parents and teachers are unwilling to grant the right of self-determination no matter the maturity of the child. As long as you live in my house and eat my food, you'll do as I say! How many homes have been disrupted by just such confrontations!

In Western culture we have for years expected our children to be docile and accepting and obedient and then, presto, overnight at the age of eighteen or twenty-one, we expect them to be fully functioning, self-directed individuals. There is no culture outside the United States, except perhaps England, which so long extends the period of childhood dependency. Some people at twenty-four and older are still dependent on their parents for a livelihood. It is most interesting to see young people wandering about Europe in an effort to "find themselves" and "declare their independence" while at the same time making regular trips to the American Express office to collect "bread" from home!

Self-direction, like any other skill, must be learned. It is basic to the functioning of individuals in a free society. In a police state or in a tightly controlled society, self-determination is not a good to be sought after and developed but a fault to be eradicated. The drill instructor means it when he says to the raw recruit, "Buster, don't try to think around here. Just do as you are told." In a society like the military, such mindless obedience might on occasion be necessary for survival, but it is hardly suitable training for responsibility. A visit to a typical "closed" classroom also makes one wonder about the ability of children to come out of such an atmosphere with any sense of self-worth or that sense of self-determination so necessary for their success and happiness in a democratic society.

Self-Discipline

The order in which these topics are discussed is important. Anyone who tries to be self-directed without being self-disciplined is a paradox. He or she may be self-willed or selfish, but this is quite different from being self-directed.

Self-discipline suggests making decisions about one's actions based on some standard of "good." People often risk their own welfare for the sake of the common good. The fireman, the policeman, the soldier in battle are all examples.

There are various definitions of what constitutes *good:*

Utilitarianism—what is *useful* is good
Relativity—what is *socially acceptable* is good
Pragmatism—what *works* is good
Existentialism—*free choice* is good
Positivism—*moral judgments* and emotional attitudes are good[3]

Thus we see a wide range of values concerning the definition of what is good. Each of us is constantly in the process of re-defining our concept of good, either because of circumstances or because of our own personal need-disposition.

Being truly self-disciplined often means denying one's self or postponing a reward in order to achieve a greater good. The parent saving for a child's education; the young person working several years to earn money to pay for college tuition; anyone trying to save for a car, a home, or a vacation all know the meaning of self-discipline or of making choices based on personal values.

Sometimes even one's physical well-being and longevity depends on self-discipline. You must stop smoking. You must lose some weight. You must stay off alcohol. All these "musts" require a high degree of will power, and sometimes people risk their very lives for lack of just such self-discipline.

One remarkable difference between life in a free society and life in a police state is the *source* of discipline. True discipline must come from *within* a person. If it is imposed from *without,* it will last only as long as someone is there representing force or sanction.

Self-Control

Self-control is a somewhat different concept from self-discipline, although the two are closely related. Self-control, like self-discipline, must come from *within.* However, until one's inner control systems have developed, some direction and discipline must come from *without* the person. Any adult who is responsible for the growth and development of young people must never lose sight of the fact that any discipline enforced from without must be designed to guide the individual toward the long-range goal of independence and self-discipline, not conformity and fear.

Discipline is not a dirty word. It is not something bitter like a dose of distasteful medicine that you must take because it is good for you. Rather, it is an organizational "frame" which allows you to get things done. Very few—almost no—human activities can proceed successfully in a state of chaos, interpersonal strife, or erratic sequence. In a learning situation the method of discipline used by the teacher can substantially affect the development of the child's ability to rationalize the consequences of his or her behavior. In a sense, teachers (and all adults who deal with young people) must be "therapists" in their approach to understanding human behavior and choosing which disciplinary methods should be employed in given situations.

While the classroom atmosphere should reflect the "ease of control" so highly prized, the teacher must attempt to assist the child to achieve the goal of self-control in several different ways:

1. The student should be allowed to see the need for control and the alternatives to his or her behavior. *This is discipline with reason.*
2. The teacher should calmly and rationally administer any corrective measure. The student's *act,* not the student's *self* should be the focal point. *This is discipline appropriate to the behavior.*
3. The class together with the teacher should establish ground rules for behavior, thus avoiding placing the teacher in the role of authoritarian dictator. *This is discipline consistent with democratic guidelines.*

Discipline is itself an important issue and will be given more attention later. Here we will concern ourselves with discipline as a function of the *self.*

There are many respectable psychologists and psychiatrists who are currently advocating "children's lib"—freedom for children in all areas of life: religious, medical, sexual, economic, educational.[4] They do not see the need for guidance toward self-direction. This attitude appears to put the whole burden for behavior on children long before they have had sufficient experience to decide which definition of good to choose. Go ahead, do as you please. If you fall down and get hurt, you'll learn how to be more careful. True, some things must be learned from experience. However, part of the adult's responsibility is to share experiences with children and thus help them grow and mature.

Surely we are all agreed that the violence and disruption and lack of civility we see in the schools is only a reflection of the same shortcomings in the larger society. However, we cannot ease our consciences by ignoring the whole problem and simply wishing it away. We must deal with it, and we must help young people to see the wisdom and necessity for self-discipline and self-control in the classroom as well as in the larger area of life.

The classroom atmosphere should reflect security in which the students have a sense of shared objectives, a feeling of belonging and of cohesiveness. Lewin, Lippitt, and White made a study of ten-year-old boys in authoritarian, democratic, and laissez-faire classrooms. Their findings demonstrated the superiority of democratic procedures in "developing individual responsibility, satisfying social relationships, constructive and friendly channeling of aggression, maintenance of work interest and the ability to continue work activities in the absence of the teacher's prodding."[5]

When students help set the standards for their own behavior in democratic and open classrooms they are taking an active part in developing their own self-control and self-discipline which in turn enhances their own positive self-concept.

Our behavior usually reflects the opinion we hold of ourselves. It is the adult's responsibility to assist young people in modifying and altering any feelings of worthlessness into positive and healthy self-images.

Finally, self-control and self-discipline should not inhibit creativity, spontaneity, or self-fulfillment. Rather, self-direction and responsibility for one's own actions should foster the skill of self-discipline and thereby enhance the ongoing process of learning. Thus, we come again to a sequence not unlike Maslow's pyramid.

SELF-CONTROL   SELF-DISCIPLINE   SELF-DIRECTION   FREEDOM!

If we have a sound base of self-control upon which to build, we are able to develop self-discipline and ultimately to achieve that state of freedom most of us aspire to, namely, being self-directed. This is the structure of creativity in its truest and fullest sense. This, likewise, is the structure of the concept of true freedom without which we all become slaves—either to ourselves or to something or someone outside ourselves.

The Case of Mrs. Karl's Seventh Grade

On Monday morning Mrs. Karl, a seventh grade teacher, telephoned the principal to say that she had a family crisis and could not come to school that day. Her younger son had fallen off his bicycle and cut a deep gash in his head. They were at the hospital.

The principal had already called for two other substitutes that morning, but since she knew Mrs. Karl's class very well, she decided to try something different. When the bell rang, the students went to their classrooms and the principal went to Mrs. Karl's room to receive the students. As soon as they were all assembled, she explained Mrs. Karl's emergency. Then she asked the students if they could handle the class themselves while she tried to find a substitute who would probably not be able to come in until noon. The class agreed enthusiastically.

The principal returned to the office and began to make some phone calls. In a very few minutes a small delegation of students from Mrs. Karl's class came to the office. The discussion went something like this:

"Mrs. Dorsa, we have discussed with the class about a substitute and they asked us to come down and see if you would let us handle our own class today. We already know what we are going to do. Mrs. Karl always has us help make our plans on Friday for the next week."

"Well, that is a bit unusual. What are your plans for today?"

"We agreed to go on working on that science center you and Mrs. Karl talked to us about last week. You know, room eight, where all the kids in the sixth, seventh, and eighth grades can go to do experiments and stuff."

"OK. If you think you can handle it, I'm willing to give it a try. I'll be around the building as usual this afternoon but, in the meantime, I want you to take the responsibility for getting yourselves to Chorus and P.E. and lunch on time and in good order."

"Gee, thanks Mrs. Dorsa. We'll try."

Several times during the morning as the seventh grades went to their special classes the principal was pleased to see Mrs. Karl's group moving in an orderly way through the building. In the afternoon, she went to several classrooms to observe, each time stopping by Mrs. Karl's room and the new science center in Room 8. Everything went well; everyone was busy, and just before the dismissal bell, the same small delegation of students came to the office.

"Here's our attendance sheet and here are our plans for tomorrow. Did we do OK?"

"You surely did. I am very proud of you, and you should be very proud of yourselves. I know Mrs. Karl will be pleased."

It was a unique day and one of those especially rewarding experiences for an administrator.

Possible Solutions

1. The principal should have assigned one of the special teachers to cancel her special classes and supervise Mrs. Karl's class.
2. The principal should have asked the teacher across the hall to keep her classroom door open and check on Mrs. Karl's students frequently.
3. The principal should have made every effort to get a substitute as quickly as possible.

Would you choose any of these solutions? If so, you may write your explanation below. However, if you would not choose any of these, you may go on to the next page and write your solution to the problem.

Your Solution to Mrs. Karl's Seventh Grade's Problem

Questions For Discussion

1. How do you think the incident relates to self-direction, self-discipline, and self-control?

2. What had Mrs. Karl done to make it possible for the students to direct their own learning?

3. How do you think the students felt about themselves at the end of the day?

4. How do you think Mrs. Karl felt when she returned to school the next day?

5. Does this sound like a phony textbook case? It is a real case. It took place in a real school which had a total enrollment in grades K-8 of 1,400 students.

Your Sample Case

If you have witnessed or experienced a case in your own school life that you think emphasizes the great importance of self-directedness, self-discipline, and self-control, describe the case and explain how you saw it handled. Did you agree with the solution? Why?

Notes

1. Robert Frost, An Informal presentation at the opening of Middlebury College, Vermont, 1959.

2. Fulton Sheen, Lecture notes in *Philosophy of Communism,* a graduate course in the Department of Philosophy, The Catholic University of America, Washington, D.C., 1941.

3. "Ethics." *Encyclopaedia Britannica,* Vol. 8, 1964 edition, pp. 775–79.

4. Richard Farson, *Birth-Rights.* (New York: Macmillan, 1974).

5. K. Lewin, R. Lippitt, and R. K. White, "Patterns of Aggressive Behavior in Experimentally Created Social Climates," *Journal of Social Psychology* (1939), 271–99.

The Self-Fulfilling Prophecy

You see, really and truly, apart from the things anyone can pick up (the dressing and the proper way of speaking and so on) the difference between a lady and a flower girl is not how she behaves, but how she's treated.

LIZA DOOLITTLE[1]

On any school day a casual observer could walk into almost any teachers' lounge in any school in any town or city in the country and hear a doomsday litany that would take the heart out of the most dedicated educator: They are just not able to do fourth grade work! I don't know how they made it through first grade without learning how to read! They are just babies who need to be told every move to make! They are really just little animals who need to be trained like animals!

Even in the sacred halls of Congress, during the House of Representatives' Committee on Education hearings for the Economic Opportunity legislation in the 1960's, one witness was at great pains to explain to the Committee that ". . . there are some people who cannot be taught anything except how to work with their hands."[2] These judgmental statements, repeated in dozens of different ways in a variety of circumstances, can all be decoded as saying to an individual: You really aren't worth very much. You really can't expect to accomplish a great deal. Even with the best intentions in the world and with the application of considerable skill, teachers often help to perpetuate a system of inequality by transmitting to students in myriad ways the message, "This is your station in society! Act, talk, perform, *learn* according to it and no more is expected of you."[3]

Novels and historical accounts of life in the antebellum South are full of colloquialisms that had as their most significant message the idea that certain individuals are simply not able to measure up or to accomplish what others can hope to achieve, simply because of the color of their skin. It is also interesting to review some of the literature of the 1850's dealing with the "natural" limitations of the female brain. So many of the arguments were used again a hundred years later in almost an identical way to attempt to prove the innate mental limitations of the Blacks.

The Theory of the Self-Fulfilling Prophecy

When Cooley and Mead developed their theory of the looking-glass self, they touched on the significant others, but it remained for Robert Merton some twenty years later to develop the theory of the self-fulfilling prophecy. Stated quite simply, the theory holds that in most situations people tend to do what is expected of them, even to the extent that a false expectation can evoke a false response or, at least, a kind of behavior that is not usual for the person involved.[4]

This is true in all phases of life. There are some people who go on year after year in a kind of "failure-complex" pattern—everything they do seems to turn out wrong. Then there are those for whom life always seems to be a rose garden. "The rich get richer and the poor get poorer." "Nothing succeeds like success." "Everything he touches turns to gold." All these homespun quotes are saying essentially the same thing, namely, that one's view of one's self goes a long way toward determining how one deals with life. The way most people behave is a direct outgrowth of the way they *think* others see them. This is especially damaging to a person who is unsure of him or herself or who has developed a poor self-image. On the other hand, a person with a strong positive self-image can be creative, original, and successful even in the face of seemingly overwhelming odds. A positive view of self gives one a tremendous advantage in dealing with life.[5]

The Teacher as Prophet

The group of significant others who most influence young learners' views of themselves are their teachers. When these significant others have developed a mental set about a learner or a group of learners, there is little that the learner(s) can do to influence the final results. Even the sympathetic teacher often errs on the side of too much empathy. Leacock, in her study of teaching and learning in city schools, discovered the phenomenon of the self-fulfilling prophecy operating as sympathetic teachers were lowering their expectations for those children who came from severely disadvantaged socio-economic backgrounds.[6]

Rosenthal and Jacobson did an interesting study of the effects of positive teacher expectations on children's achievement. They found that children who were in fact chosen by chance but who were described to their teachers as being "fast learners," showed considerable gain during one academic year—even greater progress than that of other students in the class who in fact had higher IQ's. When questioned, the teachers also described the "fast learners" more favorably with regard to their disposition, curiosity, and chances for success. When the authors looked more deeply into the teachers' attitudes, they found to their utter amazement that the teachers were upset when the other children in class made more progress than the teachers expected! One conclusion that can be drawn from this aspect of the study is that teachers resent being proved wrong in their prophecy about students and that there are hazards for the students in unpredicted intellectual growth![7] What a very sad commentary on the quality of teacher–student interactions and the kinds of self-concepts and expectations teachers often unwittingly transmit to their students.

The Permanent Label

In her book, *Spearpoint,* Sylvia Ashton-Warner is amazed at the obsession that American educators seem to have with grading, marking, and reporting. She says that in her country only commodities like meat and wool are "graded" and that "grades" do not seem appropriate for people.[8]

One of the most abused bits of administrative material is the cumulative record card. This card represents the objective and subjective judgments of teachers, year after year. Almost invariably these judgments follow a pattern of sameness that is in itself defeating: Oh, yes, I've had four of the Jones' boys and they are all alike. Don't hold out too much hope for that kid. He has been a problem since the first day he came to school. Look here! (triumphantly) John's last year's teacher said the very same things about him that I have been noticing. Etc., etc., etc. Each teacher seeks to validate his or her opinions and prophecies, the total result being that the "cum" card becomes a permanent label which stays with students all of their academic lives unless something dramatic happens to cause a change.

Prophetic Counseling

Similar to the "cum" card, much of the educational and vocational counseling that takes place in the school is affected by the self-fulfilling prophecy. It is the rare counselor, indeed, who suggests to the lower-class child that he or she has the talent to become a professional person or an artist. Usually, these children are advised to go into semiskilled professions or unskilled jobs where the pay is good, and, perhaps unsaid, the requirements are low enough for their abilities. Almost invariably the vocational expectations teachers have for children from the lower class conform to the accepted lower-class values. The same consistency seems to prevail with regard to the middle- and upper-class students who are usually urged to choose vocations which match what the teacher sees as middle- and upper-class values and career expectations.

Prophetic Discipline

Another area of school experience which reflects rather accurately the self-fulfilling prophecy is the management of discipline problems by the classroom teacher or the principal or the vice-principal. In Leacock's study, second-grade children from low-income families gave as behaviors their teachers found desirable such things as "not hollering," "doing what you're told," and "not making the teacher scream."[9] Thus, it would appear that the school begins very early to teach children their "place" in the society and sets for them those expectations which conform to their socio-economic conditions.

Prophetic Dollars

While it has always seemed oversimplistic to equate the quality of education with the dollars spent, one must ultimately come to the realization that the money which communities and nations allocate to various endeavors does reflect the value systems of the group. While there is no proven statistical relationship between quality of education and dollars spent, it does seem clear that the quality of life in any school is bound to have an effect on both students and teachers.

No one can argue that comfortable furniture, hot lunches, adequate resource materials, and well-paid teachers all have effects on the school experience and those involved in it.

Years ago, Sol Hurok proved that the general public tends to behave in a fashion consistent with the physical surroundings. Thus, he pioneered the idea of carpeted movie houses, lavishly decorated and surrounded by soothing organ music. The same psychological principle operates in any kind of physical setting.

However, more than a consideration of whether or not the paint is peeling in a school, there is the value system reflected by the priority given to the money spent—be it the $438 per pupil expenditure in Alabama or the $1,237 in New York.[10] There was a time when the old and out-dated textbooks no longer in use in a "good" school in a given district were sent over to the "poor" school—usually in the low socio-economic section of the community. This kind of "charity" is itself a form of self-fulfilling prophecy. It says to the kids in the poor school something like, some day you might be able to achieve our values, or some day you might be able to aspire to jobs and professions and homes and incomes like ours. Thus, the kinds of decisions made by school boards and school superintendents are themselves fairly good indicators of the expectations these officials hold for the children involved.

The Prophetic Curriculum

In addition to the physical condition of the school and its resources, the types of curriculum choices are another indicator of society's attempt to forecast—if not determine—the future of its students. Ability grouping in the elementary schools and tracking in the secondary schools both have a subtle but decisive effect on the vocational choices of the students. A young person who has never been in a good science lab will probably not even think of the possibility of going to medical school. One who has never had art materials or any kind of adequate art instruction might never find out whether or not he or she has a special talent for art. The same is true for every phase of human endeavor. We cannot prepare for jobs, vocations, or skills about which we know nothing. We cannot wish for those things we do not know exist. We cannot strive for those positions which have been set so far above us that we "know" we can never achieve them. Thus, the very planning of the administrative organization for teaching and the curriculum choices made by teachers and official committees all combine to forecast the ultimate result of the educational experience, namely, the life experience.

The Teacher as the Key

However, besides the disparity in money spent, besides the variation of available resources, there remains the most important factor of all:

the humanizing or de-humanizing attitude of the teacher. Truly fine teachers can be found in all kinds of schools in all parts of the country—teachers who are deeply concerned about the future of the children they teach and about the effects of the school experience on the self-image of each child. If anyone ever developed a foolproof formula for producing such teachers, all the other problems would fade into insignificance. However, it is most unfair to deliberately hamper a good teacher by not giving him or her the material tools and administrative support that will enable him or her to do the best teaching job of which he or she is capable.

All that has been said is important only in so far as it helps the teacher place emphasis on the *self* of the student and not on his or her economic, social, or even academic condition. The many curriculum meetings held each year could, in all probability, be much more fruitful if they focussed on the humaneness of the teacher-pupil relationship and the power transmitted to students by a teacher who really believes in them.

The Case of Ellen

Ellen was an unusually bright third-grade student in a small church-supported school. She was delighted when it was announced that a new art teacher was to be hired who would teach special art classes to each grade on a once-a-week basis.

At the first scheduled art class, the new teacher was nervous and uncertain of just how to begin with nine and ten year olds. The teacher herself had just completed art school and had had no experience in classroom teaching. Her first assignment was to draw a still-life which she arranged with great care—an apple on a purple velvet background. The students were somewhat baffled, but they began to try to draw.

Ellen was very frustrated because she had no idea of how to begin. However, since she was the product of a most strict home and of several years of the discipline of a church school, she was accustomed to doing as she was told. Therefore, bravely, she took up her crayons and drew something that was very, very far from the "still-life" model.

The teacher came around to each pupil, criticized, made some begin over, and in general demoralized the class. When she came to Ellen, she was completely exasperated and vented her own frustration by grabbing Ellen's poor attempt and tearing it into several parts, saying, "That's terrible! You will never be an artist!" Ellen was very upset and began to cry. The more upset she became, the more abusive the teacher became. Needless to say, the young art teacher did not keep her position very long. However, in the short time she was there she had done great damage to the self-concept of many of the students.

Ellen went through elementary school, high school, and college studiously avoiding any kind of art classes. However, when she took the Graduate Record Exam for admission to a graduate school, she was amazed when the counselor told her that her aptitude scores indicated a high potential in the field of art. However, the damage was too long-standing to be changed dramatically. Ellen found her creative outlet in writing and interior decorating, always wistfully wondering if she might have been an acceptable artist had she not been so completely convinced of her lack of aptitude in the drawing of the apple on the velvet cloth in the third grade.

Possible Solutions

1. Most of the problem could have been avoided had Ellen tried over and over again to perform acceptably.

2. The art teacher could have avoided the confrontation had she been more patient.

3. The entire situation might not have happened if the art teacher had also had some training in the art of teaching and in the problems of dealing with young children.

4. The parents should have gone to the school and complained about the methods used by the art teacher.

Would you choose any of these solutions? If so, you may write your explanation below. However, if you would not choose any of these, you may go on to the next page and write your solution to the problem.

Your Solution to Ellen's Problem

Questions For Discussion

1. Was the problem really Ellen's?

2. How does this incident point up the long-lasting effect of the self-fulfilling prophecy?

The Case of Timmy

A rather small but progressive school system in the Pacific Northwest had engaged a reading consultant to spend several days in an in-service workshop with its primary teachers. The first day's program had gone well, and the teachers were delighted with what they had learned.

During the lunch break, the consultant had noticed a small group of about 15 young children who, she was told, had just failed first grade because they simply couldn't read. They had been assigned to special remedial school for the first six weeks of the summer.

At the end of the first day, the consultant asked the curriculum director if she might have some time to work with the young nonreaders and perhaps use them as a demonstration group for the teachers in the in-service class. The plan was approved and the next day, part of the program was a demonstration with the nonreaders.

Everything went well as the consultant tried various techniques and methods with good results. Only one child did not respond to anything. He was Timmy. He was small, skinny, and black. He was in a constant state of fright and spoke only in a low whisper. The consultant was concerned and determined to try everything possible to break through to Timmy. Finally, she decided to try something different. Instead of asking Timmy to read or write, she asked Timmy to sit way off in the corner of the room and whisper any story he liked into her tape recorder. She set up the recorder and went on working with the other children.

When she went back to Timmy sometime later, he was sitting silently but smiling. She reversed the tape and as she played it back for Timmy, she lettered his story on a large sheet of newsprint. His eyes got bigger and bigger as he heard his own tiny little voice on the recorder and as he saw the consultant transfer these sounds into words on the paper. After the story was finished, the consultant and Timmy read it over again together. The consultant said, "There, Timmy! You not only wrote your own story but you read it with me." "Oh, no, Miss! That ain't my story! It came outa that box! My teacher told my mother that I cain't read or write and that's why I have to go to summer school."

Possible Solutions

1. First grade children should be made to repeat the grade if they cannot read and write at the end of the term.

2. The fact that fifteen first graders out of a rather small enrollment had "failed" first grade because of a reading problem should have been a clue to the administration that all was not well with the methods being employed.

3. Timmy obviously needed some very tender personal attention. His still whispering at the age of seven was indicative of a social–psychological problem which probably was the basis of his reading problem.

Would you choose any one or more of these solutions? If so, you may write your explanation below. However, if you would not choose any of these, you may go on the next page and write your solution to the problem.

Your Solution to Timmy's Problem

Questions For Discussion

1. Do you agree with the effort of the consultant to demonstrate that each child has some ability, no matter how small or hidden?

2. How would you have handled the situation had you been the consultant? If you were Timmy's teacher, what would you have done after the demonstration?

3. Do you think that Timmy's being black and small and frightened had anything to do with his failure?

4. How much chance do you think Timmy has of overcoming the prophecy that the teacher and his mother had so fixed in his mind?

Your Sample Case

If you have witnessed or experienced a case in your own school life that you think emphasizes the self-fulfilling prophecy, describe the case and explain how you saw it handled. Did you agree with the solution? Why?

Notes

1. George Bernard Shaw, *Pygmalion,* Act V. (New York: Brentanos, 1916), p. 208.

2. *The Congressional Record,* Tuesday, April 14, 1964. (Washington, D.C.: Government Printing Office, 1964), p. 656.

3. Eleanor Burke Leacock, *Teaching and Learning in City Schools.* (New York: Basic Books), 1969, p. 8.

4. Robert K. Merton, *Social Theory and Social Structure.* (New York: The Free Press, 1968), pp. 475–90.

5. Arthur W. Combs, *Perceiving, Behaving, Becoming.* ASCD 1962 Yearbook. (Washington, D.C.: Association for Supervision and Curriculum Development, N.E.A., 1962), p. 52.

6. Leacock, *Teaching and Learning in City Schools,* pp. 208–9.

7. R. Rosenthal and L. F. Jacobson, "Teacher Expectations for the Disadvantaged," *Scientific American,* Vol. 218 No. 4 (1968), pp. 19–23.

8. Sylvia Ashton-Warner, *Spearpoint.* (New York: Alfred Knopf, 1972), p. 125.

9. Leacock, *Teaching and Learning in City Schools,* p. 184.

10. Christopher Jencks, *Inequality.* (New York: Basic Books, 1972), p. 24.

5

The Learner as Curriculum Builder

> *Do I contradict myself?*
> *Very well, then, I contradict myself.*
> *I am large, I contain multitudes.*

WALT WHITMAN[1]

An interesting tale in Greek mythology is the story of Procrustes. According to legend, this heartless robber not only took his victims' valuables but found great delight in torturing them. His chief means of tormenting them was to make them lie down on an iron bed. If the victim's body was too long to fit the bed, Procrustes proceeded to cut off his legs; if the victim was too short, Procrustes would stretch his arms and legs out of socket to fit. Some accounts credit Procrustes with having two iron beds, one shorter than the other. (Maybe this was an early effort at providing for individual differences.)

While one can laugh or cry at the cruel inflexibility of Procrustes, it is not so easy to know how to react to the years of student "torture" by teachers and curriculum builders. Adults have always seemed to feel that they know what is best for young people and have gone about "lengthening" or "shortening" the learner to fit the plan.

There is at least one university where all efforts to revise the catalog have failed because the registrar has spent too much money having storage shelves built to the traditional size and shape of the old catalog. Is it any wonder that students feel that they have been prepackaged and programmed?

Traditionally, what has been called the "curriculum" at any level of education has usually meant that content the student must master in order to go on to the next level of schooling. Only in very rare cases, as in vocational education and in some professional schools and colleges, has the end objective of the curriculum been to prepare the student for at least a part of life—the professional part. We have only recently become aware, as we noted in Chapter 1, that "the head has a body." In the elementary and secondary schools, almost invariably the end objective of any grade level study plan is to prepare the student for the next grade level. Thus, there has developed a split-level consciousness so aptly expressed by students when they speak of life outside the school as the "real" world. Since the opposite of "real" is "unreal," one can only infer that many students view the twelve to fourteen-year curriculum as an "unreal" plan that has very little to do with their future, or even present, lives.

What Is the Curriculum?

The word *curriculum* comes from the Latin and means a course, a sequence, a continuum. It came into academic usage from the term *curriculum vitae* which means the course of one's life. In all its definitions, it has usually meant a highly personal sequence of events related to only one individual. We each have our own curriculum, whether it be a reading curriculum, a sewing curriculum, a sports curriculum, or a cooking curriculum.

Wouldn't it seem absurd if you went into a bookstore and were told that you could choose only those books marked for your age level? "Good morning. How old are you?" "Oh, the books for thirty-year-olds are on the last shelf in this row. The others are for twenty-year-olds or forty-year-olds as marked. You must choose from the proper age group." Silly as that sounds, it is exactly what we do to students when we discourage them or refuse altogether to allow them to read or learn out of their age-grade level as we have determined it. How far we have come from the highly individualized connotation of curriculum!

The term curriculum seems to most people to mean that required, structured, inflexible sequence of learning experiences determined by the teacher and the school authorities. In the vast majority of cases, the person who is to pursue this curriculum is not even known nor are the curriculum builders aware of his or her interests or goals or abilities. He is a "faceless" fourth-grader or she is a liberal arts junior who must be required to do these things before he can become a fifth-grader or she a liberal arts senior. All these arbitrary decisions about which curriculum a student must follow leave out the most important factor, namely, what the learner is like. What does he think he needs? What are his goals? Does the plan fit her needs? It is almost as if someone decided that you must wear size small clothes before you can wear size medium, then large. Even ready-to-wear that is not tailor-made needs alterations. There are very few human beings who fit the perfect size developed by clothing designers. In the same way, there are few students who "fit" the norms and achievement levels arbitrarily arrived at by the curriculum experts.

One comforting thought: regardless of the best laid plans of curriculum builders, learners generally follow their own curriculum. If it is not possible for them to do this in a classroom, then they rush to leave school at the earliest possible moment to work on their personal curriculum. Maybe this is racing a car around a drag strip, or reading "adult" literature, or exploring human sexuality, or drawing, or architectual design, or scientific investigation. The young high school scientist who developed algae flour for the production of bakery products did so at home after school hours and then finally persuaded the teacher that it was a worthwhile science project.

Make a list of all the skills required of you in any one day of normal living. Along side each skill try to identify how and where and when you learned the skill. Do you find that the majority of the things you do each day were learned somewhere other than in a classroom?

Who Should Design the Curriculum?

Since the curriculum is such a highly personalized set of choices, it seems to follow logically that the learner should have a say in deciding upon it. True, a student's choices are not always wise ones but they are, nevertheless, important. Young people, like all of us, will learn through mistakes and will find that there are some skills they need to acquire if they are going to achieve their goals in life.

In the totally open school students are allowed free choice to follow their interests wherever they may lead. Perhaps this is too extreme for American society just yet, but why not allow learners to participate in decisions affecting their own learning? Let them help design the Procrustean Bed upon which they are going to be confined for so many years!

One of the biggest problems with student participation in curriculum committees is that not only do the "adults" dominate, but even when they do not, students almost invariably choose the "right" things because they have become so indoctrinated with the idea that the schools know best.

The Language Experience approach to reading, introduced by Sylvia Ashton-Warner in her work with Maori children, is an example of a successful balance between structure and freedom of choice. Her emphasis is on the child's own words and ideas, fears and wishes. She uses the child's own verbal expressions to help each one design his or her own reader or book, and, to the child's great delight, he or she becomes an author at an age when other children are "failing" first grade reading or second grade math.[2] Not only are children participating in developing their own curriculum, but they are beginning to enjoy a positive self-concept that makes them feel worthy and able and proud.

This type of approach to teaching works best when we are open to the use of any number of vehicles. In some schools, however, dominoes or playing cards are "outlawed" as math devices, the use of dice to teach the laws of chance is frowned upon (even in cities where gambling is legal), and "unacceptable" words and social situations are not tolerated, even to demonstrate sound social or anthropological situations. Such restrictions limit teachers in their ability to set up creative and successful learning situations. Instead, they place greater emphasis on the devices and words and disregard the significance of the learning task itself.

Modalities of Learning

Just as we each have our own personal curriculum, we each have our own individual approach to learning, our own style of learning. A learning style is related to one's personal manner of sensing, responding, organizing, and interpreting the world. These components have not yet been adequately dealt with in educational research. We have spent a great deal of time and money on evaluation and ways of measuring achievement but we know very little about measuring the route by which the learner arrived at his level of accomplishment. Giving the learner a task and then telling him exactly how to do it does not reveal anything about his learning style. The teacher's directions become "the way—the only way" and any creative approach the child could have developed is nipped in the bud.

Let's listen to a typical reading lesson. Dorothy is having great difficulty with the pre-primer. She misses many words like *run, get, jump.* Yet, when she dictates a story from her own experience, she can read words like *flower, grass, petals.* She can recognize these words in her word bank as well as in context. She glows with pride. "How come these hard words are easy for me and the easy words out of the book are so hard?"[3]

Dorothy is obviously responding to clues out of her own curriculum. Does this mean that any one mode is more desirable or stronger? Maybe. What it does mean is that personal words have meaning that comes from within the learner rather than from a contrived depersonalized list.

Examples like Dorothy should cause a shift in the teacher's view of what is appropriate content. In addition, it should cause a re-focusing on the cognitive style of the learner rather than on the skills, materials and subject matter to be "covered."[4]

We all have preferences and individual styles. We use all our senses but in varying degrees of intensity depending on the problem to be solved. It is Sunday and you want to mail a package or a letter. No post office is open. You handle the package or letter in such a way as to concentrate on the *kinesthetic sense* to approximate the correct postage. Or, you are trying to describe the meaning of the word *velvet* to a blind child. It simply cannot be done without letting the child *touch* a piece of velvet. You are telling someone over the phone about the beautiful blue shirt you bought. "What shade of blue is it?" How do you answer that?

Much too often, in directing the learning of others, we ignore all these processes in our rush to get to the end product—the answer, the "right" answer, "my answer," "the only answer" or—horror of horrors—"the answer in the book!" Our modes of responding to our world are as highly individualized as are our own experiences or as the media through which we choose to respond. Yet, most teaching is done as if the only sensory receptors the learner had at his command are his eyes and ears.

Imagery, Modalities, and Successful Teaching

Perhaps it is because adults are more likely to be verbalizers that teachers assume that the verbal mode is superior to other modes of learning. How can we hope to integrate living, learning, and teaching if we do not relearn how to trust imagination, humor, and delight in new ideas. When we teach well, our minds grow alive and alert and the students themselves provide us with instant feedback concerning our talents. Their interest, their enthusiasm, their sparked intelligence all tell us when we have done a good job—that we have made learning a natural, delightful experience. The teacher and the learner are not machines in spite of the signals from our environment. Trust your imagination and that of your students. Trust the classroom as a natural space—like your own home—which allows for movement in and out, for highs and lows of interest, for moments of excitement and periods of quiet, for success and failure. Teach and learn with the rhythms of personal time.[5] Trust yourself and others. Let students explore new ways of doing things, of thinking about things. Suspect absolutes and provide the kind of home in which students can know that learning is the product of spontaneity, of genuine caring and true openness. If you can set this kind of tone in your classroom, don't worry about what research says concerning modalities. The modalities will show themselves in the accepting environment and will blossom into a richness neither you nor your students could have deliberately planned.

The Case of the Totem Pole

Sylvia was a student teacher of junior high school social studies. For eight weeks she had been assigned to a group of lower-middle-class ninth graders, about one-third of whom were Indian students.

After Sylvia had observed for only a week, the cooperating teacher became ill and Sylvia had to be in charge. The students didn't seem to take her teacher role seriously and began to be restless and disinterested. The Indian students even began to show open hostility. Four of them followed her after school one day, taunting and insulting her until she reached her apartment. When Sylvia reported the incident, the principal only shrugged and said that this wasn't a matter for school discipline since it had not taken place on the school grounds.

Now, Sylvia was beginning to be frightened. Yet, she continued to feel that somehow she should be able to reach these young people. As she was working on lesson plans, she ran across an article about a teacher in an all Indian school who had motivated her students by letting them construct a miniature village of their own tribe. The next day Sylvia took the article to her class and read it to them. Then she asked for some feedback. To her great surprise, the students loved the idea of "doing something that's not in the book." When she approached the principal, all he said was that he didn't care what she did with that class as long as it kept them out of trouble and it didn't cost any money.

Back to the class: "We have permission to do whatever we like but we don't have any money." "Let's talk about what we can do anyway!" One Indian student suggested that, since the school mascot was an eagle, perhaps they could carve one. Another student picked up that idea and suggested that they make a totem pole with the eagle on top. "Where could we get a pole?" "From the telephone company!" Sure enough, the phone company agreed to donate the pole but they couldn't deliver it. Back to the class: "Who can get the pole and bring it to school?" "My brother has a truck. We'll get it here somehow!"

The pole was delivered to the school and was on the front lawn when the students arrived the next day. It was a natural process to have one group research the history of the totem pole, one report on the specific designs of the local tribe, one consult with the art and shop teachers about materials and tools, and sketches.

The ninth-grade totem pole soon became the focal point of the whole school. Since only three weeks remained in the Spring semester, students began coming early and staying late and working during the lunch hour. Even some students who weren't in the class became involved. They had heated discussions solving problems, making decisions, checking authenticity, making designs, carving, and painting.

Finally the totem pole was finished. The students dug the hole, poured the cement, and set the pole. Parents came on closing day especially to see this famous Totem Pole.

Sylvia has gone on to another state for a permanent job but the Totem Pole still stands in front of the junior high school—a beautiful reminder that students can truly enjoy learning if they are given the chance to develop their own curriculum.

Possible Solutions

1. One solution is Sylvia's. Do you agree with it? Why?

2. Another solution would have been to request a change of student-teaching assignment to a school where she might have had better direction and administrative support.

3. On the occasion of the Indian students taunting her, Sylvia should have called the police.

4. Sylvia could have avoided all problems by just sticking to the lesson plans and demanding that students conform or fail.

Would you choose any of these solutions? If so, you may write your explanation below. However, if you would not choose any of these, you may go on to the next page and write your solution to the problem.

Your Solution to Sylvia's Problem

The Case of Pauline

A teacher of a sophomore English class in a small private boarding school had received permission to substitute a more recent biography, *Damien the Leper,* for the usual required book, *The Americanization of Edward Bok.* Therefore, she was disappointed when several students appeared disinterested. She was especially concerned about Pauline who just sat through each day's class: no reaction, no written assignments, no character sketches, nothing!

When the teacher called on Pauline deliberately to draw her into discussion, it only created more tension. When she spoke to her about not handing in any assignments, Pauline became hostile.

One day the teacher was circulating among the discussion groups and walked over to where Pauline was sitting apart from the others. There on an ordinary piece of notebook paper Pauline had made a sketch of her impression of Damien. It was beautifully sensitive, warm and loving in its disfigurement, showing all the care and concern Damien felt for his dear lepers. Pauline had not only read the book, she had made a most faithful character sketch of Damien. As soon as classes were over for the day, the teacher invited Pauline to go with her to the art store in the village where they bought paper, pastel pencils, brushes, and whatever Pauline thought she would need to make a larger color sketch.

For days Pauline worked quietly and alone. Some of the students became curious but the teacher asked that they be patient and not interfere.

At the close of the semester when the English class presented a cooperative book report on *Damien the Leper*—the history of the Hawaiian Islands, the geography, the music, the medical studies on leprosy, the dedication of the man himself—the centerpiece was Pauline's beautiful color sketch of Damien.

Possible Solutions

1. Do you approve of the teacher's handling of Pauline? If so, please comment on that.

2. The teacher could have called Pauline in for a private conference and demanded that she prepare and hand in all the required work.

3. The teacher could have gone to the head-mistress and asked that Pauline be given some counseling by a professional psychologist.

Would you choose any of these solutions? If so, you may write your explanation below. However, if you would not choose any of these, you may go on to the next page and write your solution to the problem.

Your Solution to Pauline's Problem

Your Sample Case

If you have witnessed or experienced a case in your own school life that you think indicates the importance of the student's participation in curriculum planning or of the significance of individual modalities, describe the case and explain how it was solved. Did you agree with the solution? Why?

Notes

1. Walt Whitman. "Song of Myself," *American Poetry,* edited by Karl Shapiro (New York: Thomas Y. Crowell, 1960), 69–105.

2. Sylvia Ashton-Warner, *Teacher.* (New York: Simon and Shuster, 1963).

3. Frances Minor. "The Nature of Difficulty: Clues From Children," *Urban Review,* Oct. (1974): 258–261.

4. Minor, "The Nature of Difficulty: Clues From Children."

5. Kenneth Lincoln. "Poetics of Learning," *College English* (Sept. 1974), 90–99.

SUMMARY—PART I

In the first five chapters we have considered some of the important concepts related to the central figure in the learning process: the learner.

While all living beings have basic physical needs, human beings also have emotional, social, and psychological needs. While students can hardly learn on an empty stomach, food, clothing, and shelter only form the setting in which the other needs can be met. One of the most important emotional and psychological needs is a good self-concept, an acceptance of one's self as a worthwhile human being. If students feel rejected, they may see the school as a hostile environment in which little learning can take place.

If learners develop good self-images, then it is not difficult for them to become self-directed, self-disciplined, and self-controlled! They think of their ideas—like themselves—as worthwhile and they are willing to take the responsibility for what they think and say and do.

In many cases, the teacher, the other students, and the parents have a long-lasting influence on the learner. No matter how hard the students may try to become responsible and self-directed, if the significant others in their lives do not reflect good images of them, they get caught in the triple-play trap of becoming what they think others think they are.

On the other hand, if the significant others reflect a strong positive self-image, the students can assume sufficient responsibility to become their own curriculum builders, expressing individuality in their modalities of learning.

This chapter viewed the learner as the single most important element in the learning process.

Part II

The Teacher

6 The Teacher in Focus

When I was young my teachers were the old.
I gave up fire for form till I was cold.
I suffered like metal being cast;
I went to school to age, to learn the past.

Now I am old, my teachers are the young.
What can't be molded must be cracked and sprung.
I strain at lessons fit to start a suture;
I go to school to learn the future.

ROBERT FROST[1]

The young of all living species learn the first lessons of life from adult members of their group. This is true of birds, animals, insects, and especially, human beings. Since the beginning of history—and surely before—the young have learned to hunt, to fish, to make war, to survive, to love—all within the context of the family, the group, the tribe, or in whatever pattern of social organization prevailed. Anthropologists describe a great variety of young-adult relationships, but always, regardless of time or place, there has been the imitative learning faithfully patterned after the language, behavior, and values of the adults.

While the most significant adults in a young learner's life are his parents and the elder members of his family, the human race has a long history of designating certain others as teachers.[2] Usually these tutors were chosen because of their wisdom, experience, and reputation for moral integrity. In some cases, the choice was determined by some specific skill. For example, in military education the tutor was selected for bravery and physical endurance; in oratory, he was chosen for his eloquence and forcefulness.

Since the days of the first rabbis, through the pre-Christian era and into the Middle Ages, Western civilization has valued the training and education given to the young by a qualified and respected teacher. Jesus himself was best known as a teacher as were Buddha, Gandhi, and others.

All through the ages, until the eighteenth and nineteenth centuries, such careful tutoring was usually given only to a very elite and highly selected group—the children of the very rich, those of royal blood, candidates for the church or the military. Only occasionally was a talented "commoner" brought into the ruler's palace or into the monastery to have his education subsidized. Michaelangelo is a good example, but there were many others who sought and obtained "patrons" who took the responsibility for sponsoring their education.

It was not until the early revolutionary period in Europe that education began to be seen as the right of all citizens and teachers began to be thought of as public servants. Even then, it was long understood that the teacher's rights over the child were *in loco parentis* (in place of the parent). Thus the teacher has been from the beginning, for almost every culture, the surrogate parent or, in some cases, the surrogate conscience of the nation, employed specifically to teach those values which the nation proclaims to prize but does not faithfully practice.[3]

The role of the teacher has developed into an almost indefinable list of contradictions: instructor, disciplinarian, counselor, confessor, motivator, evaluator, skills builder, behavior modifier, community helper, example setter, civic leader, baby-sitter, collector of milk money and tickets at basket ball games, attendance checker, curriculum builder, public relations person, experimenter (with no right to be wrong ever), and as long an additional list of duties as you would like to make. The teacher's role has become a kind of garbage-can role into which we throw anything that the rest of society cannot or will not take on.[4] All the while, the teacher has been expected to fill a somewhat secondary and subservient social role, just a step above that of a household servant.

As late as the 1930's, female teachers who got married were immediately dismissed from their jobs. It has never been quite clear whether morality or economics was the basis for such practice. In any case, the teacher was expected to set a very high standard of behavioral example for the students as well as the community. Much of this is specifically characteristic of the Puritan Ethic which for so long permeated American life. The "Miss Doves" are no longer with us and if they were, in all probability they would not be acceptable to a large segment of American society. There are still pockets of Puritanism where Miss Dove would fit very nicely, however. Unionism, Equal Right's Amendments, Women's Lib, Integration, Collective Bargaining, Tenure, Civil Rights, the new morality, sexual freedom—all these political and social movements have radically changed the view society once had of the teacher. In addition, these factors have all served to complicate the lives of teachers and often to distract from their primary role and function. Any teacher who is in the midst of a court case or some other kind of controversy cannot give his or her full time and attention or best efforts to the teaching act. The lives of all of us have been made almost unbearably complicated by the various State and National legislative rulings, the invasion of privacy, the strange definitions of accountability, and, in general, the overall enlargement of government. These aggravations are even more marked in the case of the professional person. At this writing, it is becoming necessary even for elementary teachers to begin to think about some form of malpractice insurance. Two court cases substantiate the fear of teachers concerning such possible action—one case involves a college student who filed suit against the college and the professor because, she claims, she did not learn anything in his class. The other involves a case against the school board of a large city school system. The parents of a recent high school graduate claim that their son was graduated without being able to read. Academic Freedom may be the next sacrificial lamb on the altar of absolute justice!

Physical and Mental Health

In this profession which still seems to expect the teacher to be all things to all people, it is especially important that the teacher maintain good physical and mental health. In addition to the "clock hours" or "seat time" required of the teacher, there are all the other "extras": parent conferences, teachers' meetings, school board meetings, PTA meetings, local, state and national professional organization meetings and committees, curriculum planning meetings, report cards and grade sheets, lesson plans, reading assignments, research and planning, emergency personnel counseling, and many other expectations which all add up to a life of full-time dedication which often leaves little or no time for rest, relaxation, or even normal living. There are few professions in modern society which require so much in return for so little. Society has taken ready advantage of the fact that most truly professional teachers derive great satisfaction from giving of themselves and their talents. There are traces of the "missionary" attitude still remaining on the part of teachers themselves as well as on the part of society and administration toward teachers.

The excessive institutionalization of the educational process has put teachers in an almost untenable position. They are probably the only professionals who are expected to function independently within a managerial structure which often does not understand or appreciate creative self-direction. Demands from students and parents on the one hand vie for attention with administrative and institutional demands on the other. Both militate against teachers' sense of personal responsibility for their own competence and excellence.

In the midst of such a demanding role, the teacher has no choice but to try to stay physically fit. This, too, is necessary in the face of sick leave policies which, though somewhat generous, often carry serious (hidden) penalties for frequent use of sick leave. In some instances, teachers are so fearful of reprisals and criticism that they neglect their general health to the detriment of all concerned. Many educational institutions are still operating on the philosophy that as long as the body is present the mind is being productive—an idea which originated with the Industrial Revolution and began to be applied to education at the beginning of the 1900's.

Reasonable rest, adequate diet, healthful exercise, lessening of tensions, some recreation, and regular medical check-ups are imperative. Anyone who is physically ill does not belong in a classroom. Preventive health care is especially important for the teacher since the attitudes of the teacher affect the lives of so many others. Some school systems, aware of the importance of preventive health care, arrange and pay for regular physical exams for their personnel. Others plan the kind of daily schedule and physical surroundings that guarantee the teacher a bit of privacy and quiet in an agreeable and attractive space each day. The time has gone when physically handicapped persons are kept out of the teaching profession. Some very inspiring and successful teachers work all their professional lives in a wheel chair or with the aid of a prosthesis of one kind or another. This is quite a different concept from physical illness or nervous disorder.

Mental health is certainly as important—if not more important—than physical well-being. The two are very closely interrelated. Sometimes in visiting classrooms one almost gets the impression that some teachers chose the profession as a revenge against society, so bitter and sadistic have they become.

Persons of weak character and bland personalities or those who give evidence of the beginnings of social maladjustment or emotional disorders should be spotted early in the pre-service education and guided out of teacher education careers. However, it must be kept in mind that there are very few really reliable predictors of success in teaching except actual teaching. Tests of social maturity should be balanced against early performance in a classroom situation and counseling should be based on both kinds of evaluation. Courses in understanding one's self, in personal mental health, in self-enhancing education should be required of the teacher candidate.

It is indeed unfortunate that most schools of teacher preparation do not have any adequate means of offering alternatives to those students who are obviously not fitted for a lifetime of teaching. Most schools of education simply do not know how or are not in a financial position to offer related career training. Demographic and economic factors are creating panic in some schools of education. Most of the teacher-training institutions were staffed to provide teachers for the explosion in education in the late 1950's and the early 1960's. Now, with reduced enrollments and budget cut-backs, administrators are at a loss to know which way to turn. One author makes some very concrete suggestions: Eliminate non-productive programs, "re-tool" the faculty, offer elective courses which appeal to non-education majors, plan programs, recruit flexible faculty, develop cooperative programs with academic departments, offer career alternatives.[5] The problem with all these suggestions is that for the most part, schools and colleges of education have become so "hardened" in their self-image that it is impossible to change. They are so mired in an era of fiscal change and uncertainty and so short on creative leadership, that one can only wonder what is the future of such institutions.[6]

One can also wonder about the mental health and sound professional leadership that can be offered by the graduates of such programs. Depressed, discouraged, hostile—in large part because of the irrelevance and dullness of course offerings and requirements—these young teachers begin their careers in a state of angry frustration which becomes deeper as they try to cope with *real* students in a *real* world for which they are unprepared.

There are few situations as personally destructive as being cast in a role for which one is totally unsuited. It is estimated that a very large percent of the people who work in the United States hate their jobs. Thus, the enormous expenditure for recreation and hobby activities. If this is true of the work force in general, then it is probably equally true of the teaching profession.

Preparation

As was noted above, most of the teachers presently engaged in elementary and secondary teaching in the late 1970's are products of a "crash" program developed in the 1950's and 1960's when there was a crying need for teachers. Because of the pressures put on teacher-training institutions during that period, not much was done to strengthen the academic background of those who were certified to teach. A few states have stood fast on the five-year program (a liberal arts degree plus one year of teacher education). In most colleges and universities, however, the requirements in professional courses constitute more than one-third of the student's entire college program.

It is a fact that hardly needs testing here that one cannot teach what one does not know. It is also generally accepted that the teachers of the United States are by and large less well educated in the liberal arts than are the members of almost any other profession. The scores on various tests—like the Graduate Record Exam—all point to the fact that many students who are preparing for a teaching career graduate without adequate background in the social sciences (especially economics and anthropology), a lack of skill in the use of the English language, and a great fear of math and science. It appears that we have spent much too much time on the "how" of teaching and far too little on the "what." We are producing mechanics rather than thinkers and creative problem-solvers. How will these teachers cope with schools of the future when they are really not ready to cope with schools of the present?

The five-year program has many advantages. In addition to another year of maturity and experience, students can become somewhat expert in at least one field of human knowledge before they try to take on the process of teaching in all or any field. Besides, a good four-year liberal arts education might serve as an eye-opener to students with regard to alternate professional opportunities they might not have heard of otherwise. Travel, a variety of work experience, and a good measure of general literacy are valuable items to have in one's background if one is thinking of teaching as a career.

Enthusiasm

Generally, most of us enjoy doing those things that we do well—whether teaching, cooking, or playing bridge. Enthusiasm and success are tightly inter-faced and have a highly integrated effect on one another. The enthusiastic teacher can often motivate even the most disinterested student and brighten the learning prospects of the most discouraged. However, to be effective, enthusiasm must be real. Students are wise in the ways of deceit.

Here, as in other areas of human relationships, the teacher usually can reflect only his or her own self-concept. Teachers who are regularly "put down" by their principals or administrators can hardly feel the enthusiasm and exhilaration for generating new ideas in their students. Enthusiasm for learning is contagious and circular; enthusiasm breeds enthusiasm and helps one to overcome the depressing effects of even the most poorly run institution. There are always ways to get around the unimaginative structure of most of our schools. One just has to be willing to take risks. The rewards are great: the heightened sense of self-actualization and the pride of seeing one's students achieve, as one student described, "more than I ever thought I could!" That's enthusiasm. That's learning. That's teaching.

The Case of Mrs. Colby

Mrs. Colby, a young woman in her middle thirties, was married and had three children, all under twelve years old. She had recently moved to a college town and enrolled in the Department of Teacher Education in the college to earn the necessary credits for that state's teaching certificate.

In all of her classes and in her relationships with the professors and younger students, she gave the impression of being a happy, carefree wife and mother; a woman who had enjoyed many advantages during her youth—vacations in Florida, private schools, golf, and tennis. In short, she presented the picture of a well-to-do young woman who had time on her hands and had decided to try teaching just to see how she would like it.

Mrs. Colby completed all the course requirements and was an excellent student-teacher. She received an appointment to teach upper grades in an elementary school in her neighborhood.

As the year progressed, she continued to be successful with her students, doing many innovative things and generally enjoying teaching. The first inkling that all was not well with her private life was when her husband went to the superintendent's office and, in a somewhat irrational tirade, demanded that she be dismissed from her job. The only reason he gave was that she had sued for divorce. The superintendent called the principal; the principal called the university professor who had been Mrs. Colby's counselor and asked for advice.

Since Mrs. Colby and her university counselor had become friends, it was not difficult for the counselor to arrange for a personal visit. In this visit, the story of an unhappy marriage, a philandering husband, a move to a new city to try to give him a new start was told. She had come to the end of her endurance with him and had returned to school in order to qualify herself for a job through which she could achieve some independence.

The university counselor reassured the principal of Mrs. Colby's stability and the incident was forgotten. Next came the divorce in which the husband attempted to cause notoriety and embarrassment. However, this was all settled, and Mrs. Colby continued to be successful in her teaching.

At one point, she remarked to her counselor, "The hours spent in the classroom have been the sanest part of my life in these months. I deeply appreciate your confidence in me."

Throughout this trying time Mrs. Colby was always alert, well-prepared, and enthusiastic in her classroom. Her students were not aware of the great effort she was putting forth to keep her personal problems from interfering with their education.

She has continued to teach and has been successful in a variety of instructional and administrative positions. She has remarried and continues to be a happy, well-adjusted person who finds great satisfaction in her work with and for children.

Possible Solutions

1. The superintendent, the principal, and the university counselor were right in supporting Mrs. Colby, regardless of her husband's attempts to discredit her.

2. Because of the general knowledge in the neighborhood of the home situation, Mrs. Colby should have transferred to a different school.

3. Mrs. Colby should have been dismissed rather than bring criticism on the school system.

4. Mrs. Colby should have received as much moral support as possible because she exhibited real emotional stability in all her professional and personal relationships.

5. When Mrs. Colby became divorced, she should have been dismissed because having a divorced teacher in the classroom indicates that the school system approves of the immoral practice of divorce.

Would you choose any of these solutions? If so, you may write your explanation below. However, if you would not choose any of these, you may go on to the next page and write your solution to the problem.

Your Solution to Mrs. Colby's Problem

The Case of Mrs. Evans

Mrs. Evans was a white teacher in an all black elementary school in a large Midwestern city. She had passed all the certifying examinations and had achieved tenure. The superintendent of the public schools recommended Mrs. Evans to the local college as a student-teacher coordinator. Accordingly, she was assigned a student-teacher majoring in elementary education.

A few days after the student was placed with Mrs. Evans, the college supervisor told his department chairman that he needed some help in evaluating the situation in Mrs. Evans' room. "There is something wrong, but I just can't put my finger on it. Perhaps if you went out there with me you could give me a clue." The next day they went to the school, visiting other student-teachers and saving a reasonable block of time to observe Mrs. Evans' room.

On entering the room, two things struck the chairman. First, the room was antiseptically clean—not a mark on the blackboard, not a picture on the bulletin board, not a pencil out of place on the teacher's desk. Second, although the room was somewhat overcrowded, there were no students sitting in the front row of seats. The student-teacher was sitting quietly in the back of the room.

As the lesson progressed, Mrs. Evans remained behind her desk. At the end of the period, the children were directed to hand in their written assignments in the usual way. The "usual way" turned out to be handing papers up the rows from back to front and placing each row's stack of papers on the empty desk at the front of the row. Then, to the great astonishment of the visitors, Mrs. Evans produced a can of spray disinfectant and sprayed all the stacks of papers before she picked them up.

When the class was dismissed, the two college professors had planned a conference with Mrs. Evans and her student-teacher. After the spray can display, there wasn't much to do except inquire why Mrs. Evans did that. Mrs. Evans readily and cheerfully explained that these children were all black and dirty and full of disease. She herself did all she could to avoid "catching their germs." That is why she never accepted a book or a piece of paper from a student, hand to hand, but had the student place it on the empty desk for spraying. It was quite evident that she found nothing unusual about this process; she had been using it for years.

Without much further conversation, the department chairman explained as carefully as possible that she had decided that the student-teacher was really misplaced in this grade level and would need to be reassigned to another school. The student-teacher was much relieved, and the three visitors left together.

As soon as the department chairman got back to her office, she telephoned the superintendent to report the incident, saying she felt something needed to be done about Mrs. Evans. The superintendent was quite casual in his reply, saying only two things: that Mrs. Evans was a good teacher who never caused any problems and that she had already achieved tenure. Since it was up to the college to place their students where they wished, he saw no reason to become involved.

Possible Solutions

1. Mrs. Evans should have been called to the superintendent's office and asked to explain her behavior.

2. The principal, the superintendent, or the chief personnel officer should have initiated some action whereby Mrs. Evans would have been required to receive some psychological counseling.

3. The college supervisor and the department chairman should not have taken the student-teacher out of this situation.

4. Mrs. Evans was well within her rights as a tenured teacher to do whatever she pleased in her classroom.

5. The college personnel should have taken some responsibility for trying to change Mrs. Evans' erratic behavior.

Would you choose any of these solutions? If so, you may write your explanation below. However, if you would not choose any of these, you may go on to the next page and write your solution to the problem.

Your Solution to Mrs. Evans' Problem

Your Sample Case

If you have witnessed or experienced a case in your own school life that you think emphasizes the physical, mental, or emotional health of the teacher, describe the case and explain how you saw it handled. Did you agree with the solution? Why?

Notes

1. Robert Frost, *The Poetry of Robert Frost,* edited by Edward Connery Lathem. (New York: Holt, Rinehart and Winston). Copyright 1928, © 1969 by Holt, Rinehart and Winston. Copyright © 1956 by Robert Frost. Reprinted by permission of the publisher.

2. Robert Coles, "Growing Up in America—Then and Now," *Time* (December 29, 1975), 27–29.

3. Henry Steele Commager, "The School as Surrogate Conscience," *Saturday Review* (January 11, 1975), 54–58.

4. Robert Hutchins, *The Conflict in Education* (New York: Harper & Bros., 1953), pp. 12–13.

5. Robert O. Riggs, "Life-Saving Prescriptions for Schools of Education," *Phi Delta Kappan* (January 1976), 333–34.

6. Riggs, "Life-Saving Prescriptions for Schools of Education," 333–34.

7

Role-Modeling: The Self-Concept of the Teacher

I slept and dreamt
That life was joy
I awoke and saw
That life was duty
I acted and behold
Duty was joy.

RABINDRANATH TAGORE[1]

In spite of the almost impossible role demands made on the teacher in America, many excellent men and women embrace the role happily and sustain it enthusiastically, combining duty with joy. Naturally, a pessimistic person will see only the negative aspects of such a role while the optimist will recognize the great potential it offers.

Role Perception

Role perception is determined by a variety of circumstances. Anyone who has known only unhappy or inefficient teachers probably has a negative perception of the role. On the other hand, anyone who has known happy, dedicated, self-actualizing teachers, will have quite a different perception of the role of teacher. In any case, definitions of role behavior are learned through two kinds of circumstances: intentional instruction and incidental learning. A teacher may have gained a concept of the role through professional reading or through such incidental learning experiences as discussions with school personnel and observing other teachers.[2] Without doubt, the strongest factor in role perception for young teachers is not *what* they were taught, but *how* they were taught.

Self-Concept

It is easy to understand that the teacher's self-concept is derived in the same way as is that of the learner—from the significant others who

93

influence or even control their lives. A teacher, whose self-concept is determined solely by the approval or criticism of the principal or other supervisor, may or may not be able to develop a healthy attitude toward him or herself. Self-approval and self-evaluation are extremely important for the teacher, as they are for any professional person.

One of the most damaging experiences for a beginning teacher is to be in a teaching situation that has unrealistic expectations or one for which he or she is totally unprepared. However, in times of economic stress, unemployed certified teachers will ignore their perceptions of themselves and accept almost any role definition offered so long as it is attached to a pay-check. The conversations that take place regularly in hiring interviews could lead one to the conclusion that teacher candidates are the least secure individuals in the whole job market. "I can teach it black or white, however you want it taught," was stated by one desperate candidate. Another, applying to a denominational school, even suggested that he would be willing to become "converted" if that would help him get the job! Is it any wonder that Hitler, when asked how he would handle the teachers of Germany in creating the new Reich, said simply, "Don't worry about teachers. They are willy-nilly anyway."

Perceiving the role is only the first part of developing a role-concept. It is in this initial process, however, that the prospective teacher should be alert to the clues he or she receives from the significant others. If some important clues are missing or if some have been misinterpreted, grave errors can result. It is for these reasons that the teacher-candidate should be prepared *to ask* as well as to answer questions in a hiring interview. What is the policy of the school with regard to field trips? Can I expect to have adequate materials to individualize my teaching? Who will supervise me? How are evaluations derived? Does the principal make it a regular practice to visit classrooms? To whom can I go for help when I feel the need for it?

Role Conflict

There are very few jobs in our society which require such difficult congeniality between independence and conformity as does teaching. Teachers must constantly be aware of their responsibility to the society and to their community, while at the same time they must maintain their own personal integrity. When we find ourselves in a situation where expectations are at variance with our own or where the significant others cannot agree with what those expectations should be, we experience conflict.[3] A teacher may feel strongly about a point of philosophy but find that the members of the school board not only disagree with him but with one another. If the point of philosophy is significant, then perhaps he should stick to it. However, if any real changes are to be made in the public schools, creative teachers must learn to refrain from swatting flies with baseball bats and to save their energies "to fight another day" for really important issues.

Teachers often find themselves in situations where various groups of significant others have conflicting expectations as to the role of the teacher. Such conflicts may be in regard to the functions teachers should perform as well as the ways in which they should operate. One of the major tasks of the teacher is to try to bring harmony, if not unity, among these various expectations. From this point of view, personal relations, public relations, and school-community relations become especially significant to the teacher.

Role Modeling

A teacher who has a confused idea of his or her own self-concept cannot help but project this to students. If one is weak and fearful and easily manipulated, the students quickly take advantage of these characteristics to control the teacher. Even if one is strong and honest and fair, there are those students who try to find a weak spot in the teacher's personality or in his or her preparation. For whatever reason, there has developed over the years an adversary relationship between teachers and students—an undercurrent of tension which can show itself openly in unpleasant ways if the teacher is not aware of its existence.

In a study of children's definition of the teacher-role, Ruth Cunningham, a psychologist, got responses such as: "The teacher is an enemy to be fought!" "He is a kill-joy who doesn't want children to enjoy their work." "The teacher is a devil, a being of power, who says that you must write your name in the upper lefthand corner—never in the upper right!" ". . . one who is never wrong." ". . . he is a person who conveys to groups of students his faith in them." "He tries to meet the interests of group members." He is called a "goal setter," a "super-conscience," a "tone giver" whose presence makes children feel good, a "hero," a "friend."[4]

Take your choice! Each teacher must choose the type of leadership to exert, the kind of model to offer to students. Again, the role definition must be *real,* the teacher's ego-concept must be *real,* the teacher must be *real.* Imitation is the highest form of flattery and the teacher must bear a great responsibility for the kinds of role-concepts students take away with them.

Traditional Roles

Images of the school teacher in American society have been varied. There was the image of the teacher as the strict schoolmaster, bending over the heads of perspiring students, rod in hand. There was the image of the puritanical school ma'am, strait-laced and humorless. There was the absent-minded professor or the teacher as a sacred object.

There have been positive images of the teacher as well. These include the teacher as the revered scholar, as the self-sacrificing idealist, or as the sympathetic advisor of youth.

Whatever the prevailing image of the teacher, at different times and in different places, it has always contained within it contradictory elements. When teachers have been feared, they have also been respected; when riduculed, also revered; when belittled, also beloved.[5] Further, as teachers themselves become more individualistic, many of the old stereotypes are broken down and discarded. It is not possible now (nor was it ever) to make valid generalizations about "the teacher" in terms of personal and social characteristics. As our society becomes more complex and as our concepts of individual rights and freedoms become more all-embracing, it will become even more impossible to generalize about the teacher.

Changing Roles

Teachers today seem to be more aware of the need to experience life more fully and to participate in a variety of roles. They are beginning to reject the concept of the teacher as the sociological stranger and, rather, are seeking to become a part of the community. No longer do teachers see themselves as a group apart; no longer do teachers feel the need to remain neutral in order to be objective in their teaching; no longer do teachers feel constrained to remain mere observers of community problems lest their effectiveness in the classroom be diminished. One university professor whose summer school contract was canceled, found himself a job as a porter in a local hotel. Other cases of teachers, professors, and even college presidents taking leave from their regular professional duties to engage in a variety of jobs have been reported as news items, not as earth-shattering landmark events.

However, for all that, society still looks to the teacher as the agent and perpetuator of middle-class morality. Parents still expect the teacher to be a better model of behavior for their children than they are themselves.[6]

Such then are a few of the theories of the teacher's role. What remains is the problem of living day-to-day in a role which makes such great personal demands. While it is true that what others expect is important to the teacher, perhaps the most meaningful criterion to apply to any role is personal integrity. Do I like myself? is a much more searching question than Do they like me?[7]

The Case of Mrs. Wills

Mrs. Wills was an English teacher in a small junior high school in a southwestern consolidated school district. She was known to several generations of students as a perfectionist and as a teacher who had little tolerance for young people. However, she was certified and tenured and both she and her husband were well known in the community and active in the local church.

When the superintendent, in an effort to bring some new ideas into the school system, engaged a consultant to work with the junior high school teachers, it soon became apparent that Mrs. Wills would have no part of any proposed curriculum changes. The superintendent advised the consultant to go ahead with the curriculum conferences and if Mrs. Wills did not wish to participate, no confrontation need be faced.

Each innovative idea that was discussed seemed to meet with Mrs. Wills' disapproval. She objected to the content of the proposals; she objected to the time set aside for curriculum meetings; she objected to everything.

The other teachers were becoming enthusiastic about field trips, special film showings, integrated social studies curriculum plans, and other new ideas. The students began to resent the fact that in most of their classes there were new and exciting things going on while in their English classes, the "same old stuff is being taught in the same old way." Student comments only served to strengthen Mrs. Wills' antagonism.

Finally, things came to a head when she refused to allow her students to attend a special film showing in the assembly hall, saying that it interfered with her teaching of Shakespeare. The film was a new color production of Macbeth.

The students were very angry when they left the building, and to the surprise of no one (except Mrs. Wills) they planned to "get even." When Mrs. Wills came into her classroom the next morning, she found to her horror that there was a pile of old, very dry, very dirty corncobs stacked on her immaculate desk. She became almost hysterical with anger. She screamed and threatened that no student would be allowed to go home until she had found out who had so insulted her. The entire day was spent in a state of high emotional excitement. There was no teaching, and no student would admit to the prank. Finally, at about five o'clock the principal came in and dismissed the students. Many of them had missed their bus home, and transportation had to be arranged.

The consultant was astounded that such teacher behavior would be tolerated but was advised not to make an issue of it. Mrs. Wills continued to teach in that school, and each school term there invariably developed some kind of confrontation with students. These incidents became famous and traditional, with each term's class trying to do something more daring than the one before. There was little English Literature learned since the emphasis was on Mrs. Wills, and the students even began to call the class "Dirty Tricks I."

Possible Solutions

1. The superintendent should have required Mrs. Wills to attend and participate in the curriculum meetings.

2. Mrs. Wills should have been dismissed from the school system.

3. Mrs. Wills should have been required to seek some psychological help (out of town if necessary) in order to help her see the degree of role conflict she was experiencing.

4. Mrs. Wills is probably one of those teachers who could have been "spotted" in preservice education and advised out of teaching as a profession.

5. Since Mrs. Wills and her husband were both well known in the district, the superintendent was right in not making any issue of her behavior.

Would you choose any of these solutions? If so, you may write your explanation below. However, if you would not choose any of these, you may go on to the next page and write your solution to the problem.

Your Solution to Mrs. Wills' Problem

The Case of Mr. McKinnon

Mr. McKinnon was a second-grade teacher in a low socio-economic neighborhood. The school was located in an agricultural community, and many of the students were the children of migrant farm workers who were not seriously concerned about education. Mr. McKinnon was a teacher with wide experience—a world traveler, the husband of a brilliant musician, and a man of substantial financial means. His teaching in this particular locale was a matter of choice without any overtones of a missionary attitude. He simply loved to teach and was convinced that the children in this area needed some exciting learning experiences.

He began his school day by arriving early in his beautiful motor home. As soon as he parked, the students were there waiting for a breakfast surprise, maybe toast and hot chocolate or warm cookies fresh from the oven. The children never tired of exploring the motor home—the beds, the bathroom, the kitchen. The greatest thing of all was to have a ride in the motor home on a field trip, sometimes even going to the seacoast to pick up shells. After breakfast, Mr. McKinnon began his classes by sitting on the floor of his classroom with his guitar, playing some familiar tune that the children recognized and could sing. Not only his own students but others gathered 'round without waiting for the late bell. Sometimes, the other students left reluctantly to go to their own classrooms for the day.

This was followed by a relaxed period of Glasser-type circle during which the children were encouraged to tell any story or relate any experience they wished. After this, Mr. McKinnon brought out a plans board, and all the children participated in listing the learning jobs they planned to accomplish that day. They then proceeded to go to the various learning centers where there was usually a student helper–director who kept track of the small computers used in individualized math or who helped students file their completed task cards.

Meanwhile, the teacher was free to circulate among the groups, to spend some time with a student who had a personal or educational problem, or even to go to the office to make a phone call to a parent or to arrange a field trip. The classroom moved smoothly with deceptive casualness—all the result of careful planning and a caring, flexible, and intelligent teacher.

The end of the school day was also a quiet time for evaluation and a sing-along. Each child was greeted by name as he or she left. Spending a day in Mr. McKinnon's classroom was a happy experience—a wholesome blend of excitement and quiet work time all without the feeling of a teacher who dominated or of children who were resentful or afraid.

Naturally, there is another side to this picture. Many teachers, unable or unwilling to give so much of themselves to their students, were critical and cynical. However, Mr. McKinnon overcame some of this by his willingness to be of help to other teachers, often acting as a resource person or, in a crisis, taking a troublesome child into his room to cool off.

Possible Solutions

1. Mr. McKinnon was really making it very difficult for the other teachers to compete with him.

2. The principal should not have allowed him to bring his motor home to the school or to serve breakfast to the students.

3. Mr. McKinnon should have been required to teach strictly according to the curriculum and the methods he learned in teacher education.

4. A teacher like Mr. McKinnon can be a great problem to the principal because he is always doing things differently and causing a great deal of jealousy among the teachers.

5. A year in this kind of classroom with this kind of teacher spoiled the children and made them unhappy with their other teachers.

Would you choose any of these solutions? If so, you may write your explanation below. However, if you would not choose any of these, you may go on to the next page and write your solution to the problem.

Your Solution to the Problem of Mr. McKinnon

Your Sample Case

If you have witnessed or experienced a case in your own school life that you think emphasizes the importance of the teacher as a role-model or the impact of role-conflict on a teacher, describe the case and explain how you saw it handled. Did you agree with the solution? Why?

Notes

1. Rabindranath Tagore, quoted in "Essay on Religion," *Time,* December 29, 1975, p. 56.

2. Theodore R. Sarbin, "Role Theory," *Handbook of Social Psychology.* Vol. I (January 1954), 223–58.

3. Francis S. Chase, and Guba Egon G., "Administrative Roles and Behavior," *Review of Educational Research.* Vol. 25, No. 4 (October 1955), 281–98.

4. Ruth Cunningham, quoted in *Hexagon,* Vol. 1, No. 2 (1964), p. 95.

5. Rosella Linskie, "Role Theory and Teachers' Expectations," *Hexagon,* Vol. 1, No. 2 (1964), 86–104.

6. Henry Steele Commager, "The School as Surrogate Conscience," *The Saturday Review* (January 11, 1975), pp. 54–57.

7. Rosella Linskie, "Role Theory and Teachers' Expectations," *Hexagon,* Vol. 1, No. 2 (1964), 86–104.

8 The Ideal Teacher

To dream the impossible dream,
To beat the unbeatable foe,
To bear with unbearable sorrow,
To run where the brave dare not go.

"THE IMPOSSIBLE DREAM"[1]

What is a teacher? That's not the question. What is an *ideal* teacher? That is the question. There are thousands of teachers in all varieties and dimensions—age, sex, marital status, disposition, experience, training, grade level assignment, subject matter emphasis, geographic location —and in all shades and variations of these dimensions.

A teacher, in the technical sense, is any person who has passed a qualifying exam, has been through a required program, or has met certifying criteria. A teacher is expected to be a fund of knowledge as well as an expert in transmitting knowledge to students.

All of the above can be said without considering the *personhood* of the teacher. However, when a student learns something in a class, it means that the student has responded to the teacher as a total person. Sometimes students learn in spite of the personhood of the teacher; sometimes their learning is enhanced by the personhood of the teacher.[2]

In any case, whatever is done in teaching is dictated in large measure by what teachers think the learners are like and what the teachers think they themselves are like.

Who Is the Ideal Teacher?

The question then is not what is a teacher. It is, what is an ideal teacher. Ideals are states of perfection toward which we all strive but seldom realize in their fullest sense. Ideally, you might wish to be beautiful in a very specific way—tall, dark, and handsome or blonde, petite, and graceful. However, as you look in the mirror each day, you are willing to compromise with the ideal and make the best of whatever qualities you have. The advertising business has been built on the realization that we are all striving to be more than we are. Applying this concept to the definition of the teacher, we can conclude that professional teachers are those who constantly strive to be better. They study and analyze their strengths and weaknesses, try to improve their relationships with others, try to understand students, attempt to improve their self-images, and, in general, try to become the kind of teacher-person whom they themselves can like.

Here is one attempt to describe the ideal teacher. Rate yourself, or some teacher you have known, on the following scale, assigning a rating of 1 to 5, with 1 indicating the highest degree of success in each particular effort and 5 the lowest degree of success.

Rating Scale for Teachers

Knowledge

1. Adequate understanding of the nature of the learner and the learning process.   1 2 3 4 5

2. Adequate understanding of the nature of self.   1 2 3 4 5

3. Good general background in content information in a wide range of fields. Some training in logic and qualitative thinking in systems organizations. Courses in basic social philosophy, social psychology, and cultural anthropology. Work in the area of comparative world cultures and international affairs. Opportunities to develop an appreciation of art, music, and other means of communication.   1 2 3 4 5

4. Specific knowledge in a specialized area sufficient to enable one to function as a member of a teaching team.   1 2 3 4 5

5. Knowledge of the current world and contemporary developments (what's happening now) as well as the cultural, economic, and social influences of society.   1 2 3 4 5

6. Knowledge of the historical, contemporary, and future issues in education; of the structures of the various levels of the institution of education; of the relationships between national, state, and local agencies.   1 2 3 4 5

7. Knowledge of various curriculum organization patterns and an awareness of the teacher's role in the development of curriculum.   1 2 3 4 5

Attitudes

1. Wholesome attitudes and relationships with other adults as well as with children. 1 2 3 4 5

2. Healthy interest in both sexes; healthy attitude toward those whose sexual drives do not fit the so-called normal pattern. 1 2 3 4 5

3. Realistic awareness of one's own capabilities, strengths as well as weaknesses, and acceptance of one's self. 1 2 3 4 5

4. Acceptance of the role of a teacher as well as related roles as a member of society. 1 2 3 4 5

5. Enough personal and inner security to permit one to grant to others the respect due them as human beings. 1 2 3 4 5

6. An attitude of eagerness for new knowledge; a curiosity and a real inquisitiveness about our fascinating universe; an excitement about learning. 1 2 3 4 5

7. A willingness to exercise freedom and to accept the responsibilities this freedom brings. 1 2 3 4 5

8. An awareness that teaching is not a giving-out-information process but a very complicated human relations process which makes great demands on one's ability to develop and perserve a well-balanced self-concept. 1 2 3 4 5

9. An awareness of the different value systems held by persons in the various sub-cultures in the United States. 1 2 3 4 5

Skills

1. Good personal study skills. 1 2 3 4 5

2. The ability to be self-directed. 1 2 3 4 5

3. The ability to direct the learning of others. 1 2 3 4 5

4. Skill in locating and using a wide variety of resources. 1 2 3 4 5

5. Skill in using the English language in all its forms—written, spoken, etc. 1 2 3 4 5

6. Good taste in manners, dress, and personal habits. 1 2 3 4 5

7. Skill in planning for the day, the week, and the semester; letting students help with this planning. 1 2 3 4 5

8. Skill in integrating subject areas; showing students how all knowledge is related and relevant. 1 2 3 4 5

9. Skill in the dynamics of human relations. 1 2 3 4 5

10. Skill in organizing, planning, and presenting a lesson in an interesting way. 1 2 3 4 5

11. Skill in motivating students to a high degree of involve-
    ment in their own learning and in their own self-evalua-
    tion. 1 2 3 4 5

If you scored 27 on this list, then you are already the ideal teacher.
If you scored 135, then you may be in the wrong profession. Most
people score somewhere in between, with a tendency toward the upper
rating. This scale can be used as a tool to discover aspects of your
background, preparation, or even personality which may need improvement before you attempt to direct the learning of others.

Becoming "Ideal"

The humanistic and caring attitudes suggested above usually develop
in the teacher who has had a well-balanced exposure to at least four
major therapeutic-type experiences: human, vocational, religious, and
recreational.* In internalizing these personal growth experiences, the
teacher becomes an expanded self—one who can embrace all kinds of
students and whose attitude determines the wholesome social climate
of the classroom.[3]

Human experience

Every one of us needs to feel that another person truly cares about
us and what happens to us. Most psychiatrists agree that our mental
hospitals are filled with people who would not be there if they had had
some therapeutic contact with another person. For some kinds of emotional disturbance, there is no medication as effective as the warm,
loving attention of someone who cares.

Integrated persons are those who have had such therapeutic human
relationships. When our relationships with friends, family, co-workers,
teachers, and students are sympathetic, caring situations, they go far
in helping us to cope with the complex demands of everyday living.
More than that, these experiences can do much toward expanding and
enhancing our concept of ourselves.

The teaching-learning process, if it is done in a humane context, can
be a vitalizing and creating experience for both the teacher and the
student. However, living in such a context is risky business—you are
always vulnerable. Those teachers who fear getting hurt often hide

---

* The four categories used in the following section are taken from Boy and Pine. The
discussion in each case is the author's.

behind notes and prepared lectures and stern exteriors. These are their barricades and they guard them defensively!

Students also build barricades: fear, distrust, self-concealment, pain. Sometimes barricades built with these materials become deep secret caves out of which the student will not venture nor allow anyone to enter. Sometimes, with the best of intentions, teachers stumble into such a cave and, unless they step lightly, can create an even bigger problem.

Vocational experience

At least two well-known psychiatrists agree on the therapeutic nature of work. Maslow and Roe both hold that "there is no single activity which is potentially so capable of providing some satisfaction to man . . . as is his occupation."[4] This is not to say that all jobs in our society are equally rewarding or equally effective in enhancing and expanding the self. However, even the most menial job can bring satisfaction if workers are allowed and encouraged to feel the value of what they are doing.

It is not the job that degrades and dehumanizes. Rather, it is the attitude the worker has toward the job. Often this attitude is the result of supervisors—the significant others who help us devise our role definition. Unfortunately, some administrators seem determined to destroy the individual's dignity, pride, and will to do a good job. This seems to be especially true in situations where the worker (teacher) is successful beyond the expectations of the administrator. Hence, we see a replay of the various themes of the self-fulfilling prophecy. It takes a very strong ego to survive some of the nit-picking administration found in many of our school systems.

How seldom does one hear praise for a teacher such as, you encouraged and valued divergent thinking, or you developed a cooperative, trusting classroom atmosphere conducive to self-direction? Rather, all too often the praise (and the merit raises) are given to those who never missed a faculty meeting, never took a day of sick leave, never had a student problem. In most instances, the teacher is rewarded for not bothering the administrator.

This attitude is bound to affect the teacher's own attitude toward students. It is extremely difficult, for example, for a teacher to put out any real effort to implement democratic practices in the classroom when the teacher has had little or no opportunity to exercise democratic rights in the relationship with administration.

Teaching can be a strong therapeutic experience but only if the teacher has the kind of administrator who extends real support—loving and caring but, at the same time, strong and effective.

Religious experience

By "religious experience" we do not mean denominational affiliation. To be human *is* to be religious because every person who lives in harmony with his or her values is exercising discipline, honesty, courage, and reflection. In creating these values, we create ourselves and thus project to others the true nature of our being.[5]

What we believe is ultimately what we are. It is always difficult to live contrary to our values. It is a role-play effort that few people can sustain for very long. Sooner or later there comes a situation when our true self becomes exposed: I can't imagine his doing a thing like that. It is so unlike him! There is nothing in her background that would have led anyone to suspect! For the most part, people who live by their values live freely and fearlessly. Those who wear masks, live with constant fear and anxiety.

This internalized valuing is the internalized expanding of self that is referred to here as a religious experience. It is not a one-time thing. It is an on-going process which if constantly evaluated and re-examined results in a higher degree of self-knowledge, self-determination, facilitating behavior, and self-acceptance. Thus, the religious human experience is not basically a particular set of beliefs but rather a strong sense of personal integration, the acting out of our beliefs in our day-to-day lives in a confusing world.

> Your daily life is your temple and your religion.
> Whenever you enter into it take with you your all.[6]

There are few professions that require greater dedication to a set of beliefs and values than does teaching. Here one's innermost philosophical, moral, and social values are constantly in view. Young children seem to have a special insight into adults, especially their teachers. They can recognize honesty almost immediately, and they are quick to detect unreal or phony values.

Truly integrated teachers are whole persons who are not afraid to examine their lives, their methods and procedures or their own philosophies. They are fully functioning individuals who are a great deal more than mechanical technicians, tinkering with children's minds in order to change their behavior. They are philosophers and humanists who are concerned with the "why" and the "what" of teaching as well as with the "how." They put these three aspects of educational thinking in their proper perspective, giving more weight to the first two than to the last.

Through all these processes, really good teachers can be said to experience religious therapy. Their morality extends to their teaching obligations, and their integrity motivates them to strive for the ideal.

Recreational experience

According to Carl Rogers, there are two kinds of recreational experiences which contribute to the expanded self. The first is what he calls "the privilege of being alone"; the other is the social activity which brings one into contact with people.[7] In the essentially selfish experience of being alone, individuals have a chance to gather up all the loose ends and to think through their goals, needs, and plans. Anne Morrow Lindbergh speaks most touchingly of this concept in her book *Gift From the Sea*. In this short but poignant account of her brief moments alone, she describes life's daily demands as tearing one's personality to tiny shreds and scattering them to the four winds. In her aloneness by the sea, she feels that she can gather together all the kaleidoscopic pieces and make of them once again a whole and integrated person.[8]

A quiet walk along a pleasant stream, a few hours of silent meditation, a drive in the country can help one to achieve that feeling of wholeness that is so necessary to effective functioning in our society.

On the other hand, there are valuable therapeutic results to be gained from socializing with others, particularly when the group is a congenial one and there is a variety of opinions and attitudes expressed. It is a mistake for teachers to socialize only with other teachers. Invariably such social situations lead to discussions of school and teaching. This is too narrow to allow for the self-expanding experiences so necessary for recreating and regenerating the self.

Recreation is a universal need. Passive activities need to be blended with participation in sports, art, music, or even intelligent conversation. Anything which keeps the mind active and expands its horizons is a worthwhile experience. Travel, reading, viewing films, entertainment, each offers a new and different view of life. This, in turn, refreshes the approach one has to teaching and enables the teacher to bring a more lively attitude to the class. Enthusiasm breeds enthusiasm and, as the cycle is completed, learning becomes exciting and interesting and worthwhile for both the teacher and the student.

Truly fine teachers all seem to have one thing in common—they sincerely enjoy the interplay of ideas, the sharpening of the mind as it contacts other minds. In short, they *enjoy* teaching and approach each day's classes with a true and abiding enthusiasm. This last is probably the magic ingredient which points one on the road to becoming the ideal teacher.

A Letter to My Favorite Teacher

Dear Miss Kellermier,

It has been many years since you were my high school chemistry teacher and we became good friends before your untimely death. However, you are still very real to me. It would hardly be possible for me to write or say anything about the ideal teacher without thinking of you.

I tried to remember all the things I would like to say to you if you and I could have a long chat about teaching and about life in general. That is how I came to decide on this letter.

First, you always trusted me and relied on me to do my very best. You made me feel proud of being your lab assistant. One of the highlights of my high school career was your selecting my chemistry notebook to go to the state accrediting agency which was evaluating our small high school. In all the years that I have been a teacher, I have tried to encourage students by trusting them and by expecting much of them as you did of me. I have known the joy of seeing some of my students' work published. Each time, I think back to that chemistry notebook.

You somehow always found time to talk to me—not as a mere student but as a person. I treasure especially the memories of long chatty walks in the spring and your telling me why you didn't like lilacs! I don't always succeed, but I do try to have time for my students. They know I can always find time to listen to their problems and to give them whatever help I have to offer. I often have small classes at my home, and I have discovered (as you did with me) that routine school problems can often be symptomatic of a deeper personal problem which needs talking about.

You were willing to express your pride in my accomplishments and thus encourage me to do more than I thought I could. I remember this

when I give a student credit for a job especially well done.

You explained to me that bright and gifted
people are not always popular and that often
one has to choose between being popular and being true to one's innermost ideals. I think of
this when I see a truly outstanding student
suffering because of jealousy or the cynicism
of classmates—or even of teachers.

You taught me to look at myself objectively
without fear of being proud of my abilities or
depressed about my shortcomings. This has
been a great benefit to me in encouraging students who do not feel sure of themselves.

You shared with me your pride in your
profession. When you stood before the class,
adjusted your pince-nez glasses and launched
into a lecture, I knew I was in the presence of
a real scholar. All these years, I have never
gone to class unprepared or tried to teach off
the cuff. I'm sure that if I did your spirit
would haunt me!

You lived with one foot in the present and
the other in the exciting, unknown future, always asking tantalizing questions. You really
opened my mind to the future and because of
that, enabled me to avoid bogging down in the
past or in the present.

You spoke lovingly and enthusiastically
about the big world and all that was yet to be
done. Thus, when the opportunity came for me
to teach and travel, I was not afraid. I went,
I learned, I grew, and always I remembered you.
I embraced difficulties and human problems and
love itself because in you I had seen a model of
the kind of open person I wanted to be.

True, not everyone sees me as you saw me or
even as I see myself, but deep down inside I
have that marvelous feeling that comes from
being an integrated whole person, not afraid
of being just what I am.

For all these gifts, I thank you. As I grow
older, they become more priceless and my memo-

ries of you seem more real. You were wise beyond your time and more honest than almost anyone I have ever known. True, I've forgotten some of the chemistry you taught but the values never change.

My most sincere thanks are daily expressed in the way I try to go about my own teaching. It is my hope that at least one of my students will be so inspired and will continue to weave the thread of excellence into the fabric of living and learning. Then I, too, will have been fulfilled.

Your loving and grateful student,

Rosella Linskie

Notes

1. Joe Darion and Mitch Leigh, "The Impossible Dream," from the musical play *Man of La Mancha,* 1965, Sam Fox Publishing Co., N.Y.

2. Arthur W. Coombs and ASCD 1962 Yearbook Committee, *Perceiving, Behaving, Becoming.* Washington, D.C: Association for Supervision and Curriculum Development, N.E.A., 1962, 1.

3. Angelo V. Boy and Gerald J. Pine, *Expanding the Self: Personal Growth for Teachers.* (Dubuque: William C. Brown, 1971), p. xi.

4. Boy and Pine, *Expanding Self,* pp. 47–66.

5. Boy and Pine, *Expanding Self,* pp. 67–86.

6. Kahlil Gibran, *The Prophet.* (New York: Alfred Knopf, 1923), pp. 77–78.

7. Carl Rogers, *On Becoming a Person.* (Boston: Houghton-Mifflin Co., 1961), p. 15.

8. Anne Morrow Lindbergh, *Gift From the Sea.* (New York: Pantheon Books, 1955), pp. 54–55, 58–59.

Summary—Part II

The three chapters in Part two have dealt with some of the more important concepts related to the teacher as a significant part of the learning process.

Good physical and mental health are essential ingredients for success in teaching as are academic preparation and personal enthusiasm. Since teachers are such significant role models, it is imperative that they be able to project positive self-images. If the model has serious defects, the process of imitation can only be destructive.

While there is no such thing as a pure *Ideal Teacher,* there are many characteristics which describe the person who is striving toward the ideal. This striving is the hallmark of a responsible professional.

The personality and attitude of teachers are as important to success as are academic and professional training. Regardless of one's high I.Q., degrees and awards or fund of knowledge, if a teacher does not have a strong healthy self-image and an open attitude toward students, he or she will probably not be successful. Students *can* learn even if teachers *can't* teach, but students cannot take away from the learning process wholesome attitudes unless these have been portrayed by the teacher. Sadly, it is often true that students learn negatively and in spite of a poor role model. When this is the case, the learning process is severely hampered.

Part three will bring together the learner and the teacher in that most important relationship—the learning process.

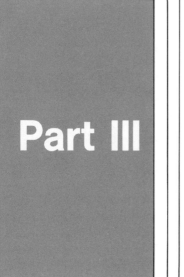

Part III

The Process

Experience, Experience, Experience!

We shall not cease from exploration
And the end of all our exploring
Will be to arrive where we started
And know the place for the first time.

T. S. Eliot[1]

You simply have to see it to believe it! There is no way to tell you how it felt! The photo really doesn't do him justice. Such comments point out how extremely difficult it is to transmit to others an experience which they have not had. Even being in the same place at the same time under the same circumstances does not guarantee that several persons will have identical experiences. If you have ever been in a courtroom and heard the testimony of two or more eyewitnesses, you know how true this can be. It is difficult to believe that they really saw the same event!

When it comes to describing persons, the variations are even greater. But the greatest differences of all are evident in interpretations of the intangible parts of an experience: How did you feel? What did you think? What was the motive?

Thus, even direct personal experience can sometimes be deceptive, depending on any number of factors such as lapsed time, the element of surprise or the mental set of the observer. Nevertheless, actual experience is more trustworthy than hearing or reading about an event. This is especially true in the learning process.

As long ago as the thirteenth century, Thomas Aquinas revolutionized the concept of the nature of learning. In his famous *Summa Theologica* he introduced two ideas that were new to the scientific mind. The first was the idea that "there is nothing in the mind that was not first in the senses," and the second was the theory of the kinship among all parts of reality—the unity of all knowledge. The second concept, the wholeness of human thought, will be discussed in Chapter 10. Here we will attempt to describe the importance of sensory intake to the learning process.

The Tabula Rasa

Some six hundred years after Aquinas, John Locke popularized the notion that the mind of the newborn babe is a "tabula rasa"—a blank tablet on which anything can be written through experience and learning. Naturally, there were philosophers and scientists who disagreed, just as there are those who disagree today.

For many years prior to Locke, even as far back as Plato, philosophers and psychologists thought that learning was really only a matter of remembering ideas which the learner had acquired before birth. This was called innate learning and claimed that the child was born with a fund of knowledge which only needed to be developed.

Aristotle taught that this development could take place in one of several ways which he called connections or associations. The first of these was *contiguity*—putting two ideas together. He believed, for example, if the child is told about elephants and peanuts at the same time, the child will in future always associate the two. The second was *similarity and contrast.* If a child can be taught that *boy* and *man* are related by degrees of *similarity,* the child can also be taught that *male* is the opposite of *female* by *contrasting* the two.

However, after all the centuries of intellectual debate, John Locke challenged the whole notion of innate ideas. His chief argument was that there is no evidence of ideas common to all people in any society and certainly not among people of different societies. He thus concluded that the mind is empty at birth and that the key to learning must be in the in-take experience through the senses. Further, he developed the theory that the mind is able not only to take in sensual experience but that it actively deals with these experiences. It compares, it categorizes, it generalizes and it discriminates among them.

One important result of Locke's work was to open the way for a new theological look at the original nature of man. If his tabula rasa theory is acceptable, then it follows that humans are not born good or bad. Rather it indicates that at birth the human organism is morally neutral and psychologically passive. Another significant result of this theory is the importance it gave to the emphasis of environmental nurture over hereditary nature. Thus, teaching becomes a matter of developing the senses rather than of training the faculties.[2]

In more recent years the same basic beliefs have been consistently supported and have become the foundation for much curriculum reform. In the 1950s, Roger Williams made the distinction between being born *equal* and being born *uniform.* Because of this, he declared, the more differences that exist in opportunities and endowments, all the more important is education's task.[3]

The philosophy of the modifying effects of the environment were largely responsible for the legislative measures of the 1960's Head Start, OEO, Job Corps, and a host of other attempts to equalize experience and thus equalize opportunities. Philosophically, none of these was designed to change the genetic heredity of children. What was needed was some improvement in the environmental experience which so greatly influences human development.

What is clear from reading the several outstanding scholars, as well as the hundreds of pages of testimony concerning the Economic Opportunity legislation,[5] is that dollars do not make all the difference. Neither do genes or lunch programs, however much these factors contribute to educational success.

In the 1970's, Christopher Jencks wrote a book entitled *Inequality.* In this work he not only supported the earlier ideas of the 1950's and 1960's but went so far as to try to answer the questions, Why are some men rich and others poor? How does the economic question influence overall cognitive development? Is the desire for education a personal value or is it an economic factor?[4] Unfortunately, these are not neat, definitive questions; therefore, there are no neat, definitive answers.

See, Hear, Feel, Touch, Taste

Thus far the word *experience* has been used frequently without any effort to define it. In its simplest connotation, experience means to see, to hear, to feel, to touch, to taste and all the other words you can think of which suggest *confronting reality.* The more sophisticated definition given by field-theory psychologists is *the interaction of a human organism with its perceived environment.* Experience is taken to include both an active and a passive element. The contact is active—we confront something and we do something with it or to it or about it. In the passive phase, we undergo certain changes or consequences, no matter how imperceptible, because of the contact. The strength of the connection between these two aspects of experience determines the value of the experience. In addition, every experience is influenced by earlier experiences and, in turn, influences future experiences.

Thus we develop an interwoven chain of active-passive contacts with reality. This is the basis for the concept of change. If life is a series of experiences through which a person continues to modify contacts with the environment, then life is a constant series of changes. When the chain is broken or if it is never begun in any meaningful way, then little change (learning) can take place. On the other hand, if the learner has rich and wide experiences the chain becomes a complicated web of interrelated concepts and ideas.

How Do Concepts Develop?

Without experience little learning can occur. How, then, does this process work? What is the mental pattern which results, in some instances at least, in a rich tapestry of knowledge?

How did you learn the meaning of the word *dog?* How did you develop the concept *dog?* How is it that you are able to identify a *dog* when you see one? The following diagram, though oversimplified, illustrates the inner-logic of experience–concept–validation, then additional experience.

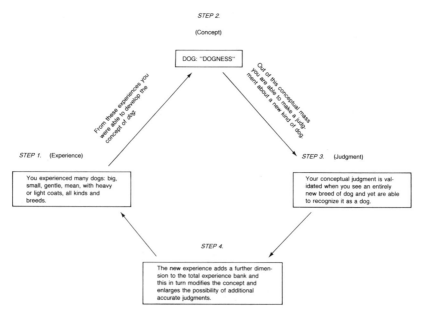

Figure 9.1

You may substitute any concept you like in place of the word *dog.* The process remains the same. Thus it is easy to see that when the teaching-learning process is conceived of as a "telling 'em" process, the

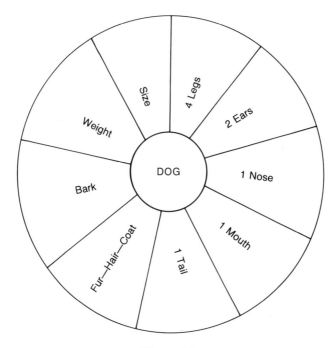

Figure 9.2

teacher is depriving the learner of a very significant part of learning and is creating a short circuit in the experience cycle.

One other aspect of concept development should be considered here. The more avenues you use in experiencing a concept and the more details you observe, relate, and interrelate, the more accurate will your ultimate concept be. For example, if some or any of the aspects of *dog* shown in the diagram above were missing from your experience, you could mistake a large cat or a small horse for a dog. Further, after you have experienced a fairly large number of dogs, you have no hesitation in declaring, "That is a dog. I never saw one exactly like it before, but I know it is a dog."

Thus, from a single, somewhat simple, experience, the mind begins to build a data bank of characteristics which can be retrieved and matched to a new experience. It seems fairly clear that the wider the sampling and the more details you relate and interrelate, the more accurate is your concept and the more accurate will be the judgments you make in a new situation. One thing to keep in mind, however, is that a concept will never be final and complete. No one can ever say that he or she knows everything about everything or even everything about any one thing. *Learning is a journey not a destination.*

From Concepts to Generalizations

We were able to see how the mind develops concepts out of experience. What is not so clear is how the mind can go from concepts to generalizations.

As it is used here, *generalization* is a stable judgment, usually tested and found accurate, about a group of concepts. If you have lived all your life on a farm, you probably have generalized *all* farms in terms of the location, soil condition, drainage, and terrain of your particular farm. There is nothing in your experience to prepare you for the tea terraces of China or the rice paddies of Japan unless you happen to be native Chinese or Japanese or have visited those countries. Thus, you might make the statement, "All the best farms are found in valleys." Well and good! However, the error lies in the use of the term *all. All* suggests that you have experienced all the farms there are in the entire world—in all kinds of climates producing all kinds of products. Until you have, you must be very careful of generalized statements. "All Mexicans are lazy" might be the mis-generalization of "I once knew a lazy Mexican." It is easy and dangerous to generalize with insufficient data. Thus we come back to step one in concept development; namely, experience.

Vicarious Experience

For many persons, experiencing the real world is limited. Handicapped persons, persons with insufficient money to travel, those in institutions of one kind or another—all of these necessarily lack exact, real, personal experiences with any but a very narrow segment of the world and its inhabitants. This lack of experience is probably the most difficult factor to overcome in the teaching–learning process. In addition to limiting the fund of knowledge, lack of experience seems to generate a lack of curiosity. You cannot yearn for those places or things about which you know nothing. It is here that vicarious or substitute experiences play an important role.

The next best thing to experiencing a different culture or social situation is to talk with others, to see pictures, or to read books about the people, places, and things you have not seen. Although Edison invented the motion picture machine specifically for the purpose of bringing new and wider experiences into the classroom, it was not until the middle of this century that audio-visual materials really began to be used to substitute for real experiences. Television, radio, educational films, books, resource persons, field trips—all these can be used by the teacher to stimulate and enrich even the most limited learning environment.

As long ago as the Middle Ages, real experience was recognized as a vital part of learning. It was then that persons were not considered truly educated unless they had made an "educational journey" and lived and studied in several countries.[6]

Without rich and varied experiences, real or vicarious, it is almost impossible to make generalizations. Even then, because the world is changing at such a rapid rate, what you thought was true (accurate) yesterday may no longer be true (accurate) today. Returning to the generalizations about farms, what about irrigation or hydroponic farming or other new developments in agriculture?

One of the aspects of modern life which is so wearing on the human spirit is the rapidity of change and the high risk of error in making judgments. About all one can do is to try to remain open to as many new experiences as possible, to develop a sound personal philosophy of life, and to remain tentative. This last is the most difficult. Yet, where is the man who said such a short while ago: "It will never fly!" or "There is nothing in space but space!"

What new experiences lie ahead? How will they change our present concepts and generalizations? What new knowledge is yet undiscovered? Perhaps that bright eccentric student in your classroom will open new doors to all mankind because you encouraged that student to ask *why*. And with the answer we may all come to know the place for the first time.

The Case of Franklin

Franklin was a young black boy from an inner city school in the mid-West. He lived all his short life in a crowded tenement, attended school in an almost totally segregated situation, and played with his friends in the crowded streets. He had never seen parks or rivers or trees.

One summer, a local university planned an outdoor education experience for children from Franklin's neighborhood. He was among those selected to go. When the school bus arrived at the university's outdoor campus, Franklin's eyes almost burst with excitement. There were grass, trees, dogs, and a river flowing along the edge of the campus.

One thing Franklin had heard about all his life but had never experienced was fishing. His uncles talked about going fishing when they were young boys in Mississippi, and Franklin had dreamed many nights about how much fun it would be. Now, here he was, right on the bank of a real wet river! He could hardly wait.

The next day one of the counselors got the group together and explained that those who wanted could go fishing with him. They had to learn to bait a hook, to cast a line, and, above all, to stay out of the river. Franklin listened carefully and learned quickly. When they went out to the river bank, he was so excited he could hardly stand it. Each child had to dig his own worms for bait and each had his own line and enough space so as not to get in the way of his neighboring fishermen. The counselor walked up and down the bank checking his young charges. After awhile, he stopped to talk with Franklin.

Franklin was having a great time but there was one thing he did not understand. He told the counselor that he did not have any trouble finding worms. As a matter of fact he had found a whole nest of worms. The problem was that the worms kept biting him as he put them on the hook. The counselor became suspicious and somewhat concerned. He questioned Franklin further and to his utter horror found that Franklin had discovered a nest of newborn copperhead snakes and had mistaken them for worms.

When the counselor found Franklin happily baiting his hook, he had already been bitten twenty-seven times. Quick action was imperative. The counselor grabbed up Franklin and tossed him in a jeep for a very fast ride to the local hospital about sixteen miles away. However, it was already too late, and, in spite of the best efforts of everyone involved, Franklin died that night of snake poisoning.

Questions for Discussion

(Try, if you can, to leave aside the legal question of responsibility and see to what extent you can relate this unfortunate incident to the topic at hand.)

1. The teacher, in preparation for the field experience, had spent time with the children trying to explain about all the new experiences they would have. The teacher did not anticipate the presence of the newborn copperheads. Can you think of anything additional the teacher could have done ahead of time?

2. Was there a factor missing in Franklin's concept of *worm?*

3. How could Franklin have had enough vicarious experience to be able to distinguish between *worm* and *snake?*

4. Should the counselor have scouted the area ahead of time to be sure there were no dangers at hand?

5. Discuss the fact that Franklin is a very specific example of a young person who literally died for lack of sufficient experience.

The Case of Cam and the Snow

Camille was a very bright four-year old who lived in south Texas. It was the Christmas season and for weeks all the TV shows featured Christmas scenes—sleigh rides, snowfall, and Santa Claus. Cam was especially fascinated with snow. She had never seen any real snow, but she thought the pictures of snow falling were beautiful.

The day after Christmas there was a massive stack of discarded paper gift wrap, tissue paper, and gift boxes. Cam's father disposed of all this by burning it in a wire container in the back yard. After all the paper was burned it left a large pile of fine white ash. No one paid any particular attention to the basket of fine white stuff until one morning Cam's mother looked out the kitchen window and saw an interesting sight. Cam had turned the wire basket upside down and was having a glorious time throwing the fine white ashes in the air and running under them as they fell. All the while she was shrieking merrily, "It's snowing! It's snowing!"

When her mother went out into the yard to see what was going on, Cam continued to role-play her own self-made snowstorm. She was terribly confused and disappointed when her mother explained to her that this was not snow. Cam insisted that it looked just like the snow on TV and that she wanted to play in the snow like the children she had seen on the Christmas shows. Her mother had quite a time trying to explain that snow is something entirely different although it may look like paper ash.

Questions For Discussion

1. How does Cam's experience illustrate the need for complete sensory experience in order to derive an accurate concept?

2. What element(s) was (were) missing in Cam's concept of snow?

3. Can you think of other situations in which the visual experience without the reinforcement of other kinds of experience might lead to error in judgment?

4. How does Cam's story illustrate the importance of cultural–social experience in the development of accurate concepts?

5. Would Cam have had the same type of problem had she lived in northern Michigan or in the mountains of the western United States?

6. List some concepts that children living in the Arctic Circle may have difficulty understanding? Select other specific geographic areas and do the same.

7. Discuss the idea that much of what we call vocabulary is derived from the conceptualization of the reality in our immediate surroundings.

Your Sample Case

If you have witnessed or experienced a case in your own school that illustrates the idea of experience as basic to learning, describe the specific situation.

If you disagree with the principle of tabula rasa, explain here why and describe which theory of learning you subscribe to.

Notes

1. T. S. Eliot, *Four Quartets,* Harcourt, Brace, N.Y. 1943, p. 39.

2. Morris L. Bigge and Maurice P. Hunt, *Psychological Foundations of Education.* (New York: Harper and Brothers, 1962), pp. 242–44.

3. Roger Williams, *Free and Unequal.* (Austin: University of Texas Press, 1956), pp. 5–7.

4. Christopher Jencks, *Inequality.* (New York: Basic Books, 1972), pp. 1–233.

5. Congressional Record, March 17, 18, 19, 20, April 7, 8, 9, 10, 13, 14. *Economic Opportunity Act of 1964.* (Washington, D.C: United States Government Printing Office, 1964).

6. Rosella Linskie, "The Field Trip as an Educational Technique," *Texas Journal of Secondary Education,* Vol. IX, No. 2, Austin, Texas, 1956. 18–31.

10 Gestalt and the Integrated Curriculum

> *The world would not function*
> *if there were not*
> *somewhere,*
> *outside time and space,*
> *a cosmic point*
> *of total synthesis.*
>
> TEILHARD DE CHARDIN[1]

Suppose you had never seen an entire automobile. The only part you had ever seen was a set of spark plugs. Would you be able to create in your mind the image of a complete car? If all you had ever seen of an elephant was a foot, could you ever develop an accurate image of the whole animal? Can you project the total picture of a clock from looking at only one small spring?

These simple examples are but a few of the thousands of illustrations of the fact that analysis of separate and discrete parts, no matter how thorough, can never provide an understanding of the whole. Rather, to comprehend the *whole,* it is necessary to analyze from the structure of the whole to the characteristics and function of the parts, not the other way around. This is a brief summary of the chief principle of Gestalt psychology.

The word *Gestalt* comes from the German and means literally "put together." There is no exact English translation. The closest we come is "form" or "shape" or "pattern" or "whole." "Whole" is the word most frequently used in psychological studies and is the one we will use in this chapter.

Chapter 9 discussed one aspect of the field theory of learning, the importance of experience. This chapter will concern itself with the second, the unity of all knowledge.

History

Gestalt theory developed in Austria at the close of the nineteenth century as a protest against the piece-meal analysis of experience which characterized the German school of Associationist thought under the teachings of Wilhelm Wundt. The situation was much like the present controversy between the Humanists and the Behaviorists over the nature of the learner and of the learning process.

By the early 1920's, Gestalt psychology had begun to be absorbed into the main stream of philosophy and psychology. Although thirty years is a short span in the history of ideas, it must be remembered that there were elements of Gestalt thought appearing as early as Aristotle and as late as some modern thinkers like Moehlman[2] and Rogers.[3]

The Whole versus the Parts

Do you remember the fun of blowing soap bubbles? No matter how large and beautiful the bubble, one pin prick and it disappeared altogether. No single part of it was left to be analyzed. Change in one tiny part of the film that composed the bubble resulted in dramatic change in the entire structure. The soap bubble is a classic example of the theory that a Gestalt is not simply the sum of its parts.

On the other hand, there are some elements in nature that do not depend for their definition on their being a part of a whole. A stack of poker chips, a bundle of straws, the seats in an auditorium each has a separate identity that does not depend on a pattern. This kind of grouping is called an *aggregate,* and changing one piece does not affect the others. However, if you think of the pile of poker chips as a *total* bet or the bundle of straws as a *single broom,* or the seats as a *pattern* of seating arrangement, then these otherwise separate things become a Gestalt. An egg by itself is a separate entity. Three eggs, shells unbroken, form an *aggregate.* An omelet is a *Gestalt.* In a true Gestalt the parts become so intermingled and fused that they are impossible to separate.

An aggregate is easily separable. For example, you can remove a link from a chain without essentially changing the nature of the link or the nature of the chain. This last distinction is important especially so as not to confuse the concept of *Gestalt* with the concept of *Set* as it is used in mathematics. Therefore, it can be concluded that the essential idea behind Gestalt is that *parts* have no identity independent of their place, role, and function in the *whole.*

Analysis versus Synthesis

Our society has become so preoccupied with evaluation, criticism, and even cynicism, that we seem to place all the emphasis on analyzing and tearing things apart without knowing how or why they should be reorganized. Riots, civil disobedience, campaign speeches rarely do anything except voice rebellion against the present state of affairs. Seldom do they also contain plans for reorganization. Analyzing is much easier than synthesizing. It takes much less talent to blow up a building or smash a car or slash a painting than it does to produce any of these.

Here is a sketch of a dissected fly.

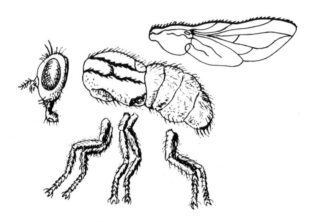

Figure 10.1 *Dissected fly.*

You can see the wings, the complex eyes, the body, the feathery legs. You can look at such a specimen as long as you like but you will never be able to define *flight* if you have never seen a fly in the air. Autopsies can only be performed on dead bodies. Only dead (static) languages can be studied with any degree of final accuracy. Latin is much easier to parse, decline, and diagram than is a living, changing language like English or Basque.

Experience and Perception

Perceiving reality is a very important facet of Gestalt. In Chapter 9, while you were *perceiving* or experiencing numerous dogs, you were also perceiving or confronting an unorganized mass of other experiences. Experiences do not occur in neat little packages. Our world is a babble of unsequenced and unrelated experiences. As you try to study, you are also listening to the radio or TV; as you drive your car, you are aware of other cars; as you cook or work in the yard, you are distracted by the telephone ringing. It is the job of the mind to sort, organize, classify, and interpret all these perceptions; to put them into patterns that have meaning; to rearrange them whenever new experiences occur. The human mind performs these complex functions as it develops its own numerous Gestalts.

Learning, Thinking, and Problem Solving

The *Elementists* (Behaviorists) have historically rejected the idea of the "wholeness" of organized experience and have held to the idea that connections among remembered items, regardless of the nature of the item, is the organizing principle of the mind. (Remember the elephant and the peanut?) Elements (experiences) are hooked together like beads on a string, and the character of an element does not change or affect any other elements or modify the whole.

In many ways, the logical extension of the elementist psychology is seen in linear computer programming. Strange things sometimes come out of the computer because it can deal only with discrete and separate items. It can select, sort, match, tabulate, and report, but it cannot produce any form of conceptual synthesis.

An example of the influence of the elementist school of thought is the vast proliferation of objective tests, programmed items, and learning kits which are concerned only with right or wrong answers. There is no provision for individualized experience or personal interpretation. The danger of this is illustrated by the story of the illiterate recruit in World War II who was given an oral examination by the Army psychiatrist. Some of the questions were: "What would happen if your tongue were cut out?" "I couldn't talk." "Right." "What would happen if your nose were cut off?" "I couldn't smell." "Right." "What would happen if your ears were cut off?" "I couldn't see." "wrong!" "Why did you say that by losing your ears you wouldn't be able to see? I'm curious about your answer." "Oh, I was thinking that without my ears, my hat would fall down over my eyes and I couldn't see."

Many times students are penalized for "wrong" answers which are wrong only in the sense that they do not relate to the test key or to the teacher's anticipated response. Using a Gestalt philosophy, one can see that associations and responses vary with the interaction of the learner with reality as well as with the test items. It is the perceptual grouping of items which relates past and present experience. The basic process in learning is not a series of unrelated hook-ups but the discovery of the structured organized wholeness of the environment. This leads to quite a different pattern of learning—not drill and memorization, but understanding and generalization. The more generalizations we develop, the easier it becomes to develop larger categories. For example, the mind can go from the idea of DOG to the idea of ANIMAL to the idea of LIVING THINGS.

One other important point is that while logic is useful in showing how ideas develop, logic is not the only system by which the mind thinks. Much human problem solving involves a reorganization of the problem material itself. A good example of this is cooking. A kitchen full of utensils, spices, and ingredients cannot guarantee that the cook will be able to put together an edible meal. All the utensils and ingredients must be arranged in proper proportions and put together into a whole. Remember, an omelet is not just three eggs.

The Integrated Curriculum

It was not until the late 1920's that Gestalt psychology became a part of American thought. Lewin,[4] Cooley,[5] and Mead[6] applied Gestalt theory to social psychology and developed ideas like role theory, the integrated personality, and reality therapy. After that, Gestalt principles were applied to education in the form of the integrated curriculum. In 1932, some elementary school systems initiated a new approach to the unified curriculum, called the Unit Approach.* Much later, in the form of the Core Curriculum, it began to influence secondary education.

Under the unified approach, the teacher was able to develop a focus (Gestalt) and explore with the students all the facets of the concept. Built into this approach was the pragmatic idea that skills be taught if, when, and to whom they were needed. A good example is again found in the kitchen. If you are in the midst of preparing a meal and discover that your paring knife is dull, the normal process is to stop and sharpen the knife. You would probably not take the time to go through the kitchen, gather up all the knives and have them sharpened just in case you may soon need a sharp knife. Thus, skills became the tools for learning and thinking, not the end object in themselves.

* A Model outline for developing an integrated unit will be found at the end of this chapter.

Cultural Universals

It was about this same time (the 1930's) that some unification in knowledge began to be attempted in higher education. Wissler[7] in sociology, Moehlman[8] in comparative education, and Katona[9] in economics developed the theory of Cultural Universals.

The theory of Cultural Universals is simply a Gestalt of all those facets of social organization that are common to all societies regardless of time or geography. Cultural Universals are generally listed as:

Art and Architecture	Geography
Economics and Industry	History
Family and Social Organization	Philosophy
Government and Political Science	Religion
Language and Education	Conflict and War

In studying any one cultural, social, or national entity, the Gestalt may look like the diagram below.

Figure 10.2

Any concept can be placed in focus at the hub, just as was demonstrated earlier in the development of the concept *dog.* In addition, a second circle can be superimposed on the Cultural Universals. This could show the curriculum areas and specific learning skills appropriate to the development of a particular segment. For example, math is helpful in interpreting some aspects of economics; language skills are necessary for almost all segments as are skills of scientific thinking and motor coordination.

One of the most exciting things about the learning process is that it is eternally unfinished and each of us can, through heightened awareness, enlarge our own Gestalt to include as much of the world as we care to. Gestalt is not a person; it is not a book; it is scarcely a system. It is one successful and rational approach to understanding, knowledge, empathy, acceptance, and, ultimately, personal happiness and fulfillment.

A Model Outline For Developing An Integrated Unit of Study

Title: _____

Age-grade level: _____

Period of study: _____
(How many days or weeks)

Author: _____

A TEACHING UNIT ON _____

I. Rationale

Why is this particular unit important or worthwhile to teach? How does it contribute to the overall sequence of the school year? Is it timely? Is it possible to motivate the children to personalize this learning? Are adequate resources available?

II. Goals and objectives

State these in general terms. In addition, specific objectives should appear in daily lesson plans. The general objectives should be categorized as those involving:

A. Knowledge
B. Attitudes
C. Skills

These then become the reference list for evaluation at the end of the period of study.

III. Motivation and initiation

Describe several alternate ways in which you may launch the unit in order to develop the highest level of motivation such as, a film, an exhibit, a field trip, or a resource person.

IV. Problem census

Sometimes called The TABA Method, this effort elicits questions from the children then encourages them to classify these questions into larger categories on subtopics for research.

List some actual questions from children and classify them into group topics.

V. Period of teacher-directed, student-directed study

The groups formed around the problem census begin to do research on their topics. List actual group topics. The teacher serves as a resource guide and a motivator, moving around from group to group to help students as the work progresses.

Periodic progress reports may be planned if the Unit runs several weeks.

VI. Integration of other curriculum areas during period of group study

Make sure that students are aware of the wide possibilities of using *all* areas to contribute to their effort. List actual learning activities that will aid each group described in IV and V above. Be sure to include *all* curriculum areas: art, math, science, music, etc., and indicate how you will integrate these. Here you may insert summary sheets like the following to give a quick overview of the whole process. Each objective should be treated.

Objectives	Enabling Learning Activities from the Primary Study Area	Integrated Activities (Math, Sci, etc.)	Resources Used	Evaluation
1. 2.	1. a. b. c. As many as needed for each objective. 2.	1. a. b. c. As many as needed. 2.	1. a. b. c. As many as needed. 2.	1. To what extent was this objective achieved?

VII. Culminating Activity

Describe how you plan to have the various groups report or share their findings with the entire class. This could be a Fiesta Day if the unit were on Mexico, or a Pow Wow if it were on Indians. Use role-playing, construction, writing, art, and any other activities that seem appropriate.

VIII. Evaluation

A. Self-evaluation. Students are urged to judge their own performance by answering questions such as: Did I do my best work? Did I help in the group? Make a list of such questions.

B. Unit Evaluation. The teacher and students evaluate the Unit in several ways.

Did we achieve our objectives? If not, why? Did we achieve other objectives than those listed? What are they? Did we notice some skills that needed additional work? Did we do this?

Did we learn something worth knowing? Did we enjoy working on the Unit? How can we improve our individual and group work in our next unit? Did this unit suggest other units we may want to develop together?

C. There is the possibility of a test or quiz. One approach is to have each research group make up a brief test on their presentation to see if they got their information across to the others in the class.

List some specific ways you may plan a test. Remember that testing is only one form of evaluation and since it checks on content, may actually be the least important.

IX. Resources to be used in the unit
(These will depend on the nature of the study groups.)
A. Persons who can help us.
B. Places we can go for information.
C. Things we can use.
   1. Books: teacher's list; students' list
   2. Realia
   3. Demonstrations or exhibits.
D. Field trips. List actual places and indicate their value in relation to the Unit.

X. How do you see this unit leading into the next unit?

Notes

1. Rev. Pierre Teilhard de Chardin, *Building the Earth,* Dimension Books, Wilkes-Barre, Pa., 1965, p. 80.

2. Arthur Henry Moehlman, and Joseph S. Roucek, *Comparative Education.* (The Dryden Press, New York, 1953).

3. Carl Rogers, *Freedom to Learn: A View of What Education Might Become.* (New York, Merrill, 1969).

4. Kurt Lewin, *Field Theory in Social Sciences,* Research Center for Group Dynamics Series. (Westport, Connecticut: Greenwood Press, 1975), Reproduction of 1951 edition.

5. Charles H. Cooley, *Human Nature and the Social Order.* (New York: Charles Scribner's Sons, 1922).

6. George H. Mead, *Mind, Self, and Society.* (Chicago: University of Chicago Press, 1940).

7. Clark Wissler, *Man and Culture.* (New York: Thomas Crowell, 1923).

8. Moehlman and Roucek, *Comparative Education.*

9. George Katona, *Organizing and Memorizing Studies in the Psychology of Learning and Teaching.* (New York: Hafner, 1967), Reproduction of 1940 edition.

11 Piaget and Developmental Learning

The child grows intellectually not so much like a leaf, which simply gets larger every day, as like a caterpillar that is eventually transformed into a butterfly.

PIAGET[1]

Is a tomato a fruit or a vegetable? As you try to answer this question your mind is going through a vast number of complicated operations. Have I ever seen a tomato? What fruits do I know? What vegetables do I know? Which of these categories does the tomato fit best? Does it belong with red things? With round things? With things to eat? With things that grow on trees? With things that grow on vines? Mentally, you are shuffling quickly through an immense catalog of concepts and categories in order to classify the word *tomato.* This task would be much more complicated, even impossible, if you had never experienced (seen or tasted) a real tomato. In an oversimplified way, this is what Piaget, the Gestaltists, and the field-theory psychologists describe as the mental process involved in learning. Although there is no research that clearly relates the work of Jean Piaget to the Gestaltist movement, there are numerous examples of similarity between the two.

From his earliest years, he was fascinated by natural sciences, and when he was only ten he published a short paper describing his careful observations of an albino sparrow. For the next ten years he did intensive research on mollusks; after publishing more than twenty papers he was considered one of the world's few experts on mollusks. Piaget's intensive study of biological development led to his study of the organism's adaptation to the environment. Among the many generations of mollusks he studied, he noticed certain structural changes in succeeding groups. These changes could only be attributed to their moving from large lakes where there was much wave activity to smaller, quieter ponds. From such studies, Piaget concluded that mental development is also largely a process of adapting to the environment and of extending biological development. Thus, from sparrows, to mollusks, to humans, Piaget progressed from biology to environment to psychology.

One of Piaget's first studies involving children was done while he was an assistant to Alfred Binet. Binet was working in a laboratory school in Paris attempting to produce a reliable standardized test. Piaget found all the minutae of item analysis, statistics, and correlations rather tedious. As the work developed, however, he became more interested in the incorrect answers that children gave to questions than to the test items themselves. He was intrigued, not with the simple right or wrong answer, but rather with the reasoning process that produced the answer. For more than two years Piaget tested and analyzed the responses of children. Thus began his monumental work in the field of the mental development of children which has made him one of the best known scholars of the twentieth century.

Piaget's Theory of Intellectual Processes

With amazing similarity to the Gestaltists, Piaget held that there are four processes basic to intellectual organization and development: *schema, assimilation, accommodation, and equilibrium.*

Schema

Even the word itself suggests the same concept as does Gestalt—diagram, plan, pattern. As children begin to confront reality, they begin to make groupings of things that seem to belong together. After a number of experiences, they are able to observe gross differences in the things around them. They can then make judgments, sort out experiences, and arrive at accurate concepts and generalizations. At first, as we saw in Chapter 9, it is difficult for young children to recognize the differences between, for example, a large dog and a small horse. In other words, as children multiply and refine their experiences, they find it easier to become more accurate in their classifications and to develop valid schema.

Assimilation

Piaget took the term *assimilation* from biology. Just as the food you eat is digested and assimilated by your body, so the experiences you have are also digested (categorized) and assimilated (fit into existing schema) by your mind. This is an on-going process involving many different experiences at the same time. As the mind assimilates more and more experiences, each schema grows larger and more complex. When the complexity causes some change in a schema, Piaget calls this new process accommodation.

Accommodation

Accommodation is the mental activity, that takes place when learners confront a new thing never before experienced. The mind, like a giant computer, begins to search through its categories or schema. If it cannot find a schema that the new thing fits exactly, then it either creates a new schema or it modifies a familiar one. Perhaps the new schema is a combination of several others. In the example of the tomato, your mind may have settled on a schema something like

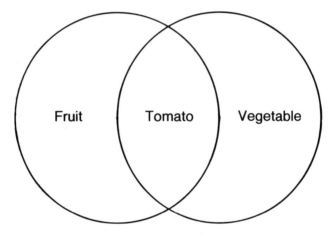

Figure 11.1

This means that the answer still is not clear but you know there is a relationship between fruit and vegetable, and somewhere there is the tomato.

Equilibrium

Piaget uses the term *equilibrium* to indicate the necessary balance between assimilation and accommodation. Both of these processes of the mind are constantly going on simultaneously. If all the mind did was assimilate and never accommodate, you would end up with a short list of large bits of knowledge with no awareness of how they are related. On the other hand, if all the mind did was accommodate, you would end up with a long list of small groups that you would be unable to relate to one another.

As the mind of the learner struggles with the great mass of unorganized experience it confronts every day, it is trying to organize: to assimilate and to accommodate. Often, among children and creative adults, their organization may be different from the one the teacher or parent or testor expected. What Piaget has shown is that there is no wrong categorizing; there is only classifying that is consistent with the thinker's own schema.

Periods of Cognitive Development

Piaget lists four periods of mental development:

1. The period of sensori-motor intelligence (0–2 years)
2. The period of preoperational thought (2–7 years)
3. The period of concrete operations (7–11 years)
4. The period of formal operations (11–15 years)[2]

While Piaget claims that the four stages are fairly typical, he warns against expecting them to be fixed and invariable. He points out that the ages at which children go through these stages vary with the individual's experience and intellectual potential.[3]

The period of sensori-motor intelligence (0–2 years)

Human infants are born with certain basic reflexes, like sucking and grasping. When an object is put into the infant's mouth, he sucks on it. When an object is put into her hand, she grabs it. They do not differentiate between a nipple or the edge of a blanket, they suck them both. Only later do infants begin to *accommodate* the sucking reflex and search for the milk-supplying nipple.

As infants mature they begin to do more differentiating, such as hand-to-mouth coordination, eye–hand coordination, perceiving objects outside themselves, becoming aware of cause and effect. Children at age two are mentally quite different from new-born infants. They have probably begun to speak, to choose, to make decisions, to try to get what they want. All these suggest that they have progressed from pure reflex acts to a form of *intentional* behavior.

The period of preoperational thought (2–7 years)

Perhaps the single most important development during the period of preoperational thought is in the use of language. From ages two to three years children begin to use words as symbols. They are able to make the transition from the concrete object to the oral symbol which represents the object. Later, they will go one step further and substitute the written symbol for the real object.

At first, even in the oral stage, the child usually begins with nouns, then action words, then sentences. Language facility develops rapidly and four year olds can understand what is said to them. Along with this increasing skill in language, comes rapid development of semi-abstract and abstract concepts.

Language helps children exchange information with others and thus begin to become socialized. It enables them to learn to internalize words and thus to begin to think. Most important, it is the key to their being able to think about their own thoughts.

Another significant aspect of the preoperational period is the development of quantitative concepts. This is evidenced by young children's growing ability to recognize conservation problems. They are becoming aware of the fact that the quantity of matter remains the same regardless of changes in shape or position. By the end of this period—approximately at 7 years of age—the child is able, after many real experiences, to begin to see the logic of the conservation of number, area, volume.

The fact that children at this period have learned to think about their own thoughts allows them to question their own judgments. Thus, the groundwork for critical thinking and evaluation has been established.

The preoperational period is one of dramatic intellectual growth and mental and social change. It is marked by the constant and rapid development of improved machinery for learning and by a move from ego-centered to socialized behavior. The 7-year-old bears little resemblance to the 2-year-old!

The period of concrete operations (7–11 years)

During the four-year period of concrete operations, most children develop skills in making logical decisions and in "decentering" their perceptions. Concepts of speed, space, time, and cause and effect begin to have meaning. The latter part of this period is held by many educators to be the ideal time to introduce history. Children younger than nine or ten years of age generally have little or no accuracy with regard to past time. "In 1492 Columbus discovered America" has very little meaning to the typical seven year old. However, the average eleven year old is interested in how many miles an hour will it go or how long does it take to get there by plane. Seriation (more or less, increasing or decreasing, long or short) also begins to have some significance and lends itself to extended forms of language development as well as to mathematical concepts and operations.

Classification and categorizing continue to become more refined, and schema increase in number, size, and complexity. The child is growing and developing and learning. Most important, learning is far more independent than before. For example, many parents and teachers are surprised that some children seem to "break down" at about the age of ten, especially in the area of reading skills. Such a breakdown indicates that earlier learning was not really conceptualized (perhaps only memorized) and responsibility for independent reading is too much for the inexperienced child.

The period of formal operations (11–15 years)

According to Piaget, the mental structure reaches maturity during the period of formal operation. All the mental processes are refined and become integrated. Theorizing, hypothesizing, and scientific reasoning are understood for the first time. There is an awareness of the difference between facts and logic and an argument can be analyzed as logical (or illogical), independent of its content.

In other words, this period is the culmination of the growth and development of all the previous stages. Its quality depends on the nature of all that has gone before and what began at birth comes to full fruition in adolescence.

Implications for the Teaching-Learning Process

Piaget's philosophy applied to the teaching–learning process helps to answer the persistent questions *when to teach* and *how to teach*.

When to teach

Readiness for learning should be a major concern of all teachers. If curriculum plans are designed without regard for the levels of mental development, the learner can only fail. Reading, for example, depends almost entirely on progression from concrete to symbolic thought. Arithmetic can only be understood when children have had experience with conservation and seriation. History and geography have no meaning without an understanding of time and space. Critical thinking can hardly be attempted until learners can think about their own thoughts. Music, dance, and gymnastics all depend on a great network of integrated motor, cognitive, rhythmic, and social skills. Piaget, however, while emphasizing the importance of developmental tasks, does not ignore the factor of individual differences. He states clearly that different individuals manifest different rates of maturation, different stores of experience, and different histories of social interaction.

How to teach

Piaget considers active interactions of the learner with the physical and social environment as the most significant school-related factors which stimulate (or retard) mental growth and development. Experience is of prime importance, and activity is a *must.* No amount of demonstration or lecturing can take the place of individual experience with reality. Here again, Piaget emphasizes consistency with children's levels of development.

Further, the attitude of the teacher toward the nature of intelligence and what constitutes learning is a powerful force in shaping the cognitive development of children. As was noted earlier, the self-fulfilling prophecy can make or break any educational theory. In last analysis, what the teachers and their students are taught to expect is largely what they will achieve.

Piaget's work of the past half-century has validated many earlier approaches and has opened the minds of educators to interest in inquiry that cannot but make an imprint on the history of ideas in the twentieth century and beyond. His emphasis on developmental learning and on individual progression stands as a monumental contradiction to the elementists, the behaviorists, and, to some extent, to the statisticians. Most, if not all, of Piaget's own work was the result of in-depth observation of a very small sampling; it was not treated statistically; it was more of the nature of testimony than of empirical, clinical experimentation.

Notwithstanding these limitations, he has made an impact on educational thinking comparable only to that of John Dewey.

The great body of literature that has developed out of his detailed notes and careful observation of his own three children has indeed changed the way most educators view the learning process.

The Case of Kim and the Ice Cubes

Kim was just two. She was a most perceptive child and began to talk at the unusually early age of ten months. It was a very hot summer and Kim's family ate out-of-doors on a number of evenings. During these family cook-outs, Kim became fascinated with the ice cubes in the various drinks. She discovered the ice bucket and had a great time picking up cubes and bringing them to anyone who was holding a glass or a cup. As the cube became colder in her hand, she would say, "Hot!" After many such experiences, she learned from her parents to say, "Cold!" Each time she said this she watched her parents to be sure they were happy with her response.

The real problem with the ice cubes came when Kim's mother put an ice cube in a shallow dish and after a little while, the cube completely disappeared. Kim was not ready to understand the melting process. When her ice cube had melted, she would look for it and then cry until one of her parents gave her another.

It was the end of the following summer when Kim was approximately three and one-half years old that she began to be aware of the relationship between the ice cubes and the little dish of water left when it melted. Quite obviously, this very intelligent child was not prepared, even at three and one-half and certainly not at two, to tackle the concept of conservation, particularly when it was complicated by a change in density as well as shape.

Questions for Discussion

1. Relate Kim's experience to a specific aspect of Piaget's theory of intellectual processes. What kind of accommodation was Kim making when she called the ice cube hot?

2. How does Kim's story illustrate the transition between Piaget's period of sensori–motor intelligence and his period of preoperational thought?

3. What aspects of conservation were present in Kim's problem in realizing what was happening when the ice cube melted?

4. Discuss how the various aspects of this case are related to other theories of developmental learning.

The Case of Scotty and the Reading Readiness Test

Scotty was completing his year in kindergarten. As is the custom, he and his classmates were given a standardized Reading Readiness Test. The teacher began with the first section of the test, called *Word Meaning.* The first three items are sample items and she went over them carefully. The second of the three appears below.*

Figure 11.2

At first, everything went well; most students understood what they were supposed to do. Then, without warning, Scotty spoke out in a loud voice. "Wow! That is some bottle of milk! I never saw one so big. I bet all the kids in this school could get a lot of milk out of such a big bottle!"

For a moment the teacher was stunned. She had been concentrating on the directions in the manual and it took her a few seconds to realize what Scotty meant. As you can see, the illustrations of the sailboat, the windmill, and the bottle of milk in item 2 are all about the same size. Such spatial inconsistencies are common in printed tests. While such items generally achieve the purpose for which they were designed, they often unwittingly present flagrant errors because of the printing requirement of fitting a given picture into a given space without regard to relative size.

---

* Metropolitan Readiness Test, Form A. (New York: Harcourt, Brace and World, 1964).

Questions For Discussion

1. Examine a complete Reading Readiness Test for other examples of disproportionate visual presentations. Explain how these could cause the same kind of confusion that Scotty indicated.

2. How is the case of Scotty a good illustration of Piaget's theory of quantitative concepts?

3. Was Scotty showing some signs of being somewhat ahead of his group? How was he indicating that he was probably already thinking at the level of concrete operations?

4. Discuss other aspects of Scotty's reaction which seem to be related to Piaget's theories.

Your Sample Case

If you have witnessed or personally experienced a case that you think relates to any aspect of Piaget's theory of developmental learning, describe the case here. How was it handled? How did you interpret it? At the time, did you understand the theory behind the incident? Would you interpret it differently now? Why?

Notes

1. Jean Piaget, *The Origins of Intelligence in Children.* (New York: W. W. Norton, 1963), p. 172.

2. Jean C. Piaget, *The Psychology of Intelligence.* (Patterson, N.J.: Littlefield, Adams, 1963).

3. Jean C. Piaget, *The Origins of Intelligence in Children.* (New York: International Universities Press, 1952), p. 329.

12 Montessori and the Orderly Mind

children . . . like rows of butterflies transfixed with a pin!

MARIA MONTESSORI[1]

These words were written by Maria Montessori after she had decided that the best preparation for working with normal children would be to visit and examine the educational systems of a number of European countries. She was astounded to see children everywhere reduced to immobility in formal classrooms.

Maria Montessori, the first Italian woman to earn a medical degree, graduated from the University of Rome in 1894. Her earliest experience in medical practice brought her into contact with little children in the slums of Rome. The *Casa dei Bambini* (children's houses) were rooms set apart in the courtyards of large tenement buildings as part of a reformed housing plan. Here she encountered children with all varieties of mental deficiencies and social deprivation. She could not endure only to treat their medical problems, and within her first year of practice she began to devise methods for educating these children. Soon, she had mentally handicapped children from the slums passing the state examinations in reading and writing. As she became more involved and more concerned, she decided to devote her career to education instead of purely to medicine. She believed that her methods which had been successful with defective children could be used with even greater success with normal children.

Thus began a career that spanned more than fifty years of productive effort in improving the educational practices of primary and elementary schools. Montessori encountered great opposition from orthodox educators but the sight of children "disciplined but annihilated"[2] gave her the strength and courage to overcome such opposition. She was so successful in her efforts that from 1900 to 1907 she held a position as lecturer on pedagogical anthropology at the University of Rome and later was appointed government inspector of schools for all of Italy. During her later years she traveled over much of the world supervising training courses in her method.

The Method

The prime concern of Montessori was to establish an air of freedom with order in the classroom. This "free discipline" allows children to develop a sense of independence and responsibility. It also helps them to learn at a very early age that true discipline comes from within one's self.

This first aspect of the Montessori Method provides for freedom of movement so long as this freedom does not interfere with the rights of others, does not transgress good manners, and does not disrupt the harmony of the group.

The second aspect is the "didactic material" designed to lead children to learning through interest and concentration. The many facets of this educational apparatus allow the teacher to demonstrate a precise way of performing the necessary movements. Then, as the children become more skilled and more self-directed, the teacher is free to give individual attention and to teach on a one-to-one basis.

The Technique

The Montessori technique, designed to follow the natural physiological and psychological development of the child, can be classified into three distinct parts: motor education; sensory education; language development. The technique is unique in that, while the source of the content for motor education is the environment, life itself, the source of the content for sensory education is carefully structured, preselected material. Both of these areas of content provide opportunities for oral and written language and basic mathematics concepts.

Motor education

Beginning with simple physical measurements—height, weight, etc. —Montessori designed school furnishings unlike any that had hitherto been used in classrooms. Tables were sturdy yet light enough for children to move and rearrange. Large and small tables were provided, making it easy to have children work alone or in small groups. Desk chairs and arm chairs were of varied sizes to allow for the comfort of children of different heights and weights. Wash-stands with basins at varying heights had upper and lower shelves for storing personal items like toothbrushes, soap, and towels. Many low storage units were available for keeping the teaching materials in order, and chalkboards were hung so that the smallest child could reach them. There were even rows of small bath tubs so that children could be bathed regularly.

The use of movable furniture allows children to seat themselves comfortably in a place and position they select. Through this activity the children learn to gain control of their physical movements and to rationalize their use of space. This ability to move about with grace and ease was considered a vital skill by Montessori.

In addition to the child-sized furniture, Dr. Montessori insisted that the classroom be colorful with large prints of the old masters for beauty and inspiration. The typical Montessori school has a large open playground and space for a garden. The outdoor areas are arranged to make it easy for the learning activities to flow out of or into the classroom and thus create an awareness of the unity of the physical world. The Montessori philosophy stresses the importance of environment. Environment can modify personality, foster development, enhance potential, and often overcome serious limitations. On the other hand, it can also stifle, depress, and destroy. In a totally unfavorable condition, even plant and animal life will die. Children, too, are subject to annihilation by inhospitable surroundings which not only make learning distasteful but often end by making children neurotic and even psychotic. Thus, we see Dr. Montessori's concern for humanism in education expressing itself at the level of the most basic and vital personal needs.

Sensory education

Unlike the structure of the Gestaltists or the individualism of Piaget, Montessori's sensory education was planned around a series of carefully designed approaches to learning. One of her strong basic concepts is that sensory experience must occur before any abstract learning can take place. In this regard, she is in close sympathy with the field-theory psychologists and with the discovery method which has recently been reintroduced into the professional literature. Thus, it can be seen that most new ideas in education are really old ideas, having been used by creative teachers before their "discovery" by clinical researchers.

Montessori makes a most applicable point concerning sensory education. She says that for most of us, impurities and adulturation in prepared foods pass unnoticed. This is true largely because our sense of taste has been dulled over the years by cigarettes, alcohol, and adulturated foods! Good clean artesian water tastes "funny" after years of drinking heavily chlorinated water. In the same vein, it is difficult to retrain the senses after one has reached adulthood. It is much easier to educate the hands to play a musical instrument during the formative period. The bones and muscles, like the mind, suffer rigidity as the result of years of lack of use and exercise. We refine our sensibilities and multiply our pleasures as we develop our sensory education. Beauty and harmony and esthetic enjoyment are the rewards of a rich sensory experience.[3]

Language development

Like Sylvia Ashton-Warner, a generation later and half-world away, Maria Montessori saw language as a natural development coming out of the rich motor and sensory experiences of children. Also, from her early medical education, she was acutely aware of the need to train children to discriminate among sounds as a precondition for learning language. Metal bells arranged in chromatic order, resonant tubes, small bars of wood, and little harps are all designed to give the child experience in tone and timbre. Rhythms and simple songs also offer a means for developing hearing and recognition of differences among sounds. In addition, Dr. Montessori used a technique called "little meditations" or lessons on silence to develop an awareness of the absence of sound and a sense of tranquility.[4]

Since language is an imitative process, parents and teachers should pronounce the sounds of the words clearly and completely when they speak to children. This listening vocabulary is the child's first exposure to language. As words develop out of sensory experience, the child begins to develop a speaking vocabulary. This is probably the most important transition children make in language development. They love rolling new words around on their tongues and making songs out of sounds they have learned, repeating them over and over again. Not only do children go through the process of naming, recognizing, and pronouncing words, but they learn to form sentences and to use comparative forms of adjectives and adverbs and tense and number forms of verbs. It is estimated that children should have a speaking vocabulary of from six to ten thousand words before they can be successful in school.

Keep in mind that some relearning necessarily takes place in the classroom. Not all children come to school speaking standard English and many come from bilingual homes. Both Maria Montessori and Sylvia Ashton-Warner see writing and reading as developing simultaneously and at a much earlier age than at the six to seven year-old level normally expected in American primary schools.

According to Montessori, all that has gone before—sensory education, motor education—is only a preparation for the skills of reading, writing, and dealing with quantities. Many refined experiences have prepared the hand to write; real life experiences have prepared the mind for conceptualizing words. In the act of writing, the mental and motor skills are synchronized into a harmonious action of communicating.

A child who has muscular problems can be extremely frustrated with writing equipment. On the other hand, a child with limited social and environmental experience, has nothing to write.

The former problem can often be alleviated by using typewriters, even as early as four or five years of age. Surely, had typewriters been available when Montessori was planning her materials, they would have been included. Only in recent years have schools of special education seen the wisdom of using electric typewriters for handicapped children. They are still not widely used with so-called normal children. Yet, here is the perfect instrument for teaching left-to-rightness, spacing, spelling, linear page arrangement, and many other complex spatial and motor skills required for writing.

The latter problem, having nothing to say, can only be remedied by enlarging the child's world through many varied and rich experiences. Experience-deprived children usually have limited language skills and almost no imagery or curiosity. Their world must be widened and opened and made available to them.

To write is to be able to combine two complex mental and sensory skills—thinking and lettering. In her didactic materials, Montessori provides boxes of alphabetical symbols. Letters are cut from sandpaper, gummed paper, and heavy board to enable children to "experience" the shape of the letters. All this is done to provide them with an ease and familiarity with writing so that when they have something to say, they do not have to be self-conscious about the motor skills but rather are able to concentrate on the ideas while the motor skills are done almost reflexively.

Do you remember the first time you drove a car? You were so preoccupied with the mechanical and motor aspects that it was difficult to be concerned about a destination. You were driving! Not to any particular place or with any particular purpose except to drive! Now, after much experience, you are hardly aware of the mechanical movements. Stop at a stop sign, signal a right or a left turn, pass only in permitted lanes. All this while your thoughts are already at your destination. "What will I say to my class today?" "Suppose the secretary can't find that file!" "I do hope the meeting won't last too long." Brake, stop, signal, turn, stop, park, lock—all done without a conscious thought. So it should be with language skills. They are tools, not ends in themselves. Nobody reads reading! You are always reading for some kind of content. The same is even more true of writing. Trying to write when you have nothing to say becomes merely an exercise in penmanship.

Throughout her discussion of language skills, Montessori stresses the many aspects of reading—recognizing colors and fine variations of shades; understanding that numbers are symbols for quantities as letters are symbols for sounds; seeing that musical notes represent certain keys to be played to produce harmony. In all these applications, she emphasizes the progression from concrete experience to abstract development to conceptualized thinking.

One aspect of Montessori's philosophy which has not had much attention is her regard for diet. Since the children in the early Montessori schools were there for very long days, two meals were served. In addition, a great effort was made to instruct the parents in the close relationship between success in learning and an adequate and nutritious diet. Montessori often said that what we sometimes think of as a bad child is a sick or hungry child.

Montessori's concept of diet was at least a half a century ahead of the biochemists and nutritionists who are now advocating multivitamin therapy for everything from learning disabilities to senility. Her "learning to do by doing," derived from her strong Aristotelian philosophy, predated John Dewey. Her didactic materials would have delighted the heart of Rousseau who believed that the young should be taught with real things. So it appears that Maria Montessori, like many scholars in many fields, was out on the cutting edge of her profession—a very lonely place to be but a very satisfying one with respect to the quality of results one is able to achieve.

The Didactic Materials *

There are many, many individual items of planned materials used in the Montessori classroom. These are available from most reputable school supply houses. In some instances, they can be constructed by the teacher or by parents or aides.

A few of the Montessori materials are pictured here as illustrations of the kind of things that are included in the category *didactic materials.*

Motor development

For motor development, the most common materials are the dressing frames.

* Illustrations from *Educational Teaching Aids Division Catalog,* Vol. 2 (A. Daigger & Co.).

DRESSING FRAMES

1. Motivate children to dress themselves.
2. Help develop independence.
3. Strengthen small fingers.
4. Coordinate finger movements.
5. Develop hand–eye coordination.
6. Are self-correcting.
7. Are attractive and attention holding.

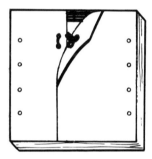

Figure 12.1 *Hook and eye frame.*

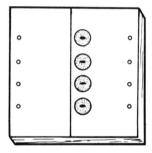

Figure 12.2 *Large button frame.*

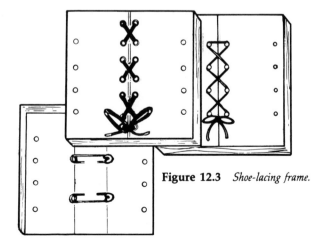

Figure 12.3 *Shoe-lacing frame.*

Figure 12.4 *Safety pin frame.*

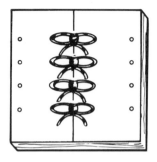

Figure 12.5 *Bow-tying frame.*

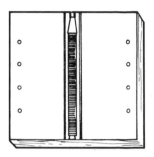

Figure 12.6 *Zipper frame.*

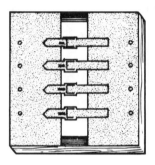

Figure 12.7 *Buckling frame.*

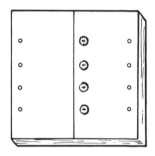

Figure 12.8 *Small button frame.*

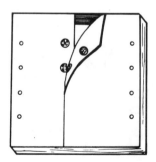

Figure 12.9 *Compression snap frame.*

Spatial development

Ideas of length, height, width, area, volume, together with the sense of touch, sight, discrimination of size and form are developed through various sets of cyclinders.

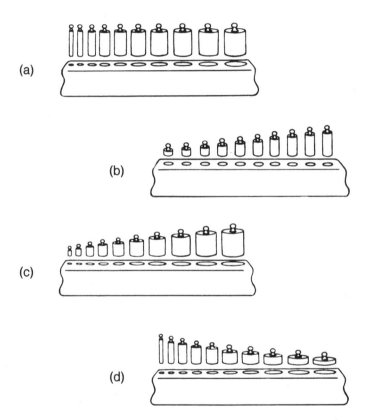

Figure 12.10 *Cylinder blocks.* **(a)** *First cylinder block. All of the cylinders are the same height; their diameters vary.* **(b)** *Second cylinder block. All of the cylinders have the same diameter; their heights vary.* **(c)** *Third cylinder block. The sizes range from the shortest cylinder, which has the smallest diameter, to the tallest cylinder, which has the largest diameter.* **(d)** *Fourth cylinder block. The sizes range from the tallest cylinder, which has the smallest diameter, to the shortest cylinder, which has the largest diameter.*

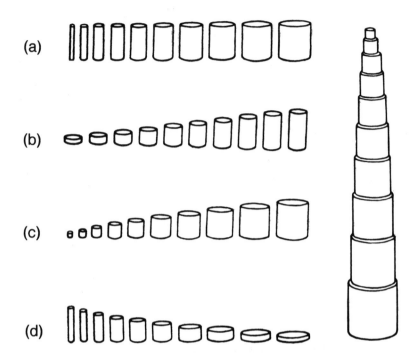

(a)

(b)

(c)

(d)

Figure 12.11 *Companions to cylinder blocks.* **(a)** *Companion to first cylinder block. The cylinders are the same height; their diameters vary.* **(b)** *Companion to second cylinder block. The cylinders have the same diameter; their height varies.* **(c)** *Companion to third cylinder block. The sizes range from the shortest cylinder, which has the smallest diameter, to the tallest cylinder, which has the largest diameter.* **(d)** *Companion to fourth cylinder block. The sizes range from the tallest cylinder, which has the smallest diameter, to the shortest cylinder, which has the largest diameter.*

Sensory apparatus

These materials teach size differentials using touch and sight.

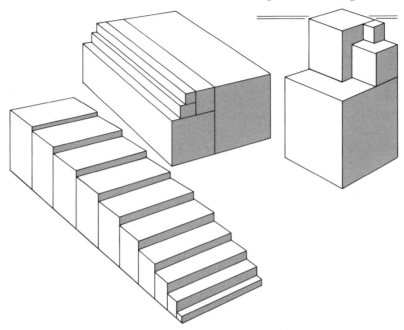

Figure 12.12 *The broad stair. This activity is slightly more difficult than the pink tower. There are ten hardwood rectangular solids, finished with nontoxic brown enamel. All pieces are the same length, but the size of the cross-section varies to give a 1 : 100 ratio. Blocks are designed according to metric measurements so that differences in height between any two can be filled exactly by one or more other blocks in the set.*

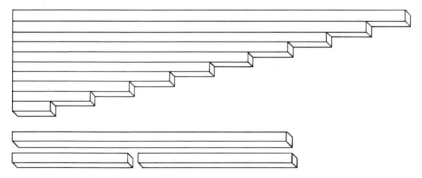

Figure 12.13 *The long stair. This activity requires the child to make the sharpest distinction among sizes. There are ten hardwood rods, finished with nontoxic red enamel. All of their cross-sections are the same size. The rods vary in length. The longest is ten times as large as the shortest. There are numerous measuring and length relationship implications.*

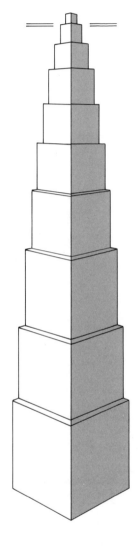

Figure 12.14 *Pink tower. This activity will help the child to learn size distinction. There are ten hardwood cubes finished with nontoxic enamel. The ratio in volume between the smallest and largest is 1 : 1000. This activity has a built-in error control.*

Color awareness

Color recognition is developed through a variety of uses of these color tablets:

1. For first experiences with color differences.
2. Appeal to the imagination of the child.
3. Demonstrate the existence of fine differences.
4. Develop color discrimination ability.
5. Increase appreciation of colors in child's environment.

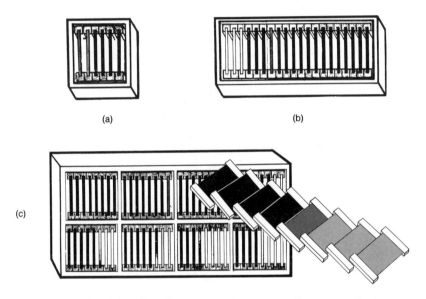

(a)

(b)

(c)

Figure 12.15 **(a)** *Color tablets.* **(b)** *First set. There are six tablets in a wooden box—two red, two blue, and two yellow.* **(c)** *Second set. This is a beautifully matched set of twenty-two color tablets, paired in eleven bright, bold colors and housed in a wooden box for storage. The tablets motivate the child to compare the colors, to match them, and to separate them into groups.*

Letters and numbers

Alphabets in manuscript and cursive writing and numbers on single or group cards with counting circles enable the child to progress smoothly from concrete to abstract (symbolic) thinking.

LETTERS

(a)

(b)

(c)

Figure 12.16 (a) *and* (b) *Large manuscript letters provide multi-sensory learning experiences.* (c) *Sandpaper alphabet.*

NUMBERS

(a)

(b)

Figure 12.17 (a) *Sandpaper numbers.* (b) *Cards and counters.*

Sound

The first experience with music is through the use of true toned bells of identical size and shape in full and half-notes. These provide a pleasant introduction to music.

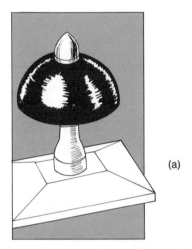

(a)

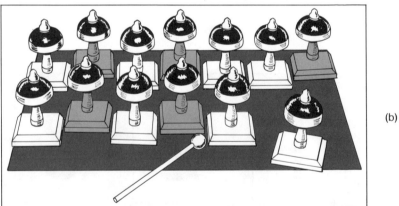

(b)

Figure 12.18 (a) *Precision bell.* (b) *Set of tuned precision bells, all the same size. The child can learn to distinguish the bells by their sound alone.*

Summary

In summary, the Montessori Method is based on these distinctive concepts:

1. From birth to the age of 6 or 7 children have *absorbent minds* that endow them with a great capacity for disciplined work and a voracious appetite for learning.

2. The *prepared environment* enables the Montessori teacher to have at hand special teaching materials that develop a child's ability to see, to feel, and to discriminate among shapes, sounds, and textures. All this sensory education is a preparation for reading, writing, and computation. In such an environment the child also learns to master simple requirements and to follow directions—skills that are critically important to the growth of general intelligence.

3. With *didactic materials* carrying the burden of the instruction, the Montessori teacher is able to operate discreetly in the background. The teacher's primary task is not information-giving but diagnosing each child's interests, level of understanding and skills, and the most fruitful line of development. Then the teacher is able to guide the children to those materials and experiences that will build on their interests and strengthen their needs. Teachers are free to teach success not failure.

The basic idea of the Montessori philosophy is that all children carry within them the persons they will become. In order to develop these physical, intellectual, and spiritual powers to the fullest, they must have freedom which is achieved through order and self-discipline. They must have liberty within limits, balancing individual freedom with collective interest. Discipline is present through the prepared environment, and in the ground rules of the class the limits to freedom are set. Children thus learn to assume responsibility for their actions.

Montessori tries to build a foundation for a lifetime of creative learning. To do this, characteristics like initiative, independence, self-confidence, persistence, a sense of order, the ability to concentrate, and an increased curiosity and a positive attitude toward exploration, discovery, and learning are developed.[5]

There are any number of current innovations in education that could have had beginnings in the Montessori philosophy—ungraded schools, programmed learning, teaching machines, Cuisenaire rods, curricula based on the discovery method of learning, the concern for the physical well-being of children, and the emphasis on good nutrition. All these developments are strikingly similar to Montessori's basic strategies.

It was Maria Montessori's one goal to introduce children to the joy of learning at an early age and to provide a framework in which intellectual and social development and self discipline could grow hand-in-hand.

The Case of Bruce

It was Thanksgiving Day in Plymouth, Massachusetts. Many families from Boston and New York and towns all around the area had come to Plymouth to enjoy the day. Museums had arranged their finest displays of the early Pilgrim days, and private homes, some built before 1776, were open to the visitors. Many residents of Plymouth dressed in Pilgrim costume. The highlight of the day was a beautifully served traditional Thanksgiving dinner in one of the authentically designed restaurants overlooking the harbor and Plymouth Rock.

One young couple had traveled from Boston with their four-year-old son, Bruce, to enjoy the day. Bruce was tired but excited and hungry when they sat down to dinner. Bayberry candles were lighted, and the marvelous odors of turkey and dressing drifted out of the kitchen.

Bruce was a bright child, and his questions soon got the attention of dinner guests at nearby tables.

"Daddy, did the Pilgrims really step on that very rock when they got off the ship?"

"Wow, I never saw such a big turkey!"

"Where do cranberries grow?"

"What is bayberry?"

"How come the candles smell so good?"

"If I blow them out can you light them again?"

"Boy, this is good pie. What is mincemeat made from?"

"Didn't the Pilgrims have electric lights?"

"Why did they wear those funny clothes?"

"I really liked the museum where they had all that stuff about whales. Some day I'll be a sailor on a whaling ship and bring you back some really big teeth!"

"Were you here when the Pilgrims landed?"

All the while Bruce's parents answered his questions clearly and honestly and in a way that helped him understand. The one answer he had difficulty with was time. The year 1620 didn't mean much to him.

After dinner, the family visited the displays in the gift shop and again Bruce was most articulate.

Meanwhile, a teacher who had been sitting at a nearby table at dinner couldn't help stopping Bruce's parents to chat about his wide vocabulary and his interest in all the experiences he had enjoyed that day. Bruce's mother explained that she and her husband spent a lot of time with Bruce and his friends just talking and that they always tried to avoid baby talk or talking down to them.

Bruce's mother was very proud of her bright young son, but as they left she said sadly, "I just don't know what will happen to Bruce when he has to go to school. I have seen some of the first-grade readers and I'm afraid there is very little in them to challenge Bruce to want to read. I am building up a library of books for him and for his baby brother so that they will always have something interesting to read. I do not want either of them to lose interest in words and especially in reading!"

Possible Solutions

1. Bruce sounds like a smart alec who had been unduly encouraged by his parents to show off. They should have told him to be quiet, especially during dinner in a restaurant.

2. The parents should have told Bruce that they would answer all his questions when they got home.

3. A pupil like Bruce will be a very big problem to the typical kindergarten or first-grade teacher because he is used to having the attention of adults and of being treated as an adult.

4. When the first-grade teacher tries to get Bruce interested in the basal reader, he will probably pay very little attention and could begin to develop poor reading habits.

5. The parents should continue to answer Bruce's questions and even encourage him to ask further questions.

6. Identify some of the Montessori principles demonstrated by this case.

Would you choose any of these solutions? If so, you may write your explanation below. However, if you would not choose any of these, you may go on to the next page and write your solution to the problem.

Your Solution to the Case of Bruce

The Case of Sherri

Sherri was a student teacher in the sixth grade. She was well prepared and sincerely interested in doing a good job. Her lessons in almost all areas were interesting, and the children were attentive and involved. The one area in which Sherri had difficulty was arithmetic. She tried very hard but became impatient and testy when the students did not follow her explanations. She seemed to have special problems with weights and measurements, area and volume, as well as with shapes and solids.

After several observations, Sherri's university supervisor sensed the problem. Sherri, herself, was not too sure of quantitative concepts and in all her math lessons she tended to verbalize rather than demonstrate. After several observations and conferences, the supervisor asked Sherri if she would be willing to try something different. Sherri was most willing.

The "something different" was an arrangement for Sherri to spend a week teaching math at a school for blind children in the same town.

At the end of her first lesson, she came out of the room to look for her supervisor. As soon as she found her, Sherri blurted out "They can't see!" The supervisor assured her that this is not unusual for people who are blind! Now and then there were a few children admitted to the school who were legally blind but who could see a little. Sherri was truly upset. She knew she had to go home and plan an entirely different approach for blind children.

The school for the blind had abundant material by way of tactile and kinesthetic shapes, forms, and surfaces. Sherri began to learn to use them and as she did, she, herself, began for the first time to develop some clear understanding of quantitative concepts. In defining a cube, for example, she had to do more than give a verbal definition. She had to give each child a cube, have the child hold it in his or her hand, feel the dimensions, and arrive at a definition from these sensory experiences. Soon, she found herself actually enjoying teaching the very math that she had been so afraid of before.

At the end of the week, her university supervisor re-assigned Sherri to her original student-teaching classroom with the reminder that she should continue to use some of the valuable lessons she had learned at the school for the blind.

Possible Solutions

1. The university supervisor should have required Sherri to enroll in additional classes in math so that she would have a firmer grasp on the material to be taught.

2. Sherri should have been allowed to go on and complete her student-teaching and be recommended for teaching with the proviso that she be placed in a team-teaching situation that did not require her to teach math.

3. Sherri should have been counseled out of the teaching profession.

4. The real first-hand experience with teaching blind children was a powerful lesson in the importance of multi-sensory experience as a background for abstract learning.

5. How does Sherri's experience relate to Montessori's philosophy of sensory-motor learning?

Would you choose any of these solutions? If so, you may write your explanation below. However, if you would not choose any of these, you may go on to the next page and write your solution to the problem.

Your Solution to Sherri's Problem

Your Sample Case

If you have witnessed or experienced a case in your own school life that you think emphasizes the importance of any or all of the Montessori principles, describe the situation and explain how you saw it handled. Did you agree with the solution? Why?

Notes

1. Maria Montessori, "Montessori System," *Encyclopaedia Britannica,* Vol. 15, Chicago, 1964. p. 761.

2. Maria Montessori, *The Montessori Method,* trans. A. E. George, 1919, quoted in *Encyclopaedia Britannica,* Vol. 15, page 761, 1964. ed.

3. Maria Montessori, *The Montessori Method.* (New York: Schocken Books, 1964), p. 221.

4. Nancy McCormick Rambusch, *Dr. Montessori's Own Handbook.* (New York: Schocken Books, 1967), p. 119.

5. Nancy McCormick Rambusch, *Learning How to Learn.* (New York: Helicon Press, 1962), p. 78.

13 | Motivation

What Makes Sammy Run?

BUDD SCHULBERG[1]

Who knows? Why do some Sammies dash and spring and leap toward success while others seem to drag through life in leaden shoes, barely able to keep up or give up trying altogether?

What is motivation? How is it that some persons are enthusiastic and vivacious and untiring in their efforts while others are disinterested and phlegmatic or even lazy? Great differences in degrees of motivation are apparent in physical and social as well as in educational activities. Often, the difference can be rooted in physical well-being (or the lack of it) or in other aspects of basic human needs.

This chapter will concern itself *chiefly* with motivation as an essential element in the learning process. However, mental activities can rarely be dealt with separate and apart from the physical and social aspects of the life of the learner.

Definition

Motivation is generally described as the desire to achieve a goal that has value for the individual. Because of this close relationship between motives and values, it seems clear that cultural mores and value systems have much to do with motivation. Material success, possessions, power, youth, and vigor are all goals that our competitive society has identified as highly desirable. Thus it appears normal to be motivated to achieve these goals. Those who reject them and substitute other goals not so favored by society are labeled deviant, strange, and non-conforming. Yet, even among those whose values appear to be the same, there are vast differences in achievement.

Education is another of those goals that society has long identified as highly desirable. At first, education was valued because it developed the complete person—the Renaissance Man. Later, after the period of Revolution, education took on a different value; namely, it became the magic door to all job opportunities. One need only to look in the yellow pages of any metropolitan area telephone book to see the long list of professional, skilled, and semi-skilled training courses that are offered. Even the typical university or community college catalogue has at least as many professional colleges and course listings as they do liberal arts or esthetic subjects.

Thus, we seem to have gone from a definition of education as a preparation for living to education as a preparation for a career. During days of unemployment, anger, hostility, and criticism are usually directed toward the liberal aspects of the educational system. There is always great emphasis on vocational and career education during times of economic depression.

In the case of either definition, there are great variations in motivation. Surely there were laggards in Aristotle's day who inspired his famous remark that "man cannot learn without pain." Today Hayakawa speaks of boredom as "the enemy of the young." Both writers were concerned with motivation.

Motivation and Learning

Motivation, like learning, is a *process*. It is a process which leads students into experiences in which they can learn. It is a process which energizes and activates students to keep them interested and alert. It is a process that keeps students' attention focused on a specific task. It is a process which helps fulfill both the need for immediate achievement and a sense of moving toward larger goals.[2]

Motivating students is not an easy task. Among other things, it requires patience, understanding, and ingenuity. Yet, every teacher knows moments of panic and dismay over not being able to motivate a child or a group of children. "I don't know what happened. I had such a good unit all planned and it just fell flat!" "How can I compete with 8-track stereo, TV, and radio?" "What's wrong with me that I can't turn these kids on?" One junior high teacher was most sympathetic toward a new student in her early fall semester English class who arrived on the first day wearing what appeared to be a hearing aid. To her great dismay, she discovered several "hearing aids" all tuned in to the World Series! Defeated? Not necessarily. She just re-worked her lesson plans around baseball for a few weeks, didn't make a big scene, and weathered the season.

There are no devices, methods, or techniques that will motivate all students in the same way or to the same degree. Motivation is as complex as personality itself. It is a blend of environments, attitudes, values, goals, and self-concepts.[3] It is as fragile as a snowflake and can evaporate before it is recognized. Students from deprived environments and with urgent basic needs can hardly get excited about the math or science "you will need to get into college." Students whose goals are as immediate as today's food or drugs or tonight's shelter, couldn't care less about a lesson in poetry. Students whose self-image projects a sullen, hostile, persecuted self are in no frame of mind to attack a theoretical problem of physics.

Children in all of the above situations are by no means exclusively those from the ghetto. The children of the elite and well-to-do have many of the same problems. Likewise, teachers in all socio-economic brackets face similar problems of motivation in the face of jarring values, unmet needs, and rising decibels of distractions.

Failure and Motivation

If "nothing succeeds like success," then nothing fails as surely as failure. We are never unmotivated. Dropouts are motivated to get out of a system that has defeated them. Suicides are motivated to try to find relief from an unbearable existence. Alcoholics and drug users are motivated to seek a fantasy state in which they do not have to face a painful situation. Think of the things you yourself have "dropped out" of and alongside each, list, if you can, the motivation for dropping out. A club, a church, a marriage, a job, an engagement, a friendship, a life-style—all these can develop circumstances that motivate you to move *away from* rather than *toward* certain experiences.

It is important to note that people are motivated not only by things as they are but by things as they perceive them to be. Perhaps even more important, they are motivated by the way they perceive themselves. This latter point was discussed earlier in Chapter 2, *Self-Concept.*

Motivation and I.Q.

Edmund Gordon, a well-known sociologist, goes beyond the consideration of the self-concept to add that motivation may play a critical role in the development of intelligence. He further suggests that the separation of feelings from thought processes may be senseless. For all learners, but especially for poor and minority children, involvement or interest in the learning task plays an especially important role.

Children do not see the relevance of curricular material if the values and attitudes they bring from home differ significantly from those presented at school. However, when instructional material emphasizes the strengths of the culture from which the youngsters come, their ability to learn appears to increase.[4]

Reading, which has had more than its share of attention during the last few decades, is hardly attractive as a skill because in many cases the materials to be read in school are so far removed from the realities of the learner. Father coming home from work in his car, carrying a brief-case, greeted by a loving wife, two clean, beautiful children, a dog, and a cat—all in a vine-covered cottage—is outside the experience of many children. Yet, we continue to ask them to struggle with reading materials filled with this sort of thing without seeming to be aware of the incongruity between those materials and their lives. That reading material must have relevance is illustrated by Faber, in his horrifying but beautifully touching book, *Naked Children.* In it, he describes how skillful children can become at feigning illiteracy while at the same time reading very efficiently those things that touch their lives—the racing form, motor magazines, the lists of arrests, and the legal decisions concerning juvenile delinquents.[5]

Goal-Setting as Motivation

In general, we are all interested in the things we ourselves plan. We work much harder on self-made goals than we ever would on goals planned for us by someone else. Participation in goal-setting carries with it a sense of pride and responsibility for the achievement of the goal. The owner of a business—large or small—works much harder than do his salaried employees or day laborers. He has much more at stake. If the venture fails, the employees can move on to other jobs, but he has invested his money, his time, his effort, and his pride. He simply cannot walk away from an unsuccessful venture. Many companies benefit greatly from the high degree of motivation they are able to develop in their employees through fringe benefits, humane working conditions, and fair administrative policies. The Japanese have been far more successful in this effort than has almost any other group. Joining a Japanese company is like becoming a member of a close-knit family, participating in benefits, helping in decision-making, and sharing substantially in profits. The Japanese employee is a participant not merely a spectator and his loyalty to his company is, in large part, loyalty to himself.

Successful teachers seem to have a special ability to involve students in goal-setting, in identifying with the learning problem, and in generating a kind of sense of personal excitement for new ideas. All of this does not necessarily imply fun, but it does suggest that learning can be a satisfying and pleasurable experience. The class plans become "our" plans, the learning problems become "our" problems, the teacher uses "us" more frequently that "you people" and there develops an attitude of "we are all in this together; let's make it work!" In such a classroom, the teacher becomes the organizer, the encourager, the resource person rather than the goal-setter, the task-master, and the all-powerful judge, jury, and executioner.

Encourage students to help with goal-setting. Don't be afraid to try "their way" even if it isn't "your way." One successful teacher begins each new school year by writing on the board two headings:

WHAT I EXPECT OF YOU	WHAT YOU EXPECT OF ME

Under each heading, the teacher and the students develop lists of attitudes and responsibilities. As the lists develop, it becomes clear that they are much the same: courtesy, respect, preparation, listening, awareness of the needs of others, fairness, punctuality, frankness, honesty, and dozens of other values that are important in the inter-personal relationships which cause a classroom to function successfully. In reviewing the lists, the students and the teacher develop the ground rules for the class, set the limits of freedom, and define the wide range of shared responsibility. A sense of mutuality begins to develop early in the school term and establishes a climate favorable to learning and— more important—a *wanting* to learn.

Competition as Motivation

Competition is probably the oldest motivational device in the history of education. "An *A* is better than a *B*." "The gold medal goes to the student with the highest grade-point average." "All students who missed more than six of the ten correct answers must do the assignment over." Sylvia Ashton-Warner, in her recent book on American education, was dismayed at the great emphasis placed on grades. She says, ". . . In New Zealand we grade mutton and wool, not people."[6]

Many psychologists have pointed out the various evils in the use of competition as motivation. Competition ignores individual differences in rates of development as well as in levels of attainment. It tends to build selfish, unsocial, and highly ego-centered attitudes. It can result in a ruthless drive for victory at the expense of another's defeat.

There are many studies on the advantages and disadvantages of competition.[7,8,9,10] However, even those noted also offered evidence that cooperation is at least as effective as competition and in many cases results in a higher level of self-esteem and self-motivation. Competition and cooperation are not mutually exclusive procedures. Competition is the hidden factor in all evaluation of whatever kind. However, there is no reason for competition to be used as the only tool for motivation. Excessive pressure to compete can be harmful to the self-concept of the individual as well as to his academic progress. On the other hand, a situation totally without competition can become stultifying and ineffectual.[11]

Teacher Variables Related to Motivation

Great variations exist among teachers as well as among students. Motivation is not a magic formula or a quick cure-all. It is not a skill possessed by all teachers to the same degree. It is possible for two teachers of equal intelligence, training, and knowledge of subject matter to differ widely in their ability to motivate students to learn. A great part of the difference can be accounted for by the effect of the teacher's personality on the learner.

One rather extensive study was made of the opinions of approximately 4,000 high school seniors concerning best-liked and least-liked teachers. The four most frequently mentioned reasons for *liking Teacher A best* were:

1. Is helpful. Explains things clearly. Uses examples in teaching. (51%)
2. Is cheerful, happy. Has a good sense of humor. (40%)
3. Is human, friendly, "one of us." (30%)
4. Is interested in and tries to understand pupils. (26%)

The four most frequently mentioned reasons for *disliking Teacher Z the most* were:

1. Is cross, crabby, sarcastic; loses temper. (50%)
2. Does not plan her work; is not clear on assignments. (30%)

3. Has "pets" and picks on certain students. (20%)

4. Is "snooty" and acts superior, even outside of class. (20%)

Notice that in each case, the causes for liking or disliking Teacher A or Z are not entirely related to teaching skills but rather to personality traits. As a matter of fact, mastery of subject matter, which is highly rated by professional specialists, ranked sixteenth on both student lists.[12]

It might easily be concluded that only normal, happy, well-adjusted people should be teachers. But what about the teachers who are successful precisely because they are neurotic? The zany, enthusiastic actor-type who can grab students' attention by just walking into the room. The compulsive-obsessional type who demands a high degree of order and precision and thus instills in students a sense of the importance of order in their lives. The perfectionist who, as some students would say, "is very easy to please—the work just has to be perfect!" but who expects (and gets) from students more than they thought they were capable of accomplishing. These and many other examples support the idea that some so-called neurotic teachers are extremely creative, highly successful, and dearly loved by their students.

Thus, we see that teacher personality is another variable—highly volatile, difficult to define, and almost impossible to capture in a job description. Yet it is that intangible something that distinguishes one classroom from another and causes a teacher to make an indelible impression that remains long after the lessons are forgot.

Just as there is no handy-dandy recipe for a good teacher, there is no infallible set of procedures for motivating learners. There are, however, some things that teachers can do to make it possible for motivation to develop. Here are a few suggestions:

1. *Be flexible.* Try to be aware of the state of readiness for learning. Be direct or indirect as the situation demands. This may be considered professional treason, but many painful confrontations could be avoided if the teacher could on occasion simply say, "To hell with it," and enjoy an open, honest conversation with students—about anything they want to talk about. It may even be a discussion of why the teacher isn't reaching them.

2. *Be perceptive.* Try to perceive the world from the students' point of view once in a while. That you are well fed, well groomed, and well organized for the day doesn't mean that they are.

3. *Know your subject.* Be prepared. Don't bluff but don't be afraid to say, "I never knew that!" You'll be surprised how much you'll learn from your students.

4. *Be consistent in expectations.* Don't let things slide one day, then crack down the next.

5. *Be creative.* Try new approaches and *demonstrate* points as you teach. Just because you understand an idea doesn't mean that your students will get it after one verbal run-through. Be willing to experiment. Why not?

6. *Listen!* Hear and try to understand what students are telling you.

7. *React.* A nod, a smile, a comment, or a light touch on the arm may be the highlight of a student's day. Don't be mawkish or patronizing. Students can spot a phony from a hundred yards.

8. *Be relaxed and informal.* Pontification is for cathedrals not for class-rooms. Try to maintain an easy conversational style without becoming too chummy. Students have only disdain for teachers who try to imitate their latest jargon or current dress.

9. *Keep your sense of humor.* Not taking yourself too seriously often makes the difference between an embarrassing situation and a bit of comic relief.

10. Above all, *keep control!* Especially of yourself but also of the class and of the learning situation.

Student Variables Related to Motivation

Just as there are unpredictable and unmeasureable factors among teach-ers and their personalities, so there are numerous variables among the students they teach. Thus, we have in the classroom the highly complex process of variables meeting variables in a volatile setting of inter-personal relationships which are constantly in a state of dynamic flux. It is a situation demanding more poise, more awareness, more common sense than almost any other human relationship.

A successful contractor who had just completed a complicated and detailed job estimate hesitated before presenting his final bid. "I know how much the steel costs, I know how much tile, concrete, wiring and fixtures cost. Now, if I only knew how much work one man can do in a day, I'd have an airtight basis for a bid!" Thus, we see the human variable with all its intricate and unpredictable facets as the key to costs of building as well as to degrees of intellectual achievement.

Student personality

A personal sense of security seems to be the most important factor in a student's successful approach to learning. It is certainly a significant element in the success or failure of an open versus a structured class-room atmosphere. Personally secure students seem to thrive in permissive, self-directed, open-ended situations. Insecure students feel threatened and frightened when there is no clearly defined structure or expected closure (final exam, for instance). The independent student can define a problem, make it his own, and go about seeking a solution while a dependent student is waiting for the teacher to tell him what to do next. Unfortunately, many of our schools are designed to keep students docile and dependent. Then, suddenly, upon graduation, overnight, they are expected to become fully functioning, self-directed, responsible adults.

Anxiety and compulsion, other-directedness, the need to excel, the need for peer acceptance—all these and a host of other personality traits create a constant kaleidoscope of challenge for the teacher. Very often a whole class seems to take on a personality composed of parts of the total mosaic of traits of the various members. Too, some class groups are dominated by the natural leader who can reinforce or destroy the teacher's efforts or even the teacher himself.

Praise versus blame

In general, praise is a much more effective motivation than is blame. Here, too, however, the teacher must be very careful not to overdo a good thing. Some teachers use praise so insincerely that students soon realize that approval from such teachers isn't worth much. "He gives everybody A's." "He doesn't even know your name but he says 'You did a great job.'" One such teacher filled out a complete semester's grade sheet without realizing that he had been given the wrong student list by the registrar. Praise is great when given sincerely. Blame is usually a waste of time. Probably the best approach is some form of reality therapy in which the teacher and student can sit down together and calmly and rationally examine a problem without blaming anyone.

Differences in learning styles

An earlier chapter discussed the importance of modalities in the learning process. "Modalities" is really only another word for learning styles. Some students learn best verbally, some visually, some physically and kinesthetically. Some students are imaginative and creative. Some are quick, some are slow. In any case, the teacher needs to become aware of the various learning styles as early as possible in order to use them and also to vary them. Otherwise, the verbally oriented student never develops any learning style except reading while the physically oriented child might not learn to read.

Knowledge of results

One very significant factor in motivation is immediate feed-back. Never, never ask students to prepare an assignment that you do not intend to read, comment on, and return as soon as possible. Everybody feels better if he knows how he is doing on a given task. "How much further do we have to go? How much longer before the test? When will the grades be out?" All such questions are indications of the eagerness to know results. In order for a student to compete against himself it is necessary for him to know how he is progressing. Such continuous evaluation is necessary to the idea of progressive goal-setting. Knowledge of a student's progress should not become a state secret; it should be shared with the student and with his parents. (More about this in a later chapter on evaluation.) Anyone is more likely to avoid errors if he knows what those errors are. In addition, it is important for the student to be able to understand not only that he made a mistake but *why*. Otherwise, there is no point to evaluation.

Providing knowledge of results is one of the very effective ways of motivating students to apply themselves to the task at hand. Such motivation is honest and fair, it is not contaminated with competition and it is not filled with blame. It simply says to the student, "Here is what you did. Can you do better?"

The Curriculum as Motivation

The content and sequence of the curriculum itself acts as a motivator, either encouraging or discouraging further effort. If the content is dull, insignificant, and irrelevant, there isn't much motivation provided. On the other hand, a stimulating lesson is the surest way of turning students on to learning.

Now we have come full circle—if the curriculum is dull and unmotivating, it is probably because the teacher is dull and unmotivating. There is no such thing as teacher-proof curricula. A poor teacher can make even the most exciting world event seem boring, whereas a lively, interested, caring teacher can bring excitement to even the most mundane piece of information.

A good teacher is a dramatist, a ham, a dreamer of dreams, and a painter of verbal pictures. He is basically an existentialist, weaving together his own personality, outlook, values, hopes, and ideals into an invigorating zest for knowledge that few students can resist.

The Case of George

George had finally finished elementary school. For him it had been a long series of failures and changing schools and constant complaints by teachers and principals. George was a good boy, very intelligent but a poor speller, a poor writer, and a terrible math student. However, he had a natural skill for anything mechanical. He had built himself a small workshop behind the family garage and the moment he got away from school each day he would rush home to his workshop. Nobody was ever sure what he was doing or making but as long as he wasn't in trouble, his parents were satisfied.

After the eight miserable years of elementary schools—public, private, Catholic, day, and boarding schools—George's mother marched him into the office of the high school principal. "Here is my son. He is 14 years old. I am trying to decide whether to raise him or kill him." The principal was a wise and patient man. His response to George's mother was, "Let me have him for at least six weeks and I'll help you decide."

As soon as classes began, the principal called George in for a long talk. They covered many topics and it soon became apparent that George had a passion for motors, for cars, for engines—for anything that turned, moved, whirred, or spun. The principal took George to the shop teacher and asked him to be George's counselor. In turn, the shop teacher contacted George's other high school teachers—especially those in English, math, and history—and explained that George was very low in achievement and could use all the motivation he could get.

Life began to look brighter for George. He spent hours in the high school auto shop, more hours in his own workshop, and even began to do some homework. At the end of six weeks, the principal called George's mother and asked her to come in for a conference. She went, expecting the worst. Imagine her surprise when the principal said, "Mrs. L., you have a very highly gifted boy. I would definitely recommend that you plan to raise him. As a matter of fact, he is going to be on the Freshmen Honor Roll." "Honor Roll! What's wrong with this school? Whoever heard of George's being on the Honor Roll?"

George was indeed on the Honor Roll, not only that six weeks but every six weeks of his four years in high school. He graduated with honors and went on to great distinction in college and later in his chosen profession—mechanical engineering.

Possible Solutions

1. Had you been one of the elementary principals who dealt with George, would you have suggested that he forget academics and go on to a purely vocational school?
2. George's father was all for getting him a work permit and letting him get a job in an auto repair shop.
3. Do you suspect that there might have been something about the elementary curriculum that turned off George's interest in school?
4. How does George exemplify the need for the teacher to be aware of varying modalities and learning styles?
5. What was probably interfering with the process of motivation in George's case?

Would you choose any of these solutions? If so, you may write your explanation below. However, if you would not choose any of these, you may go on to the next page and write your solution to the problem.

Your Solution to the Problem of George

The Case of Clara

Clara was a young teacher who had spent several years teaching in a lumber camp in the Pacific Northwest. Each summer she went to the university to earn further graduate and credentialing credits. Her professor in a social science class took great interest in her because she had lived in various parts of the world with her father, who had been an archeologist. She was a most interesting conversationalist and knowledgeable about many countries and cultures.

A problem began to develop when Clara kept going to her professor almost daily asking for more reading lists and for additional research assignments. She was so intense in her approach to summer school that her professor finally suggested they have lunch together so they could talk informally.

"Clara, you are working yourself to death. What's your hurry?" Then it all came out. Clara's father had died in the Middle East of a rare disease which she too had contracted. In her case, the disease had settled in her eyes and doctors all over the United States had examined her. The prognosis was that her condition was incurable. The medical consensus was that she would begin to lose her eyesight gradually over the next two or three years then be totally blind. She explained all this without bitterness or fear. It was only that knowing the facts, she had set herself the task of trying to learn all she could as fast as she could. She had a fantastic collection of tapes, talking books, and even a Braille typewriter. She had hundreds of color slides from all over the world and she would look at them by the hour. It was as if she were frantically storing in her memory as much knowledge of the world as it was possible to gather in the time she had left.

Clara and her professor-friend spent a most interesting summer in and out of class. Weekend trips along the coast, into the mountains, painting, sketching, photographing. It was an exhausting but exhilarating time.

Clara became totally blind three years later but was more than adequately prepared to go on teaching, writing, and living fully.

Possible Solutions

1. The professor became entirely too much involved in Clara's problem.
2. Clara would have been better off had the professor tried to keep her from being so over-motivated.
3. How does Clara's case shed new light on an unusual aspect of motivation?
4. Can you think of other causes for over-motivation?
5. How could a case like Clara become a serious peer-problem?
6. Could Clara's over-motivation have been mistaken for a fierce competitive spirit?

Would you choose any of these solutions? If so, you may write your explanation below. However, if you would not choose any of these, you may go on to the next page and write your solution to the problem.

Your Solution to the Problem of Clara

Your Sample Case

If you have witnessed or experienced a case in your own school life that you think emphasizes the importance of any or all facets of the problem of motivation, describe the situation and explain how you saw it handled. Did you agree with the solution? Why?

Notes

1. Budd Schulberg, *What Makes Sammy Run?* (New York, Viking Press, 1941).

2. Don E. Hamachek, *Motivation in Teaching and Learning.* (Washington, D.C.: National Education Association, 1973), p. 3.

3. Don E. Hamachek, *Motivation in Teaching and Learning,* p. 4.

4. Edmund Gordon, "New Perspectives on Old Issues in Education for the Minority Poor," *Information Retrieval Center on the Disadvantaged,* Bulletin 10 (Winter 1975), pp. 5–20.

5. Daniel Fader, *Naked Children.* (New York: Macmillan Co., 1971).

6. Sylvia Ashton-Warner, *Spearpoint.* (Maryland: Alfred A. Knopf, Inc., 1972).

7. J. B. Miller, "Cooperation and Competition: An Experimental Study in Motivations," *Teachers College Contributions to Education,* No. 384 (New York: Columbia University Press, 1929).

8. E. B. Hurlock, "The Use of Group Rivalry as an Incentive," *Journal of Abnormal and Social Psychology,* Vol. 22 (1927), 278–90.

9. V. M. Sims, "The Relative Influence of Two Types of Motivation on Improvement," *Journal of Educational Psychology,* Vol. 19 (1928), 480–84.

10. J. Vaughn and C. M. Diserens. "The Experimental Psychology of Competition," *Journal of Experimental Education,* Vol. 7 (1938), 76–97.

11. Walter B. Kolesnik, *Educational Psychology.* (New York: McGraw-Hill, 1963), p. 327.

12. Don E. Hamachek, *Motivation in Teaching and Learning,* pp. 9–20.

14 | Operant Conditioning

*Do men learn like animals? . . . do
animals learn like men?*

BIGGE AND HUNT[1]

Ever since Pavlov's famous dog, psychologists have engaged in a never-ending argument over the answer to this question. For almost a century psychologists have been attempting in various ways to apply the Pavlovian principles to human behavior. In his experiment, Ivan Pavlov, a Russian scientist, trained a dog to salivate at the sound of the ticking of a metronome. While he established that there was no connection between the ticking sound and the dog's mouth watering, he further tested his theory by giving the dog food each time the metronome ticked. After he had repeated this many times—delivering food as the little machine ticked—he decided to try something new. He let the metronome tick but he did not give the dog any food. However, the dog's mouth watered just the same. The sound alone was enough to stimulate the dog's taste buds and salivary glands in anticipation of food—a pure reflex action.

How many times has your own dog come running at the sound of the can opener or at the odor of cooking meat? Haven't you, yourself, felt your mouth water at the aroma of freshly ground coffee or at the smell of bread baking in a bakery? It appears that human taste buds and salivary glands also respond automatically to stimuli that has in the past given satisfaction.

This involuntary response of the glands is called an *Unconditioned Response.* The food is the *Unconditioned Stimulus.* The response of the glands to sounds and odors is the result of learning to associate them with food or drink. This action is called the *Conditioned Response.* The condition or triggering mechanism is not the food itself but something you have learned to associate with food. Thus, a certain symbolic step has been taken between the unconditioned stimulus (food) and the unconditioned response (mouth watering).

After Pavlov learned about the existence of this intermediate step, he went on to see if the response pattern was a permanent one. He found that after a while, no matter how many times he let the metronome click, if he did not give the dog food, the dog's flow of saliva decreased and then stopped altogether. Next, he tried giving the dog food only occasionally after the clicking sound. This seemed to re-establish or *reinforce* the conditioned response.

The term used for the disappearance of a response is called *extinction;* the reinforcement and re-creation of the response is called *spontaneous recovery.*

One further fact that Pavlov established is that some stimuli can be *generalized.* This means that sounds that are similar to the original stimulus cause a similar response. As the stimulus becomes more and more dissimilar, the responses cease entirely. Thus, along with *generalization* comes *discrimination.* Even your dog quickly learns the difference between the sound of your doorbell and the sound of your can opener. He usually behaves quite differently in the two situations. When the doorbell rings he probably goes to the door and begins to bark. When the can opener is operating, he might very well rush into the kitchen and get set for food. On the other hand, the sound of a doorbell or of a can opener in a television commercial can bring about responses similar to the original until the dog learns to discriminate. Thus, we see in Pavlov's experiment many of the elements and much of the terminology of learning as a physiological-psychological process.

Conditioning and Human Learning

John Watson was the first psychologist to apply the principles of conditioning to human learning. Watson believed that everything we do is pre-determined by our past experience and that behavior is simply a series of stimulus-response reactions. He believed so firmly in this theory that he once declared that he could take any group of newborn babies and condition them to become anything he wished—a doctor, a writer, a lawyer, a criminal. (Does this sound a little like George Orwell's *1984*?) Watson even went so far as to question the very existence of the human mind and of human feelings. He believed that what we call thought is merely a form of subconscious talking to one's self and that feelings are a form of glandular response to the environment.

Watson's views were accepted enthusiastically by psychologists who had grown weary of trying to examine man's consciousness or mental life. They had become convinced that studying the human mind was an unscientific effort and that it was better to examine and measure something that could be examined and measured—namely, actions and behavior—than something so invisible as the mind.

One school of educational psychology that developed out of Watson's theory was that known as the stimulus-response theory or the *S-R Psychology*. The leader of this school of thought was B. F. Skinner. He refined Watson's theories and applied them specifically to behavior control and the learning process. His theories of reward and punishment to modify connections between a stimulus and a response have become classic among theories of behavior control. Watson and Skinner became the new stars on the psychological horizon and their theories are with us to this day.

As we have seen in earlier chapters on Experience, Gestalt, Piaget, and Montessori, not all students of human learning and human nature accepted the stimulus-response theory. Later, Carl Rogers, Abraham Maslow, and even Sigmund Freud espoused a quite different approach called *humanistic psychology*.

Like most educational movements, behavior modification and operant conditioning have enjoyed at least three cycles of renewed acceptance. In the late 1970's we find once again a new interest in these theories of learning. In the modern version, the philosophy of conditioning has given rise to several innovative efforts in the teaching-learning process. The following is a brief review of seven such innovations.

Programmed Instruction

In its broadest definition, programmed instruction is as old as the printing press. For many years the basic curriculum guide for most American schools has been the textbook, outlining and defining the content material, the learning activities, and even the test items. In addition, most successful educational publishers furnish an accompanying Teachers' Manual which gives teachers detailed instructions on conducting a lesson, often even telling the teacher exactly what to say at each step of the lesson. A classic example is the teachers' manuals accompanying the various basal reading series which were popular from the mid-1940's to the 1950's.

A new twist was given to the term "programmed instruction" in the late 1950's when a novel approach resulted in programmed texts. These textbooks differed from the traditional ones in that they were not written in narrative, essay, or expository style but rather in the form of a related sequence of items. These items were discrete, specific bits of information taken from the overall content of a course and set up in a series of steps. At each new step, a single new idea or concept was introduced based on material already taught. When the learner answered or completed the item, he had readily available to him feedback in the form of the correct answer. In this way, he knew without waiting for the teacher to grade or correct his paper just where he had been right or wrong.

Usually, programmed books look something like this:

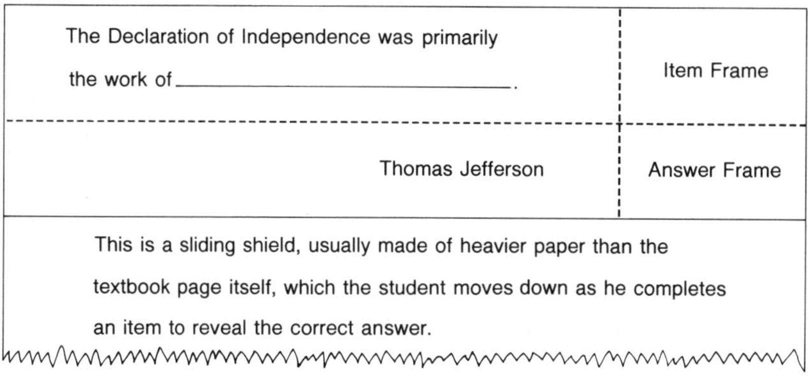

The Declaration of Independence was primarily the work of _____.	Item Frame
Thomas Jefferson	Answer Frame

This is a sliding shield, usually made of heavier paper than the textbook page itself, which the student moves down as he completes an item to reveal the correct answer.

Figure 14.1

These first programmed books were a bit more sophisticated than the simple workbooks that developed during the earlier cycle of Skinnerian influence in the 1920's and 1930's. One of the most popular series of the new programmed texts was called TEMAC in math and science and was published by Encyclopaedia Britannica, Inc.*

Teaching Machines

It was a short step from programmed instruction in book form to the teaching machine. The term was given to mechanical devices which presented programmed items. The machine usually displayed only one item at a time and, in some machines, the learner had control over the time period he required to complete the item.

Many teaching machines were developed at all levels from pre-school game-types to higher math and English grammar. Like the programmed instruction, the teaching machine could handle any discrete, specific bit of information and could also, in some instances, lead to the forming of conclusions and generalizations.

* See a sample of a learning program at the end of this chapter.

Computer-Assisted Instruction

An additional step was taken in the development of sophisticated conditioned learning when computers were invented. The student could sit at a computer terminal—much like a Western Union typewriter—and receive items from a central data bank. Then he typed in his own answers. If his answer was correct, the computer was programmed to type something encouraging like, "Good! Go on to the next item." If the answer was wrong, the computer would type an admonition like, "Re-read the item more carefully and try again. Good luck!"

Some of the newer computer-assisted instruction devices have been so well programmed that they can carry on a dialog with the student. Once he has typed in his code number and name, the computer might type out, "Good morning, Jimmy! Let's see how well you can do today. You made a fine score yesterday—60 right out of 80 items. That's good. Are you ready for item 81? Here we go!"

In one experiment, with computer-assisted instruction in math at the third-grade level, not only did students improve rapidly but they surpassed the progress of students being taught by conventional methods. Also, they accomplished much more drill in ten minutes three times a week than did the traditional classes in the regular daily class periods. Best of all, the enthusiasm was amazing. In one experiment in a school in California in which this author participated, the students watched the clock to get down to the computer center on time. Once there, seated before the keyboard, the degree of concentration was almost unbelievable. No matter that the nine other students were typing away and that the nine other computers were typing back: nothing seemed to distract the students. The math period became almost like a daily relay race with students waiting impatiently for their own ten minutes with the machine. And there was no paper work to take home, no dirty smudges to displease the teacher, and no plague of broken pencils. The children adapted easily to the left-to-rightness required by the machine and thus developed a new awareness of place value and new skills in rapid mental computation. At the end of the year, the third-graders using the computer-assisted instruction showed a gain of just under two years in achievement while the third-graders taught by conventional methods progressed just over one year. When the experiment was tried in other schools, similar results were achieved through grade six.[2]

The areas of reading skills and mathematical computation seem to lend themselves readily to Computer-Assisted Instruction. In these areas, the method has several advantages—the learner can progress at his own rate, he has more individual consideration than any one teacher can give each pupil in a class of twenty-seven students, and the feedback is immediate. This last advantage is significant in that it eliminates much remedial teaching and avoids the problem of discontinuance of learning—the painful process of re-learning something that was learned incorrectly the first time.

Learning Kits

Much of the philosophy and psychology that motivated the invention of programmed texts and teaching machines went on to develop a kind of systems approach to learning. This approach began to take the form of kits or learning packages which included a series of programmed booklets, audio tapes, small recorded discs, study prints, and detailed sets of instructions. Some courses were broken into as many as fifteen sub-units, each in a programmed booklet with all the accompanying audio-visual resources in an attractive package.

The advantages of differentiated pacing and individualized instruction remained, but as the curriculum became more and more systematized and de-humanized, students began to be "turned off." One reason for the loss of interest was the total lack of contact with a human teacher. Tests were administered by a secretary or a teacher's aide and detailed progress charts were posted on the wall of the office or the learning center somewhat in the manner of production charts for assembly-line workers. One small university in the Southwest had an especially disastrous and costly experience when it attempted to package all the pre-student teaching methods courses. After two semesters of fighting a blizzard of paper work, the students rebelled. The program was sharply curtailed, then abandoned altogether except in the areas of math and reading. Even in these two courses, regular small-group seminars were initiated and students felt some personal contact with a teacher.

There is still a serious question as to the suitability of such a self-study approach in a field like teaching, which is largely a social skill. When the learning process is not consistent with the ultimate role expectations there is bound to be conflict and disappointment. Studying teaching techniques with a learning kit is a little like trying to learn to swim from a book—without a pool. In curriculum areas where content and information are the primary objectives, such packaged approaches seem to work well. Individual self-study is an excellent approach when one is highly motivated and is seeking specific knowledge. Skills are a bit more difficult to incorporate into such a program.

Many state Master Plumbers' examinations consist of two parts—the facts and theory, administered in an objective test form, and the application, administered in a model installation form, with the applicants actually completing the installation of a total plumbing system in a scale model building.

When the object of a lesson is to develop attitudes and clarify values, then behavioral approaches become almost impossible to use. There is the dynamic of human give and take which sharpens the mind and enlivens the senses. Being alone with a learning kit is not a very humanizing experience. However, there are some students whose learning modalities are quite compatible with self-study and they do well in such programs.

Behavioral Objectives

Behavioral Objectives is the one area in which the revived philosophy of Skinner and Watson seems to have made the greatest impact on schools in the 1970's. The idea of aiming at a learning target that is *measurable* has great appeal. Teachers, so long plagued by report card problems, seem willing to try anything that would "quantify" their evaluations of students. (There will be more about this in the chapter on accountability.)

Behavioral Objectives spell out in great detail the learning expected to be accomplished—the time limits are set and the degree of acceptable success or failure is stipulated. Thus, behavioral objectives must be very specific and exact. Here is an example from math:

At the end of three weeks, the students will be able to complete all the problems in Section One on Short and Long Division with 80 percent accuracy. Any student accomplishing less than 80 percent must repeat the Section.

Such a statement contains all the elements of a behavioral objective:

1. Specific content—". . . all the problems in Section One on Short and Long Division. . . ."
2. Closure—"At the end of three weeks . . ."
3. Criteria—". . . with 80% accuracy."
4. Measurement—Pass or repeat.

Descriptive Objectives

Descriptive objectives are stated differently and have wider application. For example, here is a sample of a descriptive objective, also from math:

> At the end of the semester, the students should be able to demonstrate skill in the four fundamental operations of basic math.

This is a different kind of statement altogether. It has general content but none specifically spelled out, no hard and fast closure or criteria. These elements make it more difficult to measure.

Note that both examples are from math which is one area in which specific measurable skills can be isolated.

Try your hand at writing both kinds of objectives for an *affective* area like values or understanding or tolerance. Can you assume patriotism from a test? What is a true test of honesty? How do you measure loyalty?

Thus it is clear that the long-continuing argument over objectives is a little like discussing which is better, a knife or a fork. The answer must depend on what you plan to do with these tools. In some cases (cutting), only a knife will do. In others (eating or lifting), a fork is needed. It would seem evident that the objective like the process should be consistent with the job at hand.

Contingency Management

Contingency Management is a term used frequently in referring to the application of operant conditioning in a classroom, especially in schools for the educable mentally handicapped. The basic three-step contingency is response, stimulus, and reinforcement—in that order. In a contingency, the operant (response) is *followed* by presentation of a reinforcer (stimulus) and thus the probability of recurrence of the original operant is increased.[3]

If this three-step device is used, it is possible to bring individual behavior under precise control. "When all relevant variables have been arranged, an organism will or will not respond. If it does not, it cannot. If it can, it will."[4]

Token-Economy Programs

The token-economy (sometimes jokingly referred to as the M-and-M School of Psychology) as a behavior control originated as a technique used by behavior therapists in mental hospitals. For doing such things as dressing properly, eating in an acceptable manner, and working at useful jobs, patients can earn tokens which they can exchange like money for movies, rental of radios or television sets, cigarettes, candy, and other privileges.[5]

When the idea of token-economy is used in classrooms some very interesting things happen. To begin with, the token does not necessarily need to be a tangible thing. In some instances, merely the teacher's notice and praise is just as effective as a tangible reward.[6] In general, however, specific concrete rewards seem to be more successful with students of lesser abilities or with poor self-concepts. Increased weekly allowances are made contingent upon improved grades. Points earned for good behavior can be used to "buy" time in a play area. Reading skills are improved by the subject's being given stickers which he can later trade for a "free" activity or a snack. However, in many instances there is the ever-present problem of lack of generalization. This simply means that a child who continues to be subjected to token-economy motivation finds himself losing interest or letting his behavior disintegrate when the tokens are no longer available. This lack of generalization is probably the weakest part of the program. Apparently, when behavior changes are linked to self-enhancement, increased self-confidence, self-direction, and self-respect, then they have a chance of becoming permanent.[7]

Regardless of the techniques one uses to condition the behavior of others, there is the ever-present variable of the individual with all his own private drives and motives and concerns. In addition, the teaching-learning process depends to a very large extent on how the nature of the learner (human being) is perceived. If, as Hitler thought, all human beings are potentially docile organisms that respond to training and conditioning, then behavioral methods will be used. On the other hand, if the learner is seen as a sensitive, self-directed person, then more humanistic methods are in order. Perhaps all of us are a combination of both and need some of each to achieve our fullest potential.

Sample of a Programmed Text

This short program was prepared for use in social studies classes in the intermediate grades.

Notice that the key to any programmed material is in the careful structure of content and grammar. Each new item *must* have within it some concept linking it to the previous item. For example, while Item 4 seems to introduce a new idea, notice that the key word "curious" was used conspicuously in Item 3. In Item 6, the clue to the answer is contained in the first sentence of the item. Item 7 introduces a new term but there is a different kind of clue contained in giving the beginning consonant and the number of letters in the correct answer. In Items 10, 15, 17, 18, 25, 26, 30, 36, 39, 40, 41, 42, and 45, the answer frames suggest that there is more than one correct response.

You might compare the writing of a good programmed text to a simple task like knitting in which each new stitch is linked to and reinforced by the previous stitch.

Try completing this short program and see how well you do.

Would you like to know what makes a space capsule go? ____

1.

Yes

If you could take a rocket to the moon, do you think you could learn more about what the moon is like? _____

2.

Yes

If you are naturally curious, you probably answered _____ to both Questions 1 and 2.

3.

Yes.

There have always been people who are c - - - - - - about the world in which they live.

4.

curious

As long as man has been on the earth, he has been _____ about the things around him.

5.

curious

This curiosity first led man to discover and find out things. We can _____ new things by adding to what we already know.

6.

discover

This "finding out" and "discovering" is really the beginning of s - - - - - -.

7.

science

The atomic age is not the first age of _____.

8.

science.

There have been many ages of _____.

9.

science

As early as the 13th century, men had been interested in _____ _____.

10.

science discovery

Sailors were interested in _____ because they wanted to learn how to sail ships more safely and accurately.

11.

science

For many years people had believed the earth was _____ _____.

12.

flat

Sailors were interested in science because they were not sure if the earth was _____ or round.	13.
	flat
Even after scientists had convinced people that the earth was _____, no one had any idea that the earth is so big.	14.
	round
Because the earth is so ____, it was easy for sailors to lose their direction.	15.
	big huge
In order not to get ____, most ships sailed along the coasts where they could see the land.	16.
	lost
With no instruments to guide them, sailors traveled only along the _____.	17.
	land coast
The idea of sailing out across the ocean away from ____ seemed an impossible thing to do.	18.
	land coast
It was the Phoenicians and the Greeks who first started to use primitive charts which enabled them to sail out of sight of land and not get _____.	19.
	lost.

They also learned to use the sun and the stars as guides when they sailed out of sight of _____.	20.
	land.
These early sailors even traveled at night using the _____ as guides.	21.
	stars
In the 13th Century some Italian scientists discovered that the compass could be used to help sailors find their_____ _____	22.
	direction
The _____ itself had been invented many centuries before the birth of Christ.	23.
	compass
When the new use of the _____ was discovered in Genoa, it was nicknamed the "Genoese Needle."	24.
	compass
When the sun and stars were hidden by clouds, the captain could now find his true _____.	25.
	course direction
The little _____ would point the direction in the darkest night and the wildest storm.	26.
	needle compass

A few years later the astrolabe was invented. It could do more than the _____.

27.

compass

The word "astrolabe" is made from two words: "astro" meaning star, and "labe" meaning "to take." The two words together mean "to take your position from the _____."

28.

stars

With an astrolabe, a sailor could tell the position of his ship by checking the location of certain _____.

29.

stars

About the middle of the 14th Century, Prince Henry of Portugal used his money and his authority to build a school for _____.

30.

navigators
sailors
captains

In Prince Henry's school, sailors learned about n - - - - - - - - -.

31.

navigation

To help the sailors learn more about _____, Prince Henry built an observatory.

32.

navigation

In an observatory you can look at the sky at night and _____ _____ the position of the stars.

33.

observe
see

Prince Henry also had expert map-makers who drew new ____.	34.
	maps
He sent out ships to sail around the coast of Africa and to re-make the ____ of Africa.	35.
	maps
For all his work in improving navigation, Prince Henry was given the title "_____."	36.
	"The Navigator" "Prince Henry the Navigator"
The art of handling a ship itself was as important as the skill of _____.	37.
	navigation
The Egyptians used manpower to move their _____ over the water.	38.
	ships
Men sat in rows and used oars to _____ the ship.	39.
	move power
The Greeks found out that they could use the wind to _____ their boats.	40.
	move power

As early as the first century B.C., the Gauls abandoned _____
_____ altogether in favor of sails.   41.

manpower
rowers
oars

Another big problem in early _____ was the storage of
drinking water.   42.

travel
shipping

For many years, the only means of storing _____ was in goat-
skin bags or earthen jars.   43.

water

In these bags and jars the _____ soon became unfit to drink.   44.

water

Therefore, a ship could stay at sea only as long as the drinking
water remained _____.   45.

pure
fit to drink
uncontaminated

A new method of storing _____ in wooden casks with tight
lids kept the drinking water fresh for longer periods of time.   46.

water

This meant that ships could now sail for _____ periods of
time and still have fresh drinking water.   47.

longer

While all these things were happening, another _____ invention took place in Germany.

48.

scientific

This important scientific invention made it possible for the work of people like _____ to be read all over the world.

49.

Prince Henry
Copernicus

This scientific invention was the p - - - - - - - p - - - -.

50.

printing press

This meant that through printing and books, sailors like Columbus could learn about earlier scientific inventions and about n - - - - - - - - -.

51.

navigation

Columbus read about Prince Henry's school for _____ _____.

52.

navigators
sailors
navigation

He concluded that all new scientific discoveries are based on _____ scientific discoveries.

53.

old

He also decided that the more he knew about old discoveries, the more new _____ he could make.

54.

discoveries

After reading all the earlier books on navigation and map-making, Columbus decided that the earth is not flat but _____.

55.

round

Then he concluded that if the earth is round, he could sail all the way _____ it.

56.

around

He had a hard time convincing other people that the earth is not _____.

57.

flat

Very few people believed in him. Many people made fun of his new _____ about the shape of the earth.

58.

idea
theory

About this time, many sailors and navigators were trying to find a new route to India. They knew India was east of Europe but they did not know a good all-water route to the _____.

59.

east

Columbus argued that if the earth is round, he could reach the east by sailing _____.

60.

west

He finally convinced the Queen of Spain that by sailing west he could reach _____.

61.

India
east

Thus, it was that Columbus sailed _____ out of Palos,
Spain, one day in the summer of 1492.   62.

west

The Case of Donnie

Donnie was a handsome third-grader who was new in the school. His parents were divorced, and his father, a university professor, had great ambitions for Donnie.

Several weeks after the school term began, Donnie's teacher went to the principal with a very strange story. She said that each time she asked the children to write something or to do any kind of classroom activity which required writing, Donnie put his head down on his desk and began to cry. The principal was a bit skeptical but agreed to visit the classroom and observe the unusual behavior.

A few days later the principal went into the classroom and sat down quietly in the back of the room. The teacher and the class groups went on with what they were doing. Soon, the teacher called the children together and said, "Now, let's write some stories about our learning center activities." As if on signal, Donnie put his head down and began to cry. The principal was truly confused. He went over to Donnie, put his arm around him and said, "Donnie, what's wrong?" Donnie just cried all the harder and kept his head hidden in his hands as all the other children looked on. One pupil said, "Ah, he does that every time we have a writing lesson. He's okay. He just hates to write, I guess."

Later, the principal asked Donnie to come to the office for a talk. "Donnie, what can we do to help you? Is something bothering you?"

"No, I'm okay. I just can't write."

"Who told you you can't write?"

"My father. Everytime I try to write he yells at me and sometimes he hits me with a ruler because I don't spell right or write neat."

"Well, when you are in school nobody does that to you, do they?"

"No."

"How about writing something for me. I'm sure you can do it."

Donnie trembled and shook and struggled for a while but he wrote his name and address then looked up at the principal. "Is that okay?"

"Yes, it's very good and very neat."

"Will you show it to my father?"

"I surely will. Don't worry, Donnie, I'll talk with your father. Now you go back to your classroom and when the teacher asks you to write, remember she will be glad to help you. She won't be angry if you make mistakes."

It took an entire school year for Donnie to begin to be able to write in class. It took even longer for the father to become aware of what he had been doing to Donnie with his unrealistic demands.

Questions for Discussion

1. What behavior showed itself as a *conditioned reflex* in Donnie's case?

2. How does Donnie's reaction demonstrate the three-step contingency of *response, stimulus,* and *reinforcement?*

3. Had Donnie *generalized* his reaction to his father's attitude?

4. What processes of *discrimination* did Donnie have to learn before he was able to respond normally in the classroom?

5. Since the father was using punishment as the only response and reinforcement, what other stimuli were available to Donnie?

6. What do you think was happening to Donnie's self-concept during this continuing humiliating behavior?

7. Is there a place for praise as a response and reinforcement?

The Case of the Telephone Operators

In a southern city of some 500,000 population, a small group of long-distance telephone operators began to show signs of unrest and inefficiency. Their morale was low and there was a lot of bickering. The supervisor was experienced and well prepared to direct the work of the long-lines operators.

The summers were hot and humid and the room in which the long distance operators worked was not air-conditioned. Finally, it occurred to the supervisor that the heat and humidity might be the real problem. She observed the operators taking frequent breaks to go to the drinking fountain and complaining in general about the stools, the headphones, and the equipment. When they began to be snappy and snippy with the customers, the supervisor thought it was time for action.

She talked to the administrators of the telephone company and they approved her seeking some help. It was suggested that the local college might have some interest in the situation. The supervisor asked a member of the psychology staff to come over to see the problem at first hand.

The psychologist came and after a few hours asked if he might handle this in his own way. Permission was willingly given and the next day he arrived with a graduate assistant. They interviewed each operator and asked several questions, all indicating that the telephone company was interested in improving their working conditions. Within two days after the interviews the efficiency rate went up and the general tone of the room improved.

The following week, a crew from a local air-conditioning firm came in and began measurements for the necessary volume of air-condition needed. The efficiency and morale continued to improve. Within another week, air-conditioning equipment had been installed and the room was quite comfortable. The efficiency shot up and the operators seemed happy.

About three weeks later, the air-conditioning company manager (at the direction of the psychologist) came in and told the operators that there was some defect in the installation and that there would be some days when the room would be hot while they worked to repair the units. During the following weeks there were frequently days without air-conditioning but the efficiency and morale remained high. After about a month of such experimentation, the air-conditioning was said to be repaired and all was well.

A final series of interviews revealed that efficiency and morale remained high, even in the original conditions, because the operators were aware that something was being done for their comfort and that they were being given serious consideration as human beings.

Questions For Discussion

1. How does the case of the telephone operators illustrate the concept of *token economy?*

2. Why do you think there was no *extinction* of the improved efficiency and morale even on the days when the new air-conditioning was off?

3. To what degree was the mechanism of *contingency management* working in this case?

4. Did the supervisor show good understanding of human behavior?

5. What do you think would have happened had she called the operators together and gave them a "dressing down" instead of trying an indirect, somewhat scientific approach to solving the problem?

Your Sample Case

If you have witnessed or experienced a case in your own life that you think demonstrates any of the ideas put forth in the chapter, describe the case and explain how you saw it handled.

If you agree or disagree with the concepts of Operant Conditioning, explain here why you feel as you do.

Try to compare and contrast the philosophies of Operant Conditioning and Behavior Modification with one of the Humanistic approaches to psychology described earlier in this text; namely, Gestalt, Piaget, Montessori, or any other with which you are familiar.

Notes

1. Morris L. Bigge and Maurice P. Hunt, *Psychological Foundations of Education.* (New York: Harper and Brothers, 1962), pp. 286–87.

2. P. Suppes, and M. Morningstar, "Technological Innovations: Computer-Assisted Instruction and Compensatory Education," in F. F. Korten et al., *Psychology and the Problems of Society.* (Washington, D.C: American Psychological Association, 1970), pp. 225–27.

3. Morris L. Bigge, and Maurice P. Hunt, *Psychological Foundations of Education.* (New Ycrk: Harper and Brothers, 1962), p. 325.

4. B. F. Skinner, *Science and Human Behavior.* (New York: Macmillan, 1953), p. 112.

5. Jerome Kagan and Ernest Havemann, *Psychology: An Introduction.* (New York: Harcourt, Brace, Jovanovich, 1972), pp. 418–19.

6. H. M. Walker, R. H. Mattson, and N. K. Buckley, *The Functional Analysis of Behavior Within an Experimental Class Setting.* Quoted in W. C. Becker, *An Empirical Basis for Change in Education.* (Chicago: Science Research Associates, 1971), p. 97.

7. Robert W. Wildman II and Robert W. Wildman, *The Generalization of Behavior Modification Procedures: A Review With Special Emphasis on Classroom Applications.* (Milledgeville, Georgia: Monograph published by Central State Hospital, 1974), p. 445.

Open Schools

Open Classroom: Beauteous Beast
Delighting Some, Devouring Others.

PAT O'DRISCOLL[1]

The three-walled, open classroom is a new kind of monster. Those teachers who support it see it as a fine innovative tool for team teaching in an unconfined atmosphere. Those who do not, see it as a disruptive force which generates noise and distraction. Rarely has an educational innovation received such widely divided reaction as has the open-school concept.

In the last ten years there has been a huge volume of professional literature calling attention to the faults, inadequacies, and shortcomings of the traditional public school system. From Ivan Illich's *De-Schooling Society* to Silberman's *Crisis in the Classroom,* the critics are all agreed that something is wrong and that something must be done. There is widespread disagreement on just what should be done, however.

The chief areas of disagreement seem to focus on five general arguments—an acceptable definition of an open school; the basic assumptions justifying the open-concept philosophy; the operating principles necessary for success of the open-concept school; the role of the administrator and the teacher in such a school; and the community's expectations of its school system. These topics will be discussed in the order listed.

Definition

There is no simple explanation or pat definition of the open school. However, there seems to be in all the writings on the topic at least three recurring themes: the classroom environment, the process of teaching-learning, and the grouping of students.

Classroom environment

The physical structure has been interpreted in a hundred different ways, all leading to the conclusions that the ideal typical or "closed" school is the traditional one room with one central figure (the teacher).[2] The "open" school, on the other hand, is defined on a continuum; openness is seen in terms of degrees. The most open school, then, would be the world and life as it is lived in the world community. This is a very large, if not an impossible, order. However, a few steps down the continuum is a more realistic definition—the community school.

In this context, the community school is taken to mean any school that makes wide and continuous use of the facilities available in the community—government and public agencies, private business, all social institutions and private citizens who can help students learn about life as it is actually lived and the skills necessary for living. Field trips to museums, concert halls, art galleries, libraries, business and industrial centers are all vital to an open-concept school. In addition, the environment of the classroom itself needs to offer a varied bill of fare—learning centers, space for individual projects, and time for teacher-pupil discussions on a one-to-one basis. Resources of all kinds need to be readily at hand, not only books, magazines, and multi-media materials, but tools for construction, ovens and stoves for cooking, and even a telephone for obtaining "instant" information.*

The furniture in a truly open classroom should be selected with the variety of uses in mind: large and small tables and chairs, easels, floor mats, cushions, drawing boards, sinks, cabinets, and lots of storage places. All of this requires space. It means either designing new schools, adapting existing schools, or changing the old ideas about which "space" is "learning space." Most schools have large corridors that could be used to expand learning space and nearly all schools have huge areas of rarely used space such as cafeterias, gyms, and auditoriums. In warm, mild climates, an ideal learning space is the out-of-doors. Opening the classroom physically to the surrounding environment is a must for a truly open school.

Unfortunately, even after all this has been said, there are still those schools where the idea of movable furniture is immovable! There is no such thing as a teacher-proof classroom just as there are no teacher-proof learning materials. A narrow, closed teacher personality can make any room a "closed" room, while an interesting, enthusiastic teacher can create an open room in a windowless box. However, it is hardly reasonable to test the teacher's creativity by continuing to design windowless boxes.

Ideally, the open classroom is just that—spacious, well-equipped, and easily reached. The pod design seems to be the most popular and work-

---

* Most regional telephone offices publish a directory of toll-free numbers to libraries, government offices, and other sources of information.

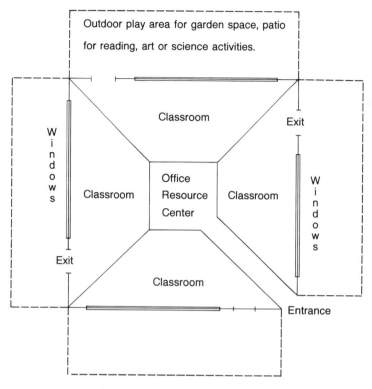

Figure 15.1

able. This is a design in which large units of space are attached to a central space which acts as office, resource library, and "nerve center" of the school. Such pods can be parts of a square, a circle, a hexagon, a pentagon, or any other suitable design. The chief idea in architectural planning is maximum convenience with maximum privacy.

In any case, while the space and the design are great facilitators, they are not the primary factors in the success of the open school concept. Here, as in any learning situation, the teacher is the key.

Teaching and learning

"We were basically trained for a closed classroom situation. Our training emphasized discipline and taught us that teaching is something you do inside four walls and a door you can close." These honest remarks from a middle-school teacher abruptly thrust into a new open-concept building, puts the finger on the crucial point, the preparation of teachers. In spite of all our professional research, our methods in teacher education have changed very little over the last forty or fifty years. Education students are still sitting in classrooms and lecture halls listening to deadly dull presentations (some of them from notes yellow with age) on individualized instruction and modular scheduling with absolutely no demonstration of either. We tell them and tell them and yet they go out and teach exactly as we taught them! Horror of horrors! If we really believed John Dewey and Marshall McLuhan and Neil Postman and Charles Silberman or even really trusted our own common sense, we'd know that the *way* we teach makes a far more lasting impression than *what* we teach. Perhaps the teacher-education institutions are not being given enough credit for the generally poor job they are doing in preparing students for teaching in the 1970's, to say nothing of the future. "The dean says we can't go." "The chairman made the schedule and handed it out. He didn't consult with anyone." "We have absolutely no money for anything." "It's never been done before." All teachers are familiar with such comments. It takes creative genius, a spirit of adventure, and real courage to take the risk of flying into the face of some of the administrative conditions that prevail in most schools and universities.

Operating as a member of a teaching team seems to generate some real fears. "Me! Teach in front of other teachers? I can't do that!" Yet, the teaching team is a real bonus, taking advantage of the various strengths, knowledge, skills, personalities, interests, and even hobbies of a group rather than limiting the teaching resource to one person. Even in the matter of style, variation among members of the team promotes experimentation and emphasizes that there are many acceptable approaches to problem-solving.

From an administrative point of view, a team is a real advantage. If one teacher is absent, there is no need for a substitute. The work continues because everyone—the team members as well as the students—have been a part of the planning. Yet, with all its advantages, members of a team need to have a strong ego and a good sense of personal worth. If they are afraid or incompetent or inadequate, the dynamics of the team causes an amount of peer pressure which few teachers can bear.

Open education is also a difficult process for students who have been accustomed to the one-teacher, one-classroom plan. There are choices to be made and responsibilities to be fulfilled. "If I choose the science center, I must stay there until I complete the experiment." "If I choose the construction center, the clean-up time always runs late and I miss part of the ball game." In addition, there is the problem of the student who has a one-track approach to learning and rejects everything except his area of special interest. In this situation, the teacher must assume the role of guidance counselor and resource person. And there are basic skills that must be mastered. Reading, arithmetic, and research techniques are crucial to the successful functioning of learning centers in an open classroom. Thus, the teacher as diagnostician needs always to be alert for signs of skills needs and plan for direct instruction when necessary. For example, if it becomes apparent that some children are having difficulties with the science center job cards, perhaps the teacher needs to re-examine the assignments to determine what is needed. If the problem is reading difficulty, then some group reading instruction might be indicated. If the problem is lack of background in a particular science concept, then the teacher needs to "back up" and begin at a less complex level.

One of the most important facts in open education is the role of the teacher. This will be expanded later in the chapter.

Grouping of students

Grouping of students in the ideal open classroom is based solely on interest—not age, size, sex, ability, reading level, or any other measures of likenesses or differences. Here, too, the teacher faces the problem of "letting children learn" rather than "telling them." In interest groups, children learn from one another, they share resources and ideas and relate to one another better without adult interference.

The emphasis in an open classroom is on the *method* of obtaining knowledge, attitudes, and skills far wider and more inclusive than one teacher could possibly present in daily lectures. Decentralizing the learning process increases and multiplies beyond measure the avenues of communication open to the learner. In a typical closed classroom, the communication is generally in one direction: *from* the teacher *to* the students.

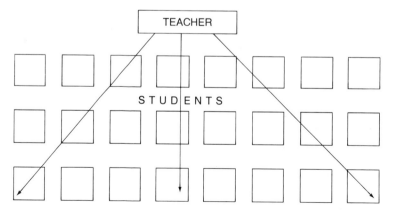

Figure 15.2

Sometimes, there is an opportunity for two-way communication when the teacher asks for or allows discussion. However, in an open classroom there is so much communication that it would be difficult even to try to diagram it—six or seven learning centers with four or five children in each center; children leaving the centers to go in search of information—to the library center or to a teacher; children going to another center just to see what's going on; large group discussions at the beginning of the day for planning and at the end of the day for evaluation; a group of children returning from a field trip eager to share their experience. Such decentralization of communication in a classroom can be very wearing on the teacher who has not yet learned to be a bit "loose." It can also be very annoying to the teacher who is accustomed to the undivided attention of the whole class of students.

One young teacher handled this very well. Each morning as the day's plans for his sixth-grade class were being developed and blocked out on the chalkboard with the names of children who had chosen various centers, the teacher blocked a period of the day he called

> MY TIME
> 10–10:30.

That meant that from 10 until 10:30 the class would stop what they were doing, gather on the floor around the teacher, and listen to him. Some days he blocked only fifteen or twenty minutes. Other days, if there was a real need, he blocked an hour or an hour and a half. If an unusual circumstance arose, he used red chalk to draw a block on the board saying something like

> SPECIAL PROBLEM TIME
> 1–1:30

However, such an "alert" was always done at least a half-hour in advance, allowing the children to finish what they were doing or to plan a good stopping point. All this was done without any screaming or yelling or hammering on the desk for attention. The red chalk on the board immediately caught the eye of the students. Other teachers have used chords on the piano, tunes on the guitar, and at least one very creative teacher uses his college mortar-board hat. He simply puts it on and sits quietly until all the children see him and gather around.

Such methods of working with groups do not develop overnight or with the speed of a miracle. They are carefully thought out and fully discussed with the students at the very beginning of the term. Without the cooperation and understanding of the students, any classroom is headed for disaster—whether it be an open or a closed room.

Basic Assumptions Justifying the Open-Concept Philosophy

There are three basic assumptions which seem to be major factors in the successful operation of an open classroom: the developmental view of learning; the fact that children learn in different ways and at different times; and the fact that children's interests are expressed in their activity and in their play.

The developmental view

While this idea was discussed fully in the chapter on Piaget, there are a few points which are specific to the open classroom. First, we really know very little about the learning process or the art of teaching. Here, practice must take precedence over theory. Yet there are some usable theories developing out of experience with open classrooms. Some of these are:

1. Teachers should assume that childhood is something to be cherished, which does not mean sentimentalized.
2. Good teachers start with the lives of their children here and now and proceed from their experiences toward more disciplined inquiry.
3. Teaching is more effective if teachers can find out where the students are by watching them in action and talking with them.
4. Learning is more effective if it grows out of the interests of the learner.
5. Both experience and theory suggest that active learning is better than passive rote.
6. Giving children choices within a planned environment helps them to develop initiative, competence, and an ability to think for themselves.
7. A good curriculum offers children knowledge worth learning. For example, it is essential that children learn reading skills but they must also see the importance of being literate, taking an interest in books, and knowing how to use them.
8. Teaching practice ought to reflect the enormous diversities among children, treating them as individuals, and proceeding when possible from their strengths rather than from their weaknesses.

9. For these reasons teachers ought to be able to set informal schedules, flexible physical arrangements, and patterns of grouping and instruction.[3]

If all these sound too, too familiar it is because it is the gospel piously preached but rarely practiced in the hallowed halls of colleges of education. Not one of these ideas, however, is meant to suggest that the open classroom is a battlefield of anarchy with the teacher standing helplessly by. They are rather meant to emphasize that the center of the education process is the _child_—not the administration, not the teacher, not the janitorial staff. No advances in building design or teacher education or the purchasing of new materials will make any difference unless all that is done is harmonious with the nature of the learner—AS HE IS, not as we would like him to be. A classroom of programmed Barbie Dolls would be easy to manipulate but dull beyond imagination. Knowledge of how children develop is essential to direct their learning effectively.

Children learn in different ways and at different times

Individual differences among children in any one group are usually larger than are differences between groups. There really is no such thing as a homogeneous group. Until a child is ready to take the next step in the developmental process, it is a waste of time to try to force it.[4]

I.Q. test scores have been discredited time and again. Social maturity test results fluctuate wildly with environmental changes. Physical growth patterns are often unpredictable. Thus it becomes critical that the teacher be aware of the individual child's "developmental age" in all areas. There is no standard third grader. He may vary from his peers in height, weight, sensory-motor skills, language development, interests or in any or all other areas of human development. Yet, there it is, _a third-grade course of study, third-grade textbooks, a third-grade teacher_—all things which seem to suggest that someone knows exactly what a _third grader_ is and how much he or she can learn in the _third grade._

The open school with larger age-grade designations (primary, intermediate, or even "family" groupings) allows for more latitude of learning concepts and facilitates learning in a more natural continuing process. Why should a fourth grader be forbidden to have access to fifth- or sixth-grade materials? Or second- or third-grade content, for that matter?

If the learning sequence as implemented in the typical American public school could be diagrammed, it would look something like this:

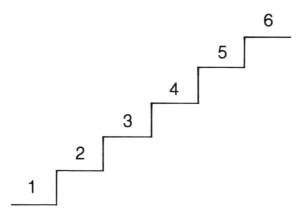

Figure 15.3

Yet, the growth and development patterns of any child do not march up in such clearly defined steps. Each child has his or her own "normal curve," own highs and lows, own continuum, and own priorities. Developmental tasks and modalities can be planned if the teacher is aware of the class as individuals rather than as a sea of nameless faces.

Children's interests are expressed in their activity and in their play

Children begin very early to develop concepts and skills through play and through what appears to adults to be random activity. Children seem to be naturally curious and from early infancy begin to try to find out about the world around them. What adults often see as destructive is only the young child's way of finding out the properties of things, what they are made of, how they work, how heavy they are, what they taste like, and what it feels like to touch them.

Play is the chief source of learning in early childhood. All kinds of materials attract young children. They seem to have a special fascination with primitive materials—water, dirt, sand, mud, rocks, and wood. Many manufactured items attract their attention. Thus, the proliferation of educational toy manufacturers marketing brightly colored and cleverly designed games, learning packages, and manipulative materials.

Anyone who has watched young children at play will surely have noticed how creative they are. A simple white cloth becomes a bridal veil, a tent, or a Roman toga, depending on which bit of imagery is at play at the moment. Two simple elongated "ears" of brown wrapping paper can turn a child into an Easter bunny or a Mexican burro. Several children, overheard as they were playing school, easily solved the problem of role. They simply said, "Mary is the teacher because she has a book." Some of this symbolism is conscious and deliberate but it can also be unconscious and therapeutic. A young child beating a doll might alert an adult to look for signs of child abuse on the child him or herself. In play children imitate, compensate, and translate. They work off aggressions and repeat situations in a somewhat selective way often acting out an experience they found painful.

Play is not just "messing around." It contains many elements of concept development and of social and emotional growth. It is the earliest form of learning and is a continuous process. It is one aspect of the child's nature that the teacher should make use of as early and as often as possible.

Operating Principles of the Open Classroom

According to the work of Beatrice and Ronald Gross and others,[5] there appear to be at least four operating principles which characterize an open classroom or an open school.

The first of these, decentralization, has already been referred to. As the term is used here it includes decentralized communication, open, flexible space divided into functional areas and easy access to resources—persons, places, and things.

The second, freedom of choice, allows the children to work in the kinds of interest groups and learning centers described earlier.

The third, a rich environment, includes all kinds of learning materials, lots of multi-media, and plenty of concrete and even primitive materials, as well as books and paper and the traditional "stuff."

The fourth, individual, one-to-one instruction and attention is possible in a situation where the teacher's entire attention is not required to control the class.

In order to implement any or all of the above, it would seem necessary to use a highly integrated and unified curriculum, one which develops and grows out of a solid understanding of developmental psychology and child growth as well as theories of learning.

Not only is an integrated curriculum a must but continuous planning for a series of integrated days would seem to offer the best approach to children's learning. Such planning can be done effectively only by teachers and curriculum experts working together with children in a real classroom on a long-term basis. Curriculum guides "written on tablets of stone and handed down" by faceless experts "up there" in the rarefied air of administrative hierarchy rarely have a chance to succeed. It cannot be emphasized enough that with young learners, practice must lead the way. When it does "internal momentum of work carries teachers and children to a point that one could not have anticipated."[6]

The Role of the Administrator and the Teacher in the Open School

The original role of the school administrator was to facilitate learning. Schools and teaching and learning existed long before Baltimore appointed the first superintendent of schools in 1864. The Industrial Revolution laid a heavy hand on education with its concept of institutionalization. The schools became "plants," the head teachers became "principals," and the chief administrative officer became the "superintendent." In some large high schools there are still time clocks for teachers to check "in" and "out." In many colleges and universities there still exists a time-clock mentality which insists that professors be in their offices at certain designated hours, regardless of the research or preparation that needs to be done away from their desks. The teaching schedule is pre-planned, the duty hours are prescribed, and then, in addition, the professional teacher is expected to write, lecture, and provide a variety of community services.

Some high school and elementary teachers are unable to take certain college courses because the teachers are required to remain in the school building until the clock strikes 4:00, regardless of the value of the classes or of the fact that their own teaching duties were completed at 3:00 or 3:15 or that they arrived at 7:00 or 7:30 A.M. Indeed, the whole clockwork structure of school administration seems to demonstrate all too clearly that as people or institutions begin to lose faith in their own worth, arbitrary regimentation sets in. If school administrators trusted themselves and their staffs, they could operate in a more relaxed and unstructured manner. Fortunately, there are some who can do this. Unfortunately, they are not typical. Happy is the teacher who is able to teach under an administrator who does not see his role primarily as that of bookkeeper or overseer. Many administrators enjoy their jobs, their students, and their teachers by becoming involved in the teaching-learning process, acting as facilitators, resource persons, and even on occasion as substitutes. A highly structured administrator can have a most unhappy experience trying to run an open school or attempting to direct the work of creative teachers.

In any school the teacher plays many roles. In an open school these roles are multiplied and increased almost by geometric progression. In an open classroom the teacher is an advisor, a supporter, an observer, a learner, a senior partner, a facilitator and, most important, a person. Many of these roles reflect the teacher's own self-concept; some of them indicate the nature of the out-of-classroom planning the teacher values; most of them are faithfully reflected in the day-to-day, on-the-spot management of the classroom. No matter how much careful planning has gone into the preparation of learning centers and the use of time and space, there are always the unexpected and unpredictable events which can catch the teacher off guard. These contingencies and the teacher's reaction to them cut through any unrealistic facade and reveal the true level of the teacher's concern for the students and for the learning process.

It is all very well to list as worthy objectives such activities as adequate planning, reflective evaluation, and diagnosis of learning problems. It is on quite another level that we must consider the teacher's interactive behavior with students—the guidance of actual learning activities, the awareness of individual problems, the honesty of person-to-person encounters and the respect for individuals as people as well as the warmth of personality. On yet another level, and perhaps the most important, there is the teacher's own personal frame of reference. If the teacher values his own philosophy of education, trusts his own ideas, accepts responsibility to the point of being willing to make decisions, and continues to explore possibilities of extending his own learning, then in all likelihood he will be a successful teacher regardless of the kind of administrative leadership offered.

Does all this sound as if the only person who can successfully operate as a teacher in an open classroom is some fantastic SUPER-PERSON? Not so! Very often teachers who may not have shown great promise in the typical pre-service education program blossom into eager creative people when given the freedom to make decisions. It is in the very area that is sorely neglected in formal teacher training—the nature of human relationships—that the teacher succeeds or fails. No matter the wealth of knowledge or the keenness of skills, unless the teacher comes across as a human being with respect, honesty, and warmth, there is little chance for open communication to develop and for real learning to take place.

If colleges of education spent more time on helping young people understand their own *personhood* and less time on formalized and structured objectives, lesson plans and curriculum guides, the schools would be happier, more productive places for all concerned—administrators, teachers, and pupils. Through an understanding of their own *personhood*, prospective teachers would begin to develop some of that self-trust and self-respect so necessary to responsible decision-making. Also, an opportunity to examine and understand one's own feelings and emotions would enable students to decide without self-prejudice or self-destruction whether or not the demanding job of teaching is a suitable one for a person with his personality.

There is something refreshing in having a student in an education class say quite honestly, "I really don't think I am cut out for this kind of profession." These students should be given credit for their sincere self-evaluation and they should be offered viable alternatives. It is a sad fact that many students spend four or five years in a teacher-education program without really examining their own fitness for the job of teaching. Then, having spent these years and much money, they feel tied to a job and a profession that they hate from the beginning. Such teachers can bring only unhappiness to themselves and to the children they teach.

What the Community Expects of Its School System

In general, American society appears to be schizophrenic about the expectations it has for education. What started out as an institution for "transmitting culture" has developed into a job-preparing, baby-sitting, problem-solving, opportunity-compensating, socially equalizing kind of social catch-all. Even when Robert Hutchins questioned the "supermarket" concept with which the schools were beginning to be identified in the late 1940's and early 1950's,[7] things weren't as bad as they are in the 1970's. Now, we have added several other dimensions—the school has become the battleground for civil rights; the substitute home, furnishing food and shelter and sometimes clothing; the family counseling service; the surrogate conscience; the medical center; and a host of more mundane jobs like driver education and learning how to fill out income-tax forms. Where will it all end? It's no wonder that academic achievement is falling by the wayside. No institution can be all things to all people. In addition, the schools are expected to operate on a solvent basis (which means as cheaply as possible). They are expected to solve all their social problems with a minimum of outside help and with absolutely no publicity. But most difficult of all, they are expected to deal with a vast dichotomy of ideals.

The parents who demand discipline and conformity also want their children to develop creativity. Honesty is highly valued in a democracy, yet most children see manipulation rewarded at home and at school. Obedience is emphasized over conscience and loyalty becomes a tool for obtaining preferred treatment. A philosophy of self-actualization is preached and written about but when the grades are in, it is competition that is rewarded. Basic facts are stressed and tested and scored but the development of a true love for learning is neglected. Docility "pays" when freedom of choice is penalized. Physical fitness is in every curriculum guide yet teachers and students alike are often required to work and study in unhealthful surroundings—poor light, inadequate ventilation, crowded classrooms, "junk food" lunches, and unsafe conditions. Team sports receive the biggest portion of the budget while many students never learn even the bare basics of nutrition or even the advantages of good posture. Good taste cannot be taught in uninspiring and decaying physical surroundings. The list could go on and on. Our schools, like the characters in Plato's *cave,* mistake shadows for substance. Authority is misused and our general pedagogical principle seems to be, "This is what you have to do; this is how you have to do it; do it and I will mark it to see if you have done it correctly, then I will reward you or punish you accordingly."[8]

If all the above sounds bitter and cynical, it is only because there are so many teachers who are saddened to see the emphasis in education change from concern with the kind of person the student will become to an exact scoring of what the student knows (or has been able to copy from someone else). All that counts is the ALMIGHTY GRADE!

Conant says that there is no such thing as "The American School"; there is only "An American School." Yet, with all the opportunities for exploring regional, ethnic, and personal differences, our schools seem to be heading for a new kind of regimentation not seen in this century. Franz Joseph of Austria was known to be proud of the fact that he knew exactly what every child in his empire was being taught at any given hour on any given day. Unfortunately, even in a democracy, there are still school administrators who are interpreting the wishes and needs and pressures of the community in just such a regimented way. In such communities, the open school doesn't have a chance. The general attitude seems to indicate that the school is only a concentration camp for pre-delinquents. If the teachers can manage a few basics as well, then everything is fine and our pious commitment to education has been fulfilled.

The Case of Richard

The new sixth-grade teacher had already heard about Richard from all the other teachers. "Wait until you have to deal with this kid!" "He is really a kook. He may be smart, but he is really a pain!" "Richard! Wow! Are you in for a different year!"

Classes began and the new teacher couldn't help being alert to Richard. He was bright, cheerful, articulate, polite—all the things teachers love about their students. It was only after the first few weeks of school when the teacher launched a new social studies unit on American history with several learning centers, that Richard came to the teacher at recess.

"Do I really have to do all that stuff? I already know all about the Revolutionary War, the French and Indian Wars, the War of 1812, the Spanish-American War. I know all about all the wars there ever were!" The teacher was a bit surprised but remained calm. "Richard, how do you happen to know all these things?"

"Well, my Dad was an Army Officer and ever since I was a little kid he taught me about the military and tactics and strategy and all that stuff."

"If you don't want to work in any of the centers I have planned, what would you like to do?"

"Do you really mean that?"

"Yes, I do."

"Well, I'd like to have my own center in the back of the room. Maybe a fort. I could build it myself and then when you are teaching about wars and history I could set up the battlefields and the armies and the kids could see how the whole thing happened. I've got every kind of toy soldier ever made and I could bring all that stuff to school if you'd let me build my fort."

"Alright. I'm willing to try. Let's find out what the rest of the class thinks about it. But remember, there is also math and science and reading."

"Don't you worry. I'll do a good job."

The teacher presented Richard's request to the rest of the class. The general response was sort of neutral and seemed to say, "What difference does it make? He never does anything anyway. All he's ever done is cause trouble." One student said, "At least he'll be in his fort all day and he won't be bothering everybody else."

Richard was there bright and early the next morning with his father and a car load of material, including a refrigerator box for the fort. Richard's father was pleased and assured the teacher that he would be ready to help in any way if Richard became a problem.

All during the school year Richard worked in his fort, coming out for math and other instruction and sometimes inviting other students to spend some time in his fort to see what he was studying. He always managed to propose math problems that had to do with military operations and his individualized reading was almost entirely history and biography of national military figures.

A number of times during the year he set up a battlefield and described what happened step by step. When he demonstrated the Battle of Shiloh, for example, he constructed dozens of miniature trees to represent the cherry orchard in which one very important skirmish took place.

The students began to go to Richard for information and soon he was no longer thought of as the class kook but the class expert. He did well in all his subjects and finished the year with a great deal of satisfaction.

Questions For Discussion

1. In what ways did Richard's teacher indicate an attitude of openness?

2. Would it have been more beneficial to Richard to have been forced to conform to the total class pattern?

3. How do you think the teacher's letting Richard build his fort affected the attitudes of the other students? Could this have created other problems?

4. Do you think this experiment in individualized learning had a good effect on Richard's self-concept? How?

5. Did the other students in the class benefit from Richard's expert knowledge?

6. Do you think Richard's request and the way the teacher handled it might have given other students some ideas about creative learning activities?

7. What do you think would have been the typical elementary principal's reaction to an arrangement like this?

The Case of Mrs. Woods

Mrs. Woods had spent many years teaching pre-school and primary children. Suddenly, she decided that she would like to end her teaching career as a college professor. She took leave and after two years of difficult struggle, she managed to obtain a Doctor of Education degree from an obscure university.

Because of her age and lack of secondary school experience, she had great difficulty getting a university position. However, she did manage to obtain a temporary contract in a small state university. The college of education had just initiated team-teaching in the integrated pre-student-teaching methods courses. Mrs. Woods was assigned to the team.

During the first planning session, Mrs. Woods insisted that she be given the area of language arts and children's literature and that she be allowed to work only with students who planned to be primary teachers. These requests were respected by all members of the team and the schedule provided for Mrs. Woods' areas of interest.

The first indication that there was a problem came when Mrs. Woods missed her first scheduled large group presentation. She called in sick. In small group lab sections, she began to have difficulties with the students. Their chief complaint was that she called them "children" and sometimes even used baby talk to embarrass a student. She emphasized a closed classroom, never allowing the team coordinator to visit and never discussing her plans with the other team members.

At the end of the semester, she had managed to avoid every large group presentation and flatly refused to teach while any other team teacher was present. She became very emotional and hostile toward some of the older students and toward the department chairman who tried to talk with her. She often broke into tears in the midst of a discussion.

It became abundantly clear that Mrs. Woods was not ready or adequately prepared for team teaching in an open classroom. The team leader suggested that Mrs. Woods be assigned separate primary methods classes. This was done but her attitude toward college students remained hostile and dominating. At the end of the year her contract was not renewed.

Questions For Discussion

1. How did Mrs. Woods' attitude indicate a lack of self-trust and self-worth?

2. Would some good strong reality counselling *before* she tried to enter the university field have benefited her?

3. Try to analyze what it was that motivated her to make such a move so late in her career.

4. What do you see as a university administrator's responsibility in dealing with such a person as a prospective candidate for Doctor of Education degree.

5. Does Mrs. Woods' behavior suggest that she probably had problems other than professional ones?

6. Is there a possibility that Mrs. Woods' deficiencies would have gone unnoticed had she not been thrust into an open-concept team-teaching situation?

7. How does Mrs. Woods' failure demonstrate the fact that open schools and team teaching are not the answer for all teachers?

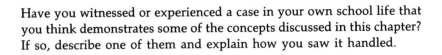

Your Sample Case

Have you witnessed or experienced a case in your own school life that you think demonstrates some of the concepts discussed in this chapter? If so, describe one of them and explain how you saw it handled.

If you agree or disagree with the principles of the open classroom, explain here why you feel as you do.

How would you characterize the typical classrooms in which you went to school? Were they predominately "open" or "closed" rooms? What about the teachers' attitudes? Were they "open" or "closed?"

Would you be comfortable teaching in an open-concept class? In a team? Why?

Notes

1. Pat O'Driscoll, "Open Classroom," *Nevada State Journal,* Reno, Nevada, June 27, 1976, pp. 14–15.

2. Eugene M. Labovitz, "Learning and Open Education," *Urban Education,* Vol. IX, No. 4 (January 1975), 356–57.

3. Joseph Featherstone, "A Unified Approach to Learning," *The Open Classroom Reader,* Charles Silberman, ed. (Random House, 1973), p. 135.

4. The Plowden Report, *Children and Their Primary Schools.* (London: Her Britannic Majesty's Stationery Office, 1970), Vol. I, pp. 518–35.

5. Beatrice and Ronald Gross, "A Little Bit of Chaos," *Saturday Review* (May 16, 1970), p. 10.

6. Joseph Featherstone, "A Unified Approach to Learning," p. 135.

7. Robert Hutchins, *The Conflict of Education.* (New York: Harper and Bros., 1953), pp. 26–47.

8. Sir Alec Clegg, "Why Did We Change?" *The Open Classroom Reader,* Charles Silberman, ed. (Random House, 1973), p. 67.

16 Evaluation

If you can look into the seeds of time,
And say which grain will grow and which will not,
Speak then to me. . . .

MACBETH

We are fast becoming a nation of accountants. There is scarcely a household, regardless of its economic level, that does not need some kind of filing cabinet for bills, receipts, canceled checks, bank statements, documents to substantiate the Income Tax Return, insurance claim forms, social security reports, detailed phone bills, unintelligible utility statements, reports of capital gains and losses, proof of expenditures for home improvements (against the day when the house may be sold at a profit), and dozens of other items.

If you are the owner of a small business, a professional self-employed person, or even a part-time waiter, the additional paper work you are required to do is daily becoming more burdensome. If you are a teacher, you must add to all the above the most difficult accounting and record keeping of all: namely, the roll book, the parent conference report, and the grade sheet. You must keep an account of attendance, assignments completed, the quality of the work done, test scores, student self-evaluations, and peer-group scores. Besides, after taking all these into account, you must be prepared to defend your own rationale for grading. If your grading average is too high (too many A's), you have trouble with administration. If it is too low, you have trouble with students and parents.

What is evaluation? How did we become so obsessed with grades and grading? Who can accurately measure what the student has learned? How does one evaluate what the teacher has taught? Whose judgment is the most valid in drawing these conclusions? What is this new phenomenon called *Accountability?* These are a few of the questions this chapter will try to answer. However, in evaluation, as in all other forms of social measurement, exactitude is elusive and conclusions must be somewhat subjective.

What is Evaluation?

In its simplest form, evaluation is the process of putting a value on a product or a process or a person. Evaluating a product is by far the easiest and most exact assessment. If you have built a table or baked a cake, it is fairly easy to determine if you have done a good job. If the table is even and sturdy and perhaps attractive, you feel satisfied. If the cake is edible and tasty and perhaps delicious, you enjoy compliments from those who eat it.

Things, like tables and cakes, are easy to evaluate and measure. There is another element even in the evaluation of tangible objects: namely, taste, design, flavor, and a number of highly personal variables. If you had envisoned a round table and the finished product came out in a slightly oval shape, you may downgrade it. If someone you serve the cake to is allergic to chocolate, the delicious, moist cake will not tempt or please.

When intangibles are evaluated, there is involved a new degree of subjectivity. What is honesty? How do you measure patriotism? How can you detect insincerity? In all such subjective judgments, the evaluator is using his own set of criteria which may or may not be valid in terms of the quality being evaluated. What is due process? In the very same incident, both the plaintiff and the defendant have a clear rationale for their respective behaviors even though the end results of those behaviors are in complete disagreement.

The practice of law, the enforcement of legal statutes, the application of formal codes of conduct are all subject to individual interpretation. It is the right to argue for your own interpretation that keeps the law schools busy producing lawyers who can take either side of a case and argue it equally well. Processes are less easily defined and, therefore, more difficult to evaluate than are products.

When we evaluate persons, then we have reached the ultimate in variability. Such an innocent remark as "He is a good student," is open to question, depending on who is making the judgment. "She is a beautiful girl," "He is a handsome man," "That's an elegant house!" are all comments that can give rise to a variety of reactions from total agreement to total disagreement.

Students who work well with one teacher can create problems for another teacher. The process of analyzing human relations and human reactions is a very nebulous one. Guidance counselors, personnel officers, and psychologists are constantly trying to identify the factors which contribute to successful functioning of individuals in any given situation.

Once again, the classroom teacher is expected to handle all these variables in such a way as to keep everyone happy. There are some guiding principles which can make the job of evaluation less difficult. First, if the teacher has involved the students in goal-setting and planning reasonable expectations, then students are less likely to resent having their performance evaluated on these criteria. Second, if the teacher is fair and firm and consistent, then students know what to expect and can work in a more secure and relaxed learning atmosphere. Third, if the teacher is well prepared and well organized, then the learning process becomes more interesting and students are more likely to respond, to participate and to put forth more effort. Fourth, if the teacher is humanistic and open in the inter-personal communication process, students develop a sense of trust and acceptance that makes honest appraisals less difficult to accomplish. Even as young children accept fair and honest discipline from their parents if it is done within the framework of family love and real concern, students of all ages develop a sense of respect for the teacher if it is clear to them that the teacher is a caring, sincere person who is interested in the students' success and accomplishment.

Evaluation has historically played a significant role in education, particularly in those systems which emphasize an elitist concept of success and thus use evaluative processes as a screening device. It has long been the practice in most European nations to administer rather strict and demanding tests at the end of the primary level of schooling—at what approximates our fourth grade. At that point, students are tested for achievement but, more important, they are screened for special skills and for possible chances of success in further academic studies. An eleven-year-old who does poorly in achievement as well as academic potential is screened out of the secondary school and sent along any one of a dozen or more technical-vocational-semi-professional tracks.

Universal compulsory education is not interpreted in any country except the United States to mean the same education and the same required achievement for everyone. Even in the Communist countries, there are early (and final) decisions made with regard to the academic future of students. The entrance exams for the major universities in the USSR are so stringent and the results can so affect one's future that students often become ill under the intense pressure. It is not uncommon to see ambulances and first aid stations around the campuses during the period when entrance examinations are being administered.

This use of academic achievement as an irreversible screening process has generally resulted in eliminating from higher education those students who come from the lower socio-economic strata of society and has caused a perpetuation of inequality of opportunity. When such criteria as the use of standard language, motivation, and acceptance of teacher-school-made goals and a docility to the system are used as yardsticks, then many potentially able students are ruled out of furthering their education.

However, the educationists emphasize, in theory at least, that the primary function of education is the full development of the individual. The assumption seems to be that talent can be developed and that the major resources of the schools should be dedicated to developing individuals, not in predicting and selecting talent.[1]

Grading

A careful examination of the report cards of any school system can be most revealing to the thoughtful observer. The various items listed and the weight given these items shows very clearly what it is that the school prizes. The report card, the grade sheet, the grade-point average report are all usually the result of testing. These results are generally spelled out in letter grades or in some other system of quantitative symbols. Grading attempts to categorize students in terms of their level of learning as compared with that of other students. Thus, the great competitive race for high marks. Grading may also be the result of subjective and personal bias on the part of the instructor. More often than not, grades are assigned as the result of the distribution of test scores on the normal curve. Such determination assumes that all classes are randomly selected and that each class represents a sufficiently large sampling. Both assumptions can be challenged very easily, particularly at the upper secondary levels where much selectivity has already taken place before the student enrolls. The very fact that a student has survived four years of high school, is motivated to seek higher education, and has the financial backing to pay the tuition in a university or junior college would seem to be a somewhat reliable selection process. Even then, many universities see the freshman semesters as the great weeding-out period.

Many schools are presently under fire for what is termed "grade inflation" and teachers who give too many high grades are severely criticized. On the other hand, recent legal decisions make it increasingly easy for students to challenge grades. Many schools have resolved the problem by adopting a simple pass-fail system of grading, which in reality is no grading at all.

One of the undesirable results of the preoccupation with grades is the widespread use of objective tests at all levels of schooling. Such tests requiring a specific *right* answer, offer the teacher and the student a sense of security by quantifying the amount of knowledge gained. In this process, the learner is restricted by the test items and the structure of the test becomes a lid on the learner's opportunity to give evidence of what he has learned.

On the other hand, when essay tests are used, the teacher is easily diverted from the content of the written answer by such things as poor spelling, weak grammatical construction, and even sub-standard handwriting. Moreover, it has been shown many times that the same test paper, presented to several readers, is evaluated differently by each reader. Thus, we return to the subjective character of the grading process.

Another factor which tends to invalidate grades is the instructor's knowledge of the student's previous performance on other tests or on earlier items in the same test.

Most sources seem to agree that no fair or impartial system of grading exists. Because of personal differences, students' perceptions, individual standards and methods of evaluation, the final results may vary dramatically. John Holt, in *The Underachieving School,* says that, at best, testing for purposes of grading seems to do more harm than good; at worst, it hinders, distorts, and corrupts the learning process.[2]

Students are aware that grades and cumulative records are almost invariably permanent and will follow them the rest of their lives. Students who feel that they have been unfairly graded and labeled often reach a frustration level which may be directed against parents, peers, teachers, school buildings, and even themselves. Many incidents of vandalism, anti-social behavior, and even suicide may have their early roots in a sense of hostility and futility developed in a grading system that the individual perceived as unfair.

Who Knows What the Teacher Has Taught? Who Knows What the Learner Has Learned?

These two questions are inseparable, chiefly because it is always assumed that what the teacher has taught is what the learner has learned. Nowhere is there any proof of the validity of such a conclusion. The teacher may have firmly in mind a precise model of the outcomes of the instruction. To achieve these outcomes, the teacher studies, prepares, and presents certain content. If, for whatever reason, the presentation is distracting, the content is inappropriate and difficult to comprehend or the presentation is too technical, students simply "tune out" the teacher and either retreat into the world of their own fantasies or, in extreme cases, set about deliberately to disrupt the class.

In order to avoid "losing" the students, teachers should always try to determine what the learners bring to the learning task. Here, an awareness of basic human needs, of cultural or ethnic differences, of developmental readiness, of immediate problems should alert the teacher to the possible success or failure of his efforts to achieve pre-planned outcomes. The wise teacher knows when to revise expectations or when to change entirely the nature of the planned learning task.

Even when the lesson planning is right on target, during each step of the teaching-learning process there is constant interaction. This interaction, if it is rich and lively and interesting, may change the direction of the lesson completely. In such a situation, the teacher needs to be ready, willing, and able to make instant judgments about the relative value of several approaches—the planned approach versus one or more suggested by the students. Such flexibility is not meant to imply an attitude of "off-the-cuff" teaching. Rather it is meant to suggest that planning for learning need not be so rigid as to rule out changes or variations in the plan. If the planning, objectives, and selection of materials are all compatible with the students' developmental level, then evaluation is more likely to be done with ease and with good results.

An effective method of inter-weaving evaluation with the teaching-learning process is to use some diagnostic evaluation *before* planning; then, during the instruction, to provide time and opportunity for feedback from students. This information is usually called *formative evaluation.* Finally, at the end of the unit or lesson or chapter is the time for *summative evaluation*—summarizing what has been learned. It is in this last activity that it becomes apparent that realistically conceived and clearly stated objectives are the key to sound evaluation. It is the simple process of deciding on a goal, working toward it, then standing back to see whether or not the goal was achieved. Sometimes, even if the stated goal was not achieved, some other unforeseen learning took place as a result of formative evaluation and teacher flexibility.

All three types of evaluation are needed if the principle of continuous evaluation is to be served. One of the best examples of the logic of the three steps is a well-planned meal. The good cook plans a menu, assembles all the ingredients, and from time to time tastes to test the seasoning, the degree of doneness, and the general quality of the dish. The final or summative evaluation is in the reaction of the diners. In the same way, a good school day begins with planning (by the teacher and with the students) and assembling materials. It provides time for "tasting" as the day progresses. Finally, it ends with a short closure period in which students and teacher review the strong and weak points and on these judgments make plans for the next day. Such a process not only has the advantage of being cooperative but it helps students begin very early to assume some responsibility for their own learning.

Most instruments of evaluation are designed as if the students learn all (and only) what the teacher has taught. There are various ways of opening the evaluative process in order to get a broader and more valid view of the students' learning. Some of these are a variety of kinds of testing—objective, essay, oral—as well as an array of instructional outcomes—concepts, inquiry, skills, attitudes. In all cases, the kind of evaluative process used needs to be consistent with the type of instructional outcome desired. If the teacher is testing skill in typing, a specific kind of test is indicated; if the skill is concept development, then an entirely different kind of test is called for. In any case, approaching evaluation from as many angles as possible enables the teacher to come closer to the truth and with this truth to be more fair in grading.

Self-evaluation is probably the most difficult for students to learn to do but, in the long run, it is the most reliable. It is the learners themselves who know what they have learned. It may not be until they are faced with the need to apply the knowledge that they really know that they have learned it.

In addition to variety in structure and content, good evaluation needs a broader base than the single judgment of the instructor. To meet this need, good teachers often use peer evaluations as well as student self-evaluations. If the peer evaluation represents a good sampling of the class and if it is balanced against the teacher's evaluation, then there is a good chance that the outcome (final grade) will be fair. However, if the teacher insists on holding the "trump" by weighting his judgment over all others, then the whole process of peer, group, or self-evaluations is a mockery. At the end of this chapter you will find a few samples of evaluative forms which enable the teacher to build a broad base for judgments and allow for a wide sampling of points of view and reaction.

Testing As Learning

One of the big advantages of programmed instruction is the immediate feedback available to the learners. They are never allowed to wander off unaware of their error. Their attention is immediately focused on whether or not their mental processes were reliable and if their judgments were accurate. This lack of immediacy is one of the problems with typical teacher-made tests. Often, students never get their test papers back. All they receive is a grade sheet from the computer with no explanation or discussion. This situation prevails either because the teacher plans to use the same test again and again or because of the test schedule. In most schools and universities, the tests are held the last few days of school. This makes it impossible for the instructor to do an adequate job of reading, much less to take the time to have conferences with the students. Enter the computer! In one state university, the final grades are due in the registrar's office three days *after* graduation. Thus it is possible to have gone through all the "pomp and circumstance" only to learn the following week that you have not graduated at all!

If testing is to serve any worthwhile purpose at all, there must be teacher-student discussion of the results. Often, in such discussions, teachers see a point of view or an interpretation of their own questions that had never occurred to them before. On the other hand, a student might be shown how he has misread a question or applied conceptual information incorrectly. Discussion should not, however, disintegrate into a haggling over grades. There are processes designed to enable students to question grades they do not understand or that they think are unfair. One such process is called *challenging a grade*. Seldom does such a process operate at the cool, cognitive level. Almost always it becomes an emotional exchange of accusations or an out-and-out attempt to intimidate the teacher. "How could I possibly have failed your course? I was never there!" "Why did you mark misspelled words? This is not an English class!" "It was necessary for me to have seven cuts out of fifteen classes. I have to work so I can afford to go to school!" Some of these arguments are so illogical that they are funny but they are also so serious that they are sad. The great grade chase is the source of constant concern for the conscientious student and the conscientious teacher as well.

True, some teachers use the grade as a big stick and in their classes students spend more time "psyching out" the teacher than in pursuing learning. The final exam is the ultimate "get-even" technique and many students are subjected to a kind of unfair predestination because they have in some way incurred the displeasure of the teacher. It is distressing to watch the glee with which some teachers prepare impossible exams and then go into the test as though it were their one big starring role on the stage of education. In such cases, testing becomes a charade, a trap, and a tool of vindictiveness. No wonder students are protective of their rights and knowledgable of the legal procedures open to them. No wonder, also, that teachers are beginning to be aware of the need for something comparable to malpractice insurance.

It is a long jump from the hand-lettered attendance cards used in the first schools in this country to the computer print-out sheets that seem to control so much of education today. If, as some educators hold, grading, marking, and reporting systems are accurate bellwethers of the kind and quality of the educational processes they report, then it seems important to ask just what it is that we expect of teachers. Are they givers of information, enforcers of discipline, substitute parents, ticket sellers for local football games, collectors of milk money and hot lunch lists, mechanics engaged in the changing of behavior by turning a few screws in the child's mind? Are they mathematicians busy all day with figures, numbers, enrollments, memos, rating scales, promotion and tenure forms, the normal curve, standard deviations, and grade point averages? How much of a teacher's time should be spent filling out forms and making reports, often the same ones, year after year? Isn't it mind-boggling to imagine anyone putting a grade on Thomas Jefferson's first draft of the Declaration of Independence or to think of Plato giving a pre-test? There is a story about an OPA official during World War II who asked Henry Kaiser how he knew when a ship was ready to launch. Kaiser replied, "When the ship weighs as much as the OPA paper work, we know she is ready to go!" Sometimes, to the serious teacher, constantly aggravated by meaningless paper work, it almost seems that the same rule of thumb (or of paper) could be used to determine when a student should graduate. For example, ten pounds for a high school diploma, twenty-five for a bachelor's degree, a hundred for a master's degree, a ton or so for the doctorate! If all this sounds sarcastic, it is only because educators and education have created a sacred cow out of the process of evaluation. It is a classic example of a common human failing; namely, that when we lose sight of our objectives we tend to double our efforts—and our paper work!

What is Accountability?

Accountability has many definitions. Some writers describe it as "the process of expecting each member of an organization to answer to someone for doing specific things, according to specific plans and against certain timetables, to accomplish tangible performance results."[3] Others see it as a negotiable relationship in which the participants agree in advance to accept specified rewards and costs on the basis of evaluation of the attainment of specified goals.[4] Another concept of accountability is based on the notion that each person in an organization is responsible for a particular function and the adequate carrying out of that function. Still another version emphasizes the adoption of business methods in the education process with performance contracts, the

Figure 16.1 *Used by permission of* Today's Education, *journal of the National Education Association. March–April 1976.*

voucher system, and other management techniques as levers for circumventing the traditional bureaucracy.

From the teacher's close-range point of view, accountability is seen as stating all learning tasks in the form of measurable objectives. Ultimately, all the variables of definition tend to insure that the public has accurate information on the goals, processes, and products of the school. Thus accountability becomes a public accounting of that which is.[5] One candidate for a local office said only last year that one of his "planks" was to be sure that his state got a dollar's worth of education for every tax dollar spent. What is a dollar's worth of education? If he or anyone else could answer that, our problems of evaluation and grading and accountability would all be solved.

The problem which arises when any or all of the above definitions of accountability are applied to the learning process is the awareness that educational *effectiveness* is not necessarily the same as *efficiency*. Effectiveness seems to connote the degree to which the school succeeds in whatever it is trying to do. Efficiency is an organization's ability to achieve certain results within a certain preconceived budget of dollars and work hours. Further, evaluation is a process which is internal to an organization while accountability carries with it the idea of external judgment.

In schools, evaluation is taken to be the responsibility of teachers, psychologists, and educational researchers. Accountability, on the other hand, tends to be the province of management, business, or finance experts. The former group invariably stresses *input*—admissions, prerequisites, and teaching. The latter stresses *output*—product, efficiency of operation and budgets.[6] It is in these several variations of perception that teachers see accountability as a threat.

Since the public school must really teach "all the children of all the people," the problem of accountability cannot be put aside lightly. The educator, when held accountable, must own up to the type of professional person he is. One author describes five types of teachers presently employed in educational institutions:

1. *The Rebel:* He is against the entire system but has no constructive suggestions for change.
2. *The Retreatist:* He just wants *out* of teaching.
3. *The Ritualist:* He has retired on the job. He repeats the same lessons with the same notes and tests year after year.
4. *The Conformist:* He goes along with whatever is the popular fad of the moment.
5. *The Innovator:* He sees the need for change and seeks to bring it about. For his efforts he is often rewarded by being denied promotion or even employment.[7]

While teachers of types one, two, and five may strongly resist the coldly calculating interpretations of accountability, they must, nevertheless, be willing to be held accountable in those areas which are crucial to the success of the teaching-learning process. Some of these have been described as: being informed in subject matter; being concerned about student welfare; understanding human behavior; implementing worthy purposes of education; the methods used in carrying out their own and society's purposes for education.[8] In any case, the accounters themselves must be held accountable for the effect of the practices they impose on teachers, students, and institutions.

Rational and reasonable accountability should call forth the best from everyone engaged in the business of education. Such accountability challenges educators to examine their purposes and their techniques in order to find better ways of making education responsible to the society that has entrusted to the schools its most precious resource—its children.

The following samples of rating scales are included here to demonstrate the advantages and disadvantages of quantitative measurement. Further, it is hoped that these examples might suggest other ways of approaching the difficult task of grading. Use your own ideas or, better still, use the students' ideas for devising other appropriate rating forms.

Samples of Rating Scales

1. Student's Self-Evaluation.
2. Students' Evaluation of Instructor—a Published Scale.
3. Students' Evaluation of Course and Instructor—an Open Evaluation.
4. Peer Evaluation of a Written Unit.
5. Peer Evaluation of a Research Paper.
6. Group Performance Rating Scale.

Note that all these scales use a Likert-type (5 point) scoring spread. Also please note that many of these can be adapted for elementary, high school, junior college, or university students.

Self-Evaluation

Name _____

(Circle the appropriate number to indicate your evaluation of each point.)

Attitude

1	2	3	4	5
A. Enthusiastic	Interested	Passive	Disinterested	Uncooperative

Effort

1	2	3	4	5
B. Unusual	Much	Average	Enough to "get by"	Very Little

Value to Me of the Required Assignments

1	2	3	4	5
C. Unusually High	High	Average	Little	None

Key

1—To a very high degree

2—To a high degree

3—To a moderate degree

4—To a low degree

5—To a very low degree

D. To what degree have I achieved my objectives in this course?   D. 1 2 3 4 5

E. To what degree can the skills practiced in this class be used in my own classroom?   E. 1 2 3 4 5

F. To what degree have I been challenged to think in new areas?   F. 1 2 3 4 5

G. To what degree am I satisfied with my accomplishments in the course?   G. 1 2 3 4 5

H. To what degree has it been possible for me to integrate the learnings in this course with my work in other courses?   H. 1 2 3 4 5

I. To what degree have I developed skill in critical thinking?   I. 1 2 3 4 5

J. To what degree has my attitude toward the teaching profession changed during this semester?   J. 1 2 3 4 5

K. To what degree have I begun to do some independent thinking?   K. 1 2 3 4 5

Self-Evaluation
(Page 2)

L. Describe what you consider to be the most valuable learning experience you have had this semester.

M. What is your own estimate of your potential as a classroom teacher?
   Excellent   Very Good   Good   Average   Fair   Poor
   Explain:

N. What letter grade would you assign yourself in this course?
   A   B   C   D   F
   Explain your choice:

   Any additional comments you wish to make may be written on a separate sheet of paper.

A Student's Rating Scale of an Instructor

Instructor's name (Please print)_____ Course_____ Date_____ Semester

Each of the qualities listed below is divided into three sections. Each section is divided into three degrees and numbered accordingly from 1 to 9, 1 being the highest degree and 9 the lowest. In rating, draw a circle around the number which best describes your instructor. Your fair and honest opinion is what really counts. Your instructor desires this rating for his own self-improvement.

Organization of Course

1 2 3	4 5 6	7 8 9
Well organized; shows thoughtful planning.	Some organization but not always clear.	Lacks organization; planning seems vague.

Preparation for Each Class

1 2 3	4 5 6	7 8 9
Shows definite evidence of careful preparation.	Shows some preparation; average knowledge of course.	Not well prepared; knowledge inaccurate at times.

Teaching Skill

1 2 3	4 5 6	7 8 9
Produces steady interest in subject; creates real desire; keeps things moving.	Teaching procedure seldom changes; student interest moderate.	Classes tend to be dry and uninteresting; class period drags.

Enthusiasm and Interest in Course

1 2 3	4 5 6	7 8 9
Keeps up steady interest and enthusiasm. Inspires interest in subject.	Appears to be reasonably interested.	Seems to teach course without enthusiasm.

Assignments

1 2 3	4 5 6	7 8 9
Students understand the tasks of each new assignment. Students know what is desired.	Sometimes rather indefinite; without clear planning.	Usually hurriedly given; rather vague; sometimes very unreasonable.

A Student's Rating Scale of an Instructor *(Continued)*

	1	2	3	4	5	6	7	8	9
Judgment of Values	Usually selects important ideals; broadens student view-points.			Sometimes overlooks important points, spending time on insignificant details.			Frequently misses important ideas; overemphasizes trivial details.		
Class Discussion and Questions	Questions challenging; demand sound thinking; discussions interesting and stimulating.			Questions rather easy and simple; memorized facts emphasized.			Discussion sometimes without purpose; discussions frequently ramble.		
Poise and Self-Confidence	Well poised; sure of himself; not easily upset.			Seems embarrassed at times; fairly self-confident.			Easily upset; uncertain as to procedure; lacks confidence.		
Examinations	Questions thought-provoking; carefully selected; clear.			Questions usually factual; require little thinking.			Examinations poorly planned and managed.		
Scholarship	Excellent mastery of subject; has broad interests.			Knowledge fair but without depth.			Knowledge frequently inadequate. Instructor seems vague.		
Ability to Create Student Interest	Usually keeps steady interest in subject; stimulates thinking.			Students have average amount of interest.			Classes drag and students are indifferent.		

A Student's Rating Scale of an Instructor (Continued)

	1 2 3	4 5 6	7 8 9
Classroom Management and Discipline	Efficient management; students orderly and attentive.	Satisfactory organization; few disciplinary problems.	Poor organization; many disciplinary problems.
Speech	Voice pleasant; speaks distinctly, fluently.	Speaks reasonably well.	Enunciation poor; makes frequent errors in speech.
Tolerance	Encourages students to express opinions even though they differ with the instructor's ideas.	At times appears to be disturbed and impatient when students oppose instructor's views.	Resents opposition; intolerant.
Sense of Humor	Possesses keen sense of humor.	Moderately humorous at times.	Shows little or no sense of humor; quite sober and serious.
Personal Appearance	Neatly and appropriately dressed; well groomed.	Appearance fair; makes average impression.	Careless in dress; untidy.
Relationship Between Students and Instructor	Attitude of friendliness; feeling of mutual interest; easily approached.	Neither ill-will nor friendliness prevails; attitude somewhat indifferent.	Considerable spirit of antagonism between students and instructor.

PRINT your criticisms of the course. These will be very helpful for your instructor's self-improvement. Do not sign your name. On the back of this form PRINT any annoying mannerisms your instructor has developed which should be corrected.

Open Evaluative Comments
(Concerning Instructor and Course)

1. I think a very warm feeling has evolved within this class.

2. I thought that there was not enough communication during the answer-and-question period. I also thought that students did not have enough time on their presentations—all of which I found extremely interesting.

3. Meeting you has also been a valuable experience. Most college courses, especially in the Education Department, are dull and very boring. Your class is the exception to the rule.

4. I really enjoyed this class and believe I learned a lot myself as did others. I think it was a definitely necessary part of my education toward becoming the teacher and the person I want to be.

5. I think a few good films should be shown throughout the session—perhaps in the evenings. These should be advertised and posted ahead. I would suggest a good one on the most populous minority groups—African American, Asian American, Chicano, native American, and any others available. There are some excellent filmstrips but they are not available in the Resource Center. If money is available, some up-to-date ones should be purchased.

6. I really enjoyed everything we've done. I know it has helped me. I got a lot of new and different ideas from everyone. I do think the class is a valid requirement because it exposes you to new ideas.

7. This was really a great class. I came in with a negative attitude but I changed my mind real fast. Thank you for helping to make my summer profitable as well as enjoyable.

8. I'm really happy with this class. I only regret that time is such a factor in summer school. I've learned a lot that I feel I will use in the classroom or gymnasium when I begin teaching.

9. This has been an interesting class and a good learning experience to which I've tried to put a lot of effort into. I intend to teach Special Education in high school.

10. This is the only course of this kind I have had and I feel I learned a lot.

11. Wish there had been more time for a question-and-answer period after presentations. The class was very enjoyable and informative. In my personal opinion, the day of kite-making and flying should have been dropped and replaced with discussion. We can fly kites at any time, but this class is available only once. The field trip was interesting but rather far if the school doesn't furnish transportation.

12. I feel I did learn a lot in this class. Things were brought up in here that would not crop up in any other setting. I suppose I resented giving up a day of learning for a day of playing simply because the class was so informative.

13. Overall an excellent, stimulating course. My one objection was some of the factual questions on mid-terms.

Which of the foregoing (the prepared scale or the open comment) would you prefer to use?

Which of these do you feel gives the teacher more usable feedback?

Peer Evaluation of a Written Unit

Title of the Unit: _____

Student Author: _____

Student Reader: _____

Key

1—To a very high degree
2—To a high degree
3—To a moderate degree
4—To a low degree
5—To a very low degree

Circle the appropriate number to indicate your evaluation of each point.

I. Format

    A. To what degree is the unit neat and well typed?   A. 1 2 3 4 5
    B. To what degree is writing in the unit grammatically
       correct?   B. 1 2 3 4 5
    C. To what degree is the unit well organized?   C. 1 2 3 4 5
    D. To what degree is the typed unit "visually" planned
       so as to be easy to read and to comprehend?   D. 1 2 3 4 5

II. Content and Organization

    E. To what degree are the objectives clearly stated?   E. 1 2 3 4 5
    F. To what degree do the objectives include content,
       attitudes and skills?   F. 1 2 3 4 5
    G. To what degree is there clear differentiation be-
       tween content and the teaching of content?   G. 1 2 3 4 5
    H. To what degree are there sufficient activities listed?   H. 1 2 3 4 5
    I. To what degree does the section on resources for
       teaching seem to offer sufficient reference material
       for both teacher and students?   I. 1 2 3 4 5
    J. To what degree are the activities and resources suit-
       able to the subject matter and grade level?   J. 1 2 3 4 5
    K. To what degree is there evidence of adequate re-
       search on the part of the Student Author?   K. 1 2 3 4 5
    L. To what degree is there evidence of the integration
       of other subject areas in the curriculum?   L. 1 2 3 4 5
    M. To what degree are there sufficient and suitable
       evaluative techniques suggested?   M. 1 2 3 4 5

*N. To what degree is the unit "teachable"?	N. 1 2 3 4 5
O. To what degree does it readily suggest other good teaching units?	O. 1 2 3 4 5
P. To what degree do you find the unit interesting and challenging?	P. 1 2 3 4 5

III. How would you evaluate the *overall* quality of the written unit? Take into consideration format as well as content and organization. *Circle one.*

Superior   Excellent   Very Good   Good   Average   Poor

IV. Make any other comments you feel appropriate to express your reaction to the written unit.

Each unit is evaluated by approximately five or six student readers as well as by the instructor. The scores are then averaged. Thus, each student author knows which of his or her peers have read the work and can then have a meaningful discussion with them.

---

* If you do not find the unit "teachable," please explain why.

Peer Evaluation of a Research Paper

Title: _____

Author: _____

Reader: _____

Key

1—To a very high degree
2—To a high degree
3—To a moderate degree
4—To a low degree
5—To a very low degree

Circle the appropriate number to indicate your evaluation of each point.

I. Format

    A. To what degree is the paper neat?   A. 1 2 3 4 5
    B. To what degree is the paper attractive?   B. 1 2 3 4 5
    C. To what degree does grammar conform to good usage?   C. 1 2 3 4 5
    D. To what degree is the style of writing forceful?   D. 1 2 3 4 5

II. How would you evaluate the overall quality for the *form* of the paper? You should consider appearance, grammar and organization. Circle one.

SUPERIOR EXCELLENT VERY GOOD GOOD AVERAGE POOR

A+   A   B+   B   C   D

III. Content

    E. To what extent is there a clear statement of the problem?   E. 1 2 3 4 5
    F. To what degree is there clear organization of ideas?

                                          F. 1 2 3 4 5
    G. To what degree is there evidence of adequate research?   G. 1 2 3 4 5
    H. To what degree does the bibliography seem to be adequately representative of a good reading list on the topic?   H. 1 2 3 4 5
    I. To what degree are the conclusions and implications valid (consistent with the main discussion of the paper)?   I. 1 2 3 4 5
    J. To what degree has the writer evidenced creative thinking in arriving at conclusions and implications?   J. 1 2 3 4 5

IV. How would you evaluate the over-all quality of the *content* of the paper?

SUPERIOR   EXCELLENT   VERY GOOD   GOOD   AVERAGE   POOR

A+   A   B+   B   C   D

Each research paper is evaluated by approximately five or six student readers as well as by the instructor. The scores are then averaged. Thus, the student author knows which of his peers read his work and can then have a meaningful discussion with them.

Group Performance Rating Form

Instructions: Circle the statement under each question which most accurately describes your feelings about the question with regard to your group.

1. To what extent did the participants act as a unified group, rather than a disjointed collection of individuals?

Acted completely unified	Fairly well unified	Somewhat unified	More disjointed than unified	Completely disjointed

2. How free did you feel to bring up objections and partly formulated suggestions during this discussion?

Felt very hesitant	Felt somewhat hesitant	Felt moderately free	Felt very free	Felt completely free

3. How well satisfied are you with the decision(s) made by the group?

Completely satisfied	Fairly well satisfied	Just satisfied no more	Slightly dissatisfied	Very dissatisfied

4. Although you may or may not be in agreement with the particular decision(s) reached at this meeting, how satisfied are you with the way it was arrived at?

Completely satisfied	Fairly well satisfied	Just satisfied no more	Slightly dissatisfied	Very dissatisfied

5. How strongly are you willing to support the plans developed by your group?

Complete support	Moderate support	Limited support	Very little support	No support

The Case of Burns

Burns was an extremely bright fifth-grader. He came from a family that had somewhat above average income and who valued rich experiences for their children. Burns' older sister had studied in Europe for a year and the prospect was that he, too, when he reached college age would have a year's study abroad.

Burns' teacher was a very sincere young woman who had been well trained and who enjoyed involving her students in the planning for teaching-learning. However, there had been a recent confrontation in a School Board meeting over the idea of accountability and teachers were warned that they should always be ready to justify grades. The principal had argued for more tests, particularly objective tests which could be scored without any question of right or wrong. This was difficult for Burns' teacher but at the end of one unit on the USSR, she decided to try. She spent much time constructing what she thought was a fair, complete, and reasonable test.

At the end of the unit, she administered the test. When she took the papers home to grade, she was amazed at how poorly Burns had done on the test. She went back over the items, trying to reconstruct her own original thinking and, more than that, trying to understand why such a bright, articulate, and well-informed student had done so poorly.

As she was about to give up, she noticed a tiny bit of writing in the bottom right-hand corner of the page. It said, "Dear Teacher, Please look on the back. I wrote some things I learned about the USSR that you didn't ask on the test. Sincerely, Burns." There he had written a whole page of facts and generalizations that he had found interesting but which had not been included on the objective test.

Questions For Discussion

1. Should the teacher have given Burns any credit for his additional essay part of the test?

2. How does this case illustrate the idea that the structure of the test itself puts a lid on the amount of learning a student can give himself credit for?

3. Did the fact that Burns took the initiative and went on to elaborate what he had learned indicate that he realized that the test was inadequate in its coverage?

4. How would Burns have been discriminated against had the teacher chosen to ignore his additional material and made the score on the objective portion his only grade?

5. What would be the attitude of most teachers toward a student who would take such liberties with a test form?

The Case of the "Hot Seat"

Mr. Johnson was a very creative teacher. He always said that he'd rather do anything than write out report cards because they were such an inadequate representation of the students. After struggling with his ideas for several years he hit upon a solution that he decided was worth trying. When he presented it to his sixth-grade class, they were enthusiastic about trying it.

Here is how it worked. Several days before report cards were due in the principal's office, Mr. Johnson organized his day so that each of his twenty-seven students had an assigned conference period with him. During this conference, the students were asked to submit all their work for the grading period, suggest a grade appropriate to their accomplishment, and be ready to discuss it with Mr. Johnson. Many of the students thought this was going to be a big "push over" and a neat way to get easy A's.

The first conference day arrived and each student knew when he or she was scheduled for a talk with Mr. Johnson. The learning center plans had all been completed the day before and the students had agreed to call on Mr. Johnson only in case of dire necessity. When the class arrived that morning, they saw that Mr. Johnson had arranged his desk in a corner with an extra chair for the student conference. Immediately the student chair was named the "hot seat." As the students kept their conference appointments, the discussions centered on how well they had done, what they could have done better, what the weak spots were in their work, etc. For the first hour or so, everybody was so busy trying to listen in that not much work was done in the centers. But as the day went on, normal work began and the conferences continued. Each student presented his or her work and self-evaluation and also was asked to help fill out the actual grades. That was the real shocker. Most of the students acted as though they thought grades were some magic thing plucked out of thin air. To their great amazement, most of their grades coincided with Mr. Johnson's. In cases where they did not, further discussion was needed.

At any rate, at the end of the day, the students knew exactly what grade they would see on their report cards in every subject. Moreover, they all felt a new sense of pride and importance in having been asked to give their own opinions of how well or poorly they had done.

When the report cards went out to the parents later in the week, there were no calls from the parents of Mr. Johnson's students. The pupils themselves were able to explain how the grades were derived and why they were fair marks.

The hot seat became a permanent part of Mr. Johnson's classroom and the following year one prankster brought bright green paint and a leather strap to make the chair look like a real hot seat. Mr. Johnson took this all in good humor and continued to use the technique—and the green chair!

Questions For Discussion

1. What do you think of Mr. Johnson's idea?

2. Have you ever been a student in a class that used anything similar in terms of self-evaluation?

3. How did Mr. Johnson's plan indicate his respect for his students and his attitude of trust in them?

4. Do you think this was just an easy way to keep the teacher from having to fill out report cards?

5. If the only person who really knows what the learner has learned is the learner, then wouldn't it be logical to expect the learner to be able to grade himself?

6. Do you think the students who are asked to do such self-evaluation need some training in being objective and honest about themselves?

Have you witnessed or experienced a case in your own school life that you think demonstrates some of the concepts discussed in this chapter? If so, describe one of them and explain how you saw it handled. Did you agree with what was done?

Why is it so difficult for teachers to be "fair" in their grading of students' work?

Have you ever had the experience of having a piece of work of which you were especially proud badly down-graded by a teacher? What was the reason? Did it have to do with the work itself or was there some other factor operating?

How will emphasis on accountability cause teachers to spend more time on testing than on teaching?

Notes

1. Benjamin S. Bloom, J. Thomas Hastings, George F. Madaus, *Handbook on Formative and Summative Evaluation of Student Learning.* (New York: McGraw-Hill, 1971), p. 6.

2. Robert L. Wondrash, "Accountability." (Unpublished research paper, University of Nevada, Reno, 1976), p. 9.

3. Leslie H. Browder, *Emerging Patterns of Administrative Accountability.* (New York: McCutchan Publishing Corp., 1971), p. 384.

4. R. W. Hostrop, J. A. Mecklenburger, and J. A. Wilson, *Accountability for Educational Results.* (Connecticut, Linnet Books, 1973), p. 51.

5. William Demont and Roger Demont, *Accountability: An Action Model for the Public Schools.* (Chicago: ETC Publications, 1975), pp. 2–4.

6. R. W. Hostrop et al., *Accountability for Educational Results,* p. 45.

7. I. David Welch, Fred Richards, and Anne Cohen Richards, *Educational Accountability: A Humanistic Perspective.* (Denver: Shields Publishing Co., 1973), p. 29.

8. Ibid., pp. 238–40.

9. Russell M. Eidsmore, *A Student's Rating Scale of an Instructor.* Sioux City, Iowa: Morningside College Press, 1966.

Summary—Part III

The eight chapters in Part III have dealt with the heart of the education process—the teaching-learning relationship.

Chapter 9 emphasized the importance of first-hand experience with the environment and described in some detail how valid concepts can be developed only out of a wide knowledge of reality.

Chapter 10 used the Gestalt theory as a model for the integrated curriculum. It emphasized the importance of the "wholeness" of knowledge and defined cultural universals as a useful tool for understanding the universe.

Chapter 11 attempted to describe and explain the developmental theory of learning by using the important work of Piaget. It attempted to apply Piagetian theory by answering *when* and *how* to approach the teaching-learning of any new concept.

Chapter 12 went into some detail to describe the significant work of Dr. Montessori. It also pointed out that many innovations in education can be traced to the tenets of Montessori's philosophy—open schools, individualized learning, the discovery method, the "new" concern for nutrition as a factor in learning and many others.

Chapter 13 explored the concept of motivation as an essential element in the learning process. It emphasized the highly individual nature of motivation and pointed out that the curriculum itself can help or hinder this important process.

Chapter 14 tried to simplify some of the complicated concepts of behavioral psychology and its applications for curriculum. It also described the use of operant conditioning as a control device in many schools.

Chapter 15 went into some detail to describe the current attitudes toward open schools. It also attempted to define the changing roles of administrators and teachers in the open-concept school.

Chapter 16 discussed evaluation, not merely as the technique for arriving at grades but from the philosophical point of view of accountability and the effects this concept will undoubtedly have on schools and teachers and students.

To summarize, Part III tried to highlight some of the more significant psychological and philosophical elements affecting the operation of educational institutions. It would be foolish to assume that everything that needs to be said has been included here. There is much, much more. It is to be hoped that the offerings in this section will be the beginning of a serious thought process out of which the reader will evolve his or her own theory of education.

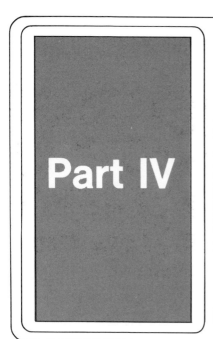

Part IV

The Never-Ending Odyssey

17 | Learning for Living a Lifetime

I'll stop teaching when I stop learning.

GREGOR PIATIGORSKY[1]

When you compare the normal span of a human life to the life expectancy of a star, a lifetime is just a flash—a burst of brilliance and it's all over! There is hardly time for identifying a beginning or an ending; a growing, learning process or a declining, aging process. Human living is an infinitesimal, single piece of *time.*

Yet, knowing this, we have, nonetheless, compartmentalized our lives into rigid segments determined in large part by the calendar. Begin school at age six—no earlier and no later! Graduate from high school at eighteen. From college at twenty-two. From university or professional school at twenty-five or twenty-six. If you are not firmly set in a work pattern by the age of thirty, you are considered something less than ambitious, perhaps even somewhat unstable. "Finding one's self" is usually equated with fooling around, wasting time and money, and producing nothing.

From thirty to sixty-five is the long, unbroken period of intense production. A short vacation here and there, a constantly increasing burden of economic and social responsibility. With a little luck, perhaps some kind of sabbatical leave, but even then one must return with a product—a paper, a book, a research report. It is not acceptable to come back simply refreshed and rested and better informed about the human condition.

Before you realize what has happened, your sixty-fifth birthday is upon you. In many educational and business institutions, you are automatically retired. In educational institutions it is rare that consideration is given to the creativity, maturity, and social flexibility the senior faculty member can bring to students and staff alike. In some universities there is a post-retirement appointment to a position like resident scholar or senior consultant. In most institutions, however, pinching pennies and people, the policy is to increase the teaching load and ". . . get all we can out of him before he retires." This kind of attitude is guaranteed to make most sixty-five-year-olds only too happy to pack up and get out. What happens after sixty-five? Collapse? Heart attack? Stroke? Actually, it is true that the sudden release from unbearable

287

pressures and frustrating tensions can cause serious physical problems. This is a rather dismal litany of a life. However, it is all too often precisely the kind of thing that happens in our assembly-line culture in which people become obsolete before their time. Years of experience are not valued or respected, the wisdom of age is disregarded and the aging themselves are seen as problems. Our cult of youth has over-looked the fact that many people considered "too old" have the young-est ideas of all. The aging and the young of our society seem to have much more in common than either group has with the eternally busy, pushy, frantic, buck-chasing, power-hungry middle-age group.

What does all this have to do with education? What role does learning play in this drama of an all-too-brief existence? How do the truly creative people survive, some seeming almost to be re-born, as if life had reserved its greatest rewards until last?

Ending or Beginning?

A young college senior talking with his professor just after graduation expressed grave doubts about his readiness for the future. "Here I am! A B.A. degree in history and a teaching credential! Yet I feel as if I am still too ignorant to go out and teach!" The professor, still holding the graduation program in hand, showed it to the student. "What does the heading say?" "It says 'Fiftieth Annual Commencement.'" "That's right. It says commencement—not the end of anything but the begin-ning. So it is. If the university has done its job well, you are now equipped to 'commence' your real education. Nobody guaranteed to teach you everything about everything in twelve years of public school and four years of college. Your real learning begins now and continues as long as you breathe the breath of life!"

Somehow, in our rush to achieve the great American dream, we overlook the fact that society is waiting with a calendar, checking off our years, just waiting to put a big "X" through year sixty-five! Does this need to be so? No. One educator came up with an article entitled, "Six Hundred and Twenty-Five Ways to Postpone Old Age."[2] All of his ideas involved mind-stretching, money-making, recreational, and service opportunities.

There are always some who have resisted new ideas and who have looked forward for years to that magic date when they can be released from jobs they can hardly endure, from students whom they consider an intrusion, and from demands that make them feel inadequate. For them, there is really nothing more to say. Their aim in life was merely to survive until the regular arrival of the retirement check each month. It is the others, those urgent, generous, life-giving people for whom this chapter is intended. People like Frank Story of Dallas, Texas, who, at eighty-four is a substitute foreign-language teacher in the high school from which he retired in 1961. Or like Henry Steele Commager of Amherst who at seventy-three writes off-handedly of ". . . lectures at the Royal Academy, the British Academy, the Royal Library in London and Copenhagen in June and July . . . then back to teach three seminars and read proof on a book and write another before preparing 15 broad-cast scripts for the winter. Otherwise, I'm living the life of Riley!" Or someone who emulates Carl Sandburg who wrote some of his most touchingly beautiful verse at age eighty-five. Or another Grandma Moses, whose paintings, some done when she was one hundred and one, are still considered classic Americana. Winston Churchill, Albert Schweitzer, and Frank Lloyd Wright seemed not to have the time to get old. These wonderful human beings—it is they and countless others like them who keep on learning and teaching and giving and living. If you are one of them when you are older, count yourself lucky. You can be if you plan ahead! One of the most charming comments this author received from a student at the end of one school term was from a bright vivacious young woman who wrote on her final term paper this little note: "Thanks to a super person from a future super person!" There is no doubt she will make it!

Re-tooling and Re-education

Alvin Toffler and the other futurists describe the fact that all persons presently in the work force may face the very real possibility of needing to retrain themselves at least two or even three times in their careers. Many professionals and semi-professionals are in jobs that simply did not exist fifteen or twenty years ago. So much for acquiring one skill and staying with it for a lifetime. So much for fixed and secure re-sponses. So much for carefully defined and protected ego boundaries.

Aside from job changes, there is the whole area of change in social organization. How do you define a family? Now; how will you in the future? What is happening to sex roles? Now; what will happen in the future? How do you plan a functional city? Now; how will you in the future?

Even with the thinking of scholars who are on the cutting edge of social development, we continue to teach and to play out our own personal, social, and professional roles as if this is it! Once you have obtained a higher degree, there is no need for further study. Would you be willing to go to a surgeon who had not learned any new techniques since he graduated in the 1940's or the 1950's? Would you let a blacksmith work on your new sports car? Do you need a lamplighter to come around each evening to light the street lamps? These examples are no more inappropriate than seeing teachers year after year go through the same class notes, assignments, and exams. Much of the bibliography they use is more than ten years old. But it is worse still to see them personally unwilling to entertain new ideas or to develop innovative changes.

Aging and Creativity

How does one reconcile the wisdom of aging with the concept of creativity? It's very simple. Older scholars have arrived at an enviable state indeed. They have the inner security to think their own thoughts and to express them. They have a lifetime of experience on which to draw for solutions to present problems. They have lived through countless evolutions of ideologies and educational theories and classroom practices. They no longer need to descend into the pit of competition. They have established their own worth and are no more in need of defense than is Pike's Peak! True, they may feel the stings of sarcasm from younger, insensitive, ambitous colleagues. However, they recognize this (or we might hope they do) as expression of insecurity and frustration or even downright jealousy.

Truly self-actualized senior educators generally exhibit at least three characteristics.

First, they are not swept away by every fad that blows across the face of education. They can be eclectic because they have a storehouse of philosophy which will assist them in making choices. They can be themselves. They have long since enjoyed status and respect and reputation. No need to wear masks or play roles or bow in obsequious obeisance to the powers that be. They have learned that there is no truly reliable security except inner security and that integrity and self-respect do not have a dollar value. They may not have economic riches, but they have a different kind of wealth—one they have earned and can enjoy. The remembrances of success, the sense of pride in their students' accomplishments, the awareness of their self-worth. These are the golden coins that they can take out and polish and savor even when the retirement check is woefully inadequate. Maslow suggests that the peak experiences of life—the tragedies, the triumphs, the crises—are the moments we should treasure. These are the times for the life-long learner when real learning takes place. While such experiences are largely emotional, they are also cognitive.[3]

Second, self-actualized people of any age are nearly always engaged in generativity not stagnation. Their minds, long accustomed to being sharpened on the stone of other (maybe brighter) minds, are keen and acute. They are busy generating new ideas, new projects, new experiences. Not for them the stagnation of the status quo or the "finished" life. No rocking chair, no quiet fishing cottage, no retreat into a retirement home. They continue to be "where the action is," whether this is in the field of public service, continuing education, or self-fulfillment.

Third, they truly care about what happens to the next generation. They are concerned about environment, values, and particularly about the quality of education that they see being fashioned for the next generation.

All of these are traits of persons who have made the journey from the need for environmental support to self-support; from dependence on other-approval to self-approval; from the need to receive affection to the need to give it. They love themselves in a broad philosophical sense and have reached that "centered" place where they are truly free. In that freedom they become mirrors for others less confident, less secure, less productive. When these others look into their eyes, they feel their own beauty and worth and thus experience a good feeling about themselves. There is no cognitive or behaviorable or measurable explanation for this. It is simply a kind of overflow of a humanistic spirit that allows those who are mature and serene to look at people the way they look at sunsets—they are there, they are unique and they need no "touching up."[4]

How Does One Begin?

How does one go about becoming such a self-actualized person? Is there a formula? Is it possible to change? What transforms a drone into a creator? How can one become accustomed to variety in human values and human expression? What has our own education done to prepare us?

It is generally believed that we change as we grow older—become more crochety, more argumentative, more self-centered, more set in our ways. Not so, say the psychologists. Instead, as we age we simply cease to sustain our masks and our status-role costumes. Like the Emperor with no clothes, we are "bare" to the bone—our own real selves just as we have always been, without the benefit of concealing academic robes or status positions. A mean young man will almost surely develop into a mean old man, no matter that he has been able to control or even conceal his true personality for many years.

Gregor Piatigorsky answered many of these questions when he said, "Start early in life to look for your best quality. Stick to it. Develop it. The best fruit ripens slowly. Old wood burns best. Old wine tastes best. An old fiddle sounds sweeter. . . . fall in love . . . with an apricot tree, a human voice . . . Michelangelo's Moses."[5]

All of this seems to say, get out of yourself, savor the world, make friends, read, develop new skills, enjoy the opportunities to learn new things, keep in touch with the young. All of these come easier if you have built lifetime habits of curiosity about the world, about people, and about ideas. If you have never ventured over the next mountain, it may be impossible to look beyond it to range after range of unexplored life. Seek out new experiences. Never think, "Oh, I could never do that!" Try it! You may like it! Try new foods, new cultures, even new modes of dress and religious thought. Absolutes are paralyzing. Prejudice is confining. Daily routines are deadening. Being alone can be a treat for the soul but loneliness is a miserable state.

Where Does One Begin?

Self-actualization is not something to be delayed until retirement and old age. It is a quality that sheds an aura of youth around even the very old and helps people of all ages to see life clearly—as it is, rather than as they wish it to be. It allows one to make fair judgments of others—real or phony. It permits somewhat accurate predictions of the future coupled with an ability to enjoy the present. It supports a healthy humility which accepts without arrogance or annoyance the fact that there is always more to learn. It moves one to dedication to some worthy work and to a set of values in which accomplishment is exciting and pleasurable. It is almost always marked by creativity, spontaneity, and a sharp sense of humor. Finally, it enhances one's own feeling of courage, a willingness to go it alone, so necessary in the lonely moments of creation and, if necessary, to stand up for a new idea or a treasured value.

People should be encouraged very early in life to think seriously about their own value systems and their own philosophy. Sometimes it is a fruitful exercise to have students in college or university or even high school write a full description of themselves as they will be and what they think their accomplishments will be when they are forty or fifty. It is amazing that so many complete this task by casting themselves in the same mold they are already in. Some few daring souls take marvelous flights into the future but, unfortunately, they comprise a minority. Another experiment that causes young people to stop and think about themselves is to propose a situation in which they will be part of a group sent to colonize a space platform and to organize a whole new society. Invariably, the society they propose is exactly like the one they live in. Still another is to ask them to write a detailed description of the specific changes that will probably take place in any one institution like education, religion, or family organization. Again, most of the responses are simply duplications of what already exists. In fields like communication, travel, and housing, however, there is a wider range of imagination. Perhaps this only proves that tangible, outward parts of our culture are easier to change than are the intangible, valuing parts. Whether we like it or not, change is the only constant of our times. Unless we are able to make peace between our closely held values and the inevitable adaptations of the future, then we can look forward to a lifetime of frustration and unhappiness.

What Has Our Educational System Done To Prepare Us For a Lifetime of Learning?

Unfortunately, in a large number of cases, the answer is "very little." As was demonstrated earlier, each step in the educational ladder is generally viewed as preparation for the next step. Very little attention is given to developing habits and attitudes that will assist in expanding our world. Somehow, the school system has only a very limited vision of its scope of responsibility. The first-grade teacher is responsible *only* for getting you ready for second grade; the college supervisor is responsible *only* for getting you through student-teaching; the French professor is responsible *only* for getting you through the prescribed course of study for one year. This thinking prevails until the day someone hands you a diploma when the whole system seems to breathe a sigh of relief and is definitely finished with you. Unless, of course, they need you as a loyal alumnus for a donation.

Often, instead of helping students develop a love for reading, for example, schools make the reading task so difficult, so complicated, and so clinical that as adults they are "turned off" to books because of their repeated experience with failure in school. The same could be said of math, creative writing, art, or almost any other curriculum area. In one high school it has long been the custom to use as punishment for misbehavior a "sentence" of so many hours in the library. You can be sure that adults who remember sitting many dull hours in the library as punishment will not be likely to have an interest in exploring the great variety of learning and mind-expanding opportunities their local public library has to offer.

The larger failure is in the short-sighted view the school has of its own role. Truly educated persons must be more than doctors, lawyers, teachers, or electronics experts. They must also be fully functioning human beings and responsible citizens. One General Electric executive put it very well when he said to this author, "We are delighted to send you our semi-skilled staff for classes. Please *do not* try to teach them our methods of working the assembly line. We will do that. Please *do* teach them something to think about while they are working the assembly line!"

The Seven Cardinal Principles of Education, published by the Commission on the Reorganization of Secondary Education in 1918, identified seven objectives for the education of every American. These were listed as health, command of fundamental processes, worthy home membership, vocation, citizenship, worthy use of leisure time, and ethical character. While these principles in somewhat original interpretation were reaffirmed by the NEA Bicentennial Panel in 1976, it is clear that they suggest little by way of meeting the increasing need for lifelong education.

Health needs to be expanded to include mental and emotional health, nutrition, use of drugs, as well as the health of the total environment.

Command of the fundamental processes can no longer be interpreted merely as the "Three R's." Some of the fundamental processes of the 70's and 80's include a new definition of literacy as well as a new concern for human relationships, the ability to make choices, and skill in decision making.

Worthy home membership needs to take into account the current state of the economy, which almost requires that both parents have earning power. It must also look at the changing roles of women and an acceptance of the various new definitions of family and affinity groups.

Vocational education must be so planned so as not to "lock" people into jobs that are changing and are daily becoming obsolete.

Citizenship requires more than voting, paying taxes, and meeting military obligations. There is the concept of true patriotism with an awareness of the weaknesses of our government coupled with the willingness to be creatively critical of our leaders. There is the further concept of the global community and of loyalties and responsibilities that transcend traditional love of country.

Worthy use of leisure time seems almost naïve in an era of limited leisure. What about the thousands of fathers and mothers who not only need to work but must also take on a second or even third job to meet the demands of an uncontrolled inflation? What about the hours required to meet the increasingly complicated bookkeeper role that has overwhelmed us all? Sunday afternoon would be a lovely time for a walk along the river. Instead, at least one Sunday afternoon each month must be given to paying the bills, balancing the checkbook, and keeping records for the Internal Revenue Service.

Ethical character is one value that has taken a severe beating during this decade. The models held up for the young are often anything but ethical. The careless substitution of wrong for right, of expediency for integrity, has eroded respect, responsibility, and regard for the rights of others.[6]

We may have come a long way in the imperfect vehicle we fashioned sixty years ago. There have been many successes along the way and we should be justly proud of them. It is imperative, however, that the schools take a long hard look down the road and build some new vehicle which includes values like world peace, attention to neglected human rights, and the development of a more humane society.

What Opportunities Are Open to Everyone?

Opportunities are everywhere. Ideas are free; library cards don't cost much; travel is becoming available at reasonable cost. Community colleges are offering a full range of courses from interior decorating to fly casting. Whether one is interested in learning for leisure or preparing for a new career, opportunities abound. All it takes is a little asking around. In all this urgency to keep informed, one should not neglect the efforts necessary to keep fit. Young people who neglect nutrition can hardly expect to be hale and hearty in their late years. Eating and exercising properly are like thinking—they become a part of our lives and serve us in good stead when we need them. Good physical and mental health are usually mutually supportive. Neglect one and the other suffers. Try to find time for both.

Ulysses, returning home from the Trojan Wars, tired and grown old, is reported by Tennyson to have said, "Though much is taken, much abides; and though we do not have that strength which in old days moved heaven and earth, that which we are, we are . . . heroic hearts made weak by time and fate but strong in will to strive, to seek, to find, and not to yield."

Like Ulysses, each of us soon finds that those learnings which endure are the ones in which we discover ourselves and with which we are able to feel a sense of integration with the universe. Our formal educational tasks require that we use only a small part of our potential. There is so much more that is there just waiting to be called up.

The truly educated person is at home in any part of the world. He has stretched his boundaries both mental and physical and by seeking new experiences, taking new risks, and trying new things, he has established a large and interesting environment for himself. At any age he will be a leader, a motivator, a teacher.

Piatigorsky's quote, with which this short chapter began, reads: "I'll stop teaching when I stop learning." There is an additional thought with which to close this chapter—and this book—"I'll stop learning when I stop living."

Notes

1. Gregor Piatigorsky, quoted in "Retirement? It's a a Second Chance!" by Jean Landon Taylor, *Phi Delta Kappan,* June, 1976, 652.

2. Berlie J. Fallon, "The Case Against Retirement," *Phi Delta Kappan* (June 1976), 649.

3. Harold C. Lyon, Jr., "Humanistic Education for Lifelong Learning," *International Review of Education,* Vol. 20, No. 24 (1974), 502.

4. Lyon, "Humanistic Education for Lifelong Learning," 505.

5. Jean Landon Taylor, "Retirement? It's a Second Chance," *Phi Delta Kappan* (June 1976), 653.

6. Harold G. Shane, "The Seven Cardinal Principles Revisited," *Today's Education* (Sept.-Oct. 1976), 57–73.

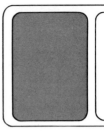

Additional Readings

Ahlfeld, Kathy. "The Montessori Revival: How Far Will It Go?" *Nation's Schools* 85:1 January 1970: 75–78, 80.

Allport, Gordon. *Becoming.* New Haven, Conn.: Yale University Press, 1955.

Ascare, D. and Axelrod, S. "Use of Behavior Modification Procedures in Four 'Open' Classrooms,' " *Psychology in the Schools* 10 (1973): 243–248.

Ashton-Warner, Sylvia. *Spearpoint.* New York: Knopf, 1972.

Ashton-Warner, Sylvia. *Teacher.* New York: Simon and Shuster, 1963.

Ayllon, T. and Azrin, N. H. *The Token Economy: A Motivational System for Therapy and Rehabilitation.* New York: Appleton-Century-Crofts, 1968.

Bakan, Rita. "Malnutrition and Learning," Michigan State University, East Lansing Center of Urban Affairs, 1973.

Bandura, A. *Principles of Behavior Modification.* New York: Holt, Rinehart and Winston, 1969.

Barth, Roland S. *Open Education and the American School.* New York: Agathon Press, 1972.

Barth, Roland S. "Should We Forget About Open Education?" *Saturday Review,* November 1973: 58–59.

Bauer, Francis C. "Guidance and Psychiatry." In *The Interdisciplinary Roots of Guidance.* Edited by Thomas C. Hennessey. Bronx, N.Y.: Fordham University Press, 1966.

Birch, Herbert G., and Grotberg, Edith H. *Designs and Proposals for Early Childhood Research: A New Look: Malnutrition, Learning and Behavior.* Office of Economic Opportunity, Office of Planning, Research and Evaluation, 1971.

Birnbrauer, J. S., Wolf, M. M., Kidder, J. D. and Tague, C. E. "Classroom Behavior of Retarded Pupils With Token Reinforcement," *Journal of Experimental Child Psychology,* 2 (1965): 219–235.

Blank, Marion and Rose, Susan A. "Some Effects of Testing Methodology on Children's Cross-Modal Performance," *Developmental Psychology,* January 1975: 120.

Borich, Gary D. *Evaluating Educational Programs and Products.* New Jersey: Educational Technology Publications, 1974.

Borton, Terry. _Reach, Touch, and Teach._ New York: McGraw-Hill, 1970.

Boy, Angelo V. and Pine, Gerald J. _Expanding the Self: Personal Growth for Teachers._ Dubuque, Iowa: Brown, 1971.

Bradley, Curtis H. "Competence Motivation Reconsidered: The Construct of Intentionality," _Journal of Industrial Teacher Education,_ Vol. 12, No. 3.

Bridgman, P. W. _The Way Things Are._ Cambridge, Mass.: Harvard University Press, 1959.

Brown, G. I. _Human Teaching for Human Learning: An Introduction to Confluent Education._ New York: Viking, 1971.

Bruner, Jerome S. _Toward a Theory of Instruction._ New York: Norton, 1969.

Bussis, Anne M. and Chittenden, Edward A. "Toward Clarifying the Teacher's Role." In _Open Education: A Sourcebook for Parents and Teachers._ Edited by Ewald B. Nyquist and Gene R. Hawes. New York: Bantam Books, 1972, pp. 117–136.

California Teachers Association, _Accountability and the Curriculum,_ Research Resume No. 46, California, 1971.

Calvano, Michael A. "Predicting the Use of Imagery as a Mediation Strategy," _AV Communication Review,_ February 1974: 269–278.

Campbell, David N. "Accountability—Behavioral Objectives: The Grand Charade," _Today's Education,_ March-April, 1976.

Cass, J. "Teachers and Change," _Saturday Review,_ November 1973: 53.

Combs, Arthur W. "Perceiving, Behaving, Becoming," _Yearbook of the Association for Supervision and Curriculum Development._ Washington, D.C.: Education Association, 1962, p. 85.

Coombs, Arthur W. and Snygg, Donald. _Individual Behavior: A Perceptual Approach to Behavior,_ Rev. ed. New York: Harper & Row, 1959.

Conroy, Pat. _The Water is Wide._ New York: Houghton Mifflin, 1972.

Corcoran, D. W. J. _Pattern Recognition._ Penguin Books, 1971.

Darland, D. D. "The Profession's Quest for Responsibility and Accountability," _Phi Delta Kappan,_ September 1970: 41–44.

Dean, General James. Informal lecture before PTA of the American School in Yokohama, Japan, September 1950.

DeChardin, Pierre Teilhard. _The Phenomenon of Man._ New York: Harper & Row, 1957.

Demont, Bill and Roger. _Accountability: An Action Model for the Public Schools._ Illinois: ETC Publications, 1975.

Dreikurs, Rudolph. _Psychology in the Classroom._ Harper & Row, 1957.

Duval, Shelly and Wicklund, Robert A. *A Theory of Objective Self-Awareness.* New York: Academic Press, 1972.

Eckstein, Gustav. *The Body Has a Head.* New York: Harper & Row, 1970.

Elkind, D. "Children's Discovery of the Conservation of Mass, Weight and Volume: Piaget's Replication Study II," *Journal of Genetic Psychology,* 98 (1961): 219–227.

Elkind, D. "Giant in the Nursery," *The New York Times Magazine,* May 26, 1968: 25.

Ellis, Willis. *A Source Book of Gestalt Psychology.* London: Routledge and Kegan Paul, 1950.

Farley, Frank H. and Rosnow, Jan M. "Student Analyses of Motivation and School Learning," *The Journal of Experimental Education,* Vol. 43, No. 3, 1975.

Featherstone, J. *Schools Where Children Learn.* New York: Liveright, 1971.

Featherstone, J. "The British and Us: Open Schools I," *The New Republic,* September 11, 1971: 20–25; idem, "Tempering a Fad: Open Schools II," *The New Republic,* September 25, 1971: 17–21.

Fitts, William H. *Self Concept and Self Actualization.* Nashville, Tennessee: Fitts, 1971.

Flavell, J. *The Developmental Psychology of Jean Piaget.* Princeton, N.J.: D. Van Nostrand, 1963.

Furth, Hans G., and Wachs, Harry, *Thinking Goes to School.* New York: Oxford University Press, 1975.

Frymier, Jack R. "Development and Validation of a Motivation Index," *Theory Into Practice,* 9 (1970): 56–85.

Galloway, C. G. and Mickelson, N. I. "Modifications of Behavior Patterns of Indian Children," *Elementary School Journal,* 72 (1971): 150–155.

Gamow, George. *Mr. Tompkins in Wonderland.* Macmillan, 1946.

Gergen, Kenneth J. *The Concept of Self.* New York: Holt, Rinehart and Winston, 1971.

Gibran, Kahlil. *The Prophet.* New York: Alfred Knopf, 1923, pp. 77–78.

Ginsburg, Herbert, and Opper, Sylvia, *Piaget's Theory of Intellectual Development.* Englewood Cliffs, N.J.: Prentice-Hall, 1969.

Giusti, Joseph P. and Hogg, James H. "Teacher Status: Practitioner or Professional?" *Clearing House,* November 1973: 182–185.

Goldschmid, M. L. "Different Types of Conservation and Nonconservation and Their Relation to Age, Sex, I.Q., M.A. and Vocabulary," *Child Development,* 38 (1967): 1229–1246.

Goodlad, John I. "A Perspective on Accountability," _Phi Delta Kappan,_ October 1975.

Goodman, P. _Compulsory Mis-Education and the Community of Scholars._ New York: Vintage, 1962.

Green, Donald Ross. _Educational Psychology._ Englewood Cliffs, N.J.: Prentice-Hall, 1964.

Greer, Mary and Rubinstein, Bonnie. _Will the Real Teacher Please Stand Up?_ Pacific Palisades, Calif.: Goodyear, 1972.

Grothe, Barbara Ford. "Transforming Curiosity into Learning Skills." In _Elementary Curriculum._ Edited by Robert E. Chasnoff. New York: Pitman, 1964, pp. 161–164.

Gussow, Joan D., "Bodies, Brains and Poverty: Poor Children and the Schools," _IRCD Bulletin,_ Vol. VI, No. 3, September 1970.

Gwedy, Patricia A. "What Research Tells Us About Spelling," _Elementary English,_ February 1975: 233–236.

Hall, R. V., Lund, D., and Jackson, D. "Effects of Teacher Attention on Study Behavior," _Journal of Applied Behavior Analysis,_ 1 (1968): 1–12.

Harper, Ralph. "Significance of Existence and Recognition for Education," _Modern Philosophies and Education._ 54th Yearbook of the National Society for the Study of Education, edited by N. B. Henry, Chicago, 1955, pp. 245–247.

Hartman, George W. _Gestalt Psychology._ New York: Roland Press, 1935.

Hayman, John L. and Napier, Rodney N. _Evaluation in the Schools: A Human Process for Renewal._ California: Brooks/Cole, 1975.

Hendrick, I. "Work and the Pleasure Principle," _Psychoanalytical Quarterly,_ 12 (1943):311–329.

Highet, Gilbert. _The Art of Teaching._ New York: Vintage, 1954.

Hooper, I. H. "Piagetian Research and Education." In _Logical Thinking in Children._ Edited by I. E. Sigel and F. H. Hooper. New York: Holt, Rinehart and Winston, 1968, pp. 423–434.

Horton, Claude G. _Humanization of the Learning Environment._ United States Educational Resources Information Center #ED 066 929, 1972.*

Hunt, David E. and Sullivan, Edmund V. _Between Psychology and Education._ Hinsdale, Illinois: Dryden Press, 1974.

* For additional information, ERIC contains numerous references to periodical materials for a fuller treatment of Montessori and many facets of philosophy and psychology related to the Montessori Method.

Jacobson, Edith. *The Self and the Object World.* New York: International Universities Press, 1964.

Kallen, David J., *Nutrition, Development and Social Behavior.* U.S. Department of Health, Education and Welfare, 1973.

Katz, David. *Gestalt Psychology.* Roland Press, 1950.

Kazdin, A. E. and Bootzin, R. R. "The Token Economy: An Evaluative Review," *Journal of Applied Behavior Analysis,* 5 (1972):343–372.

Kelley, Earl C. *Education for What Is Real.* New York: Harper Brothers, 1947.

Kirk, Samuel A. *Educating Exceptional Children.* Boston: Houghton Mifflin, 1972.

Kline, Lloyd W. *Education and the Personal Quest.* Columbus, Ohio: Charles E. Merrill, 1971.

Knapp, Joan. *A Selection of Self Concept Measures.* United States Educational Resources Information Center #ED 080 534, 1973.

Koch, L. and Breyer, N. L. "A Token Economy for the Teacher," *Psychology in the Schools,* 11 (1974):195–200.

Laswell, Harold. *The Social Process.* Encyclopaedia Britannica Films, Wilmette, Illinois, 1956.

Lawson, Tom E. "Instruction and the Structure of Content," *Educational Technology,* May 1974: 27–28.

Lee, Dorris M. and Allen, R. V. *Learning to Read Through Experience,* 2nd ed. New York: Appleton-Century-Crofts, 1963.

Leeds, Leslie and Martin, Jeff. *Montessori and the Orderly Mind.* Unpublished research paper, University of Nevada, Reno, 1976.

Leonard, George B. *Education and Ecstasy.* New York: Delacorte, 1968.

Lillard, Paula Polk. *Montessori—A Modern Approach.* New York: Schocken Books, 1972.

Lindberg, Anne Morrow. *Gift From the Sea.* New York: Pantheon Books, 1955, pp 54–55, 58–59.

Linskie, Rosella. "The Field Trip as an Educational Technique," *Texas Journal of Secondary Education,* Winter 1956.

Lowenberg, Miriam E., Ph.D; Todhunter, E. Neige, Ph.D.; Wilson, Eva D., Ph.D.; Feeney, Moira C., Ph.D.; and Savage, Jane E., Ph.D. *Food and Man.* New York: John Wiley & Sons, 1968.

Lyon, Harold C., Jr. *Learning to Feel—Feeling to Learn.* Columbus, Ohio: Charles E. Merrill, 1971.

Madsen, C. H., Becker, W. C., and Thomas, D. R. "Rules, Praise, and Ignoring: Elements of Elementary Classroom Control," *Journal of Applied Behavior Analysis,* 1 (1968):139–150.

Marx and Hillix. *Systems and Theories in Psychology.* McGraw Hill, 1973.

Maslow, Abraham H. *Motivation and Personality.* New York: Harper & Row, 1954.

Meehan, Trinita. "An Informal Modality Inventory," *Elementary English,* September 1974: 901–904.

Menninger, William. "Recreation and Mental Health," *Recreation and Psychiatry.* New York: National Recreation Association, 1960, p. 8.

Menninger, William. "The Meaning of Work in Western Society." In *Man in a World at Work.* Edited by Henry Borow. Boston: Houghton Mifflin, 1964.

Mitchell, Allee J., "Who in the World?" *National Association for the Education of Young Children Conference.* Atlanta, Georgia, November 15, 1972.

Montagu, Ashley. *Man in Process.* New York: World Publishing, 1961, pp. 192–217.

Montagu. *On Being Human.* New York: Hawthorn Books, 1950.

Montessori, Maria. *The Absorbent Mind.* Trans. by Claude A. Claremont. New York: Holt, Rinehart and Winston, 1967.

Mucchielli, Roger. *Introduction to Structural Psychology.* New York: Funk and Wagnall, 1970.

Neil, Marion. "Cognitive Style: A New Aspect to Instructional Technology," *New Directions for Community Colleges,* Spring 1975: pp. 73–80.

Neisser, Ulric. *Cognitive Psychology.* New York: Appleton-Century-Crofts, 1966.

O'Leary, K. D. and Drabman, R. S. "Token Reinforcement Programs in the Classroom: A Review," *Journal of Abnormal Child Psychology,* 1 (1973):127–138.

Orem, R. C. *A Montessori Handbook.* New York: G. P. Putnam's Sons, 1965.

Orem, R. C. *Montessori Today.* New York: Capricorn Books, 1971.

Perelle, Ira B. "Auditory and Written/Visual Stimuli as Factors in Learning and Retention," *Reading Improvement,* Spring 1975: pp. 15–22.

Piaget, J. *The Origins of Intelligence in Children.* New York: International Universities Press, 1952.

Piaget, J. *Judgment and Reasoning of the Child.* New York: Harcourt, Brace and World, 1928.

Piaget, J. *The Child's Conception of Number* London: Humanities Press, 1952.

Piaget, J. *The Child's Conception of Physical Causality.* New York: Harcourt, Brace and World, 1930.

Piaget, J. *The Child's Conception of the World.* Paterson, N. J.: Littlefield, Adams, 1963.

Piaget, J. *The Language and Thought of the Child.* New York: Harcourt, Brace and World, 1926.

Piaget, J. *The Mechanisms of Perception.* New York: Basic Books, 1969.

Piaget, J. "Three Lectures." In *Piaget Rediscovered.* Edited by R. E. Ripple and U. N. Rockcastle. Ithaca, N.Y.: Cornell University Press, 1964.

Piaget, J. and Inhelder, B. *The Child's Conception of Space.* London: Routledge and Kegan Paul, 1956.

Ponty, Maurice. *The Structure of Behavior.* Boston: Beacon Press, 1963.

Postman, Neil and Weingartner, Charles. *The Soft Revolution.* Dell, 1971.

Prescott, Daniel. "Emotion and the Education Process." *American Council on Education,* 1938.

Randolph, Norma and Howe, William. *Self-Enhancing Education.* Palo Alto, California: Sanford Press, 1966.

Rich, H. Lyndall. *The Effects of Teaching Styles on Students' Behavior as Related to Social-Emotional Development.* Washington, D.C.: National Center for Educational Research and Development, February 1973.

Roe, Anne. *The Psychology of Occupations.* New York: John Wiley & Sons, 1956.

Rogers, Carl R. *Freedom to Learn.* Columbus, Ohio: Charles E. Merrill, 1969.

Rogers, Carl R. *On Becoming a Person.* Boston: Houghton Mifflin, 1961.

Rogers, Vincent, ed. *Teaching in the British Primary School.* New York: Macmillan, 1970.

Rosenthal, Robert and Jacobson, Lenore. *Pygmalion in the Classroom.* New York: Holt, Rinehart and Winston, 1968.

Roueche, John E. and Herrscher, Barton R. *Toward Instructional Accountability,* California: Westinghouse Learning Press, 1973.

Russell, E. W. "The Power of Behavior Control: A Critique of Behavior Modification Methods," *Journal of Clinical Psychology,* 30 (1974):111–136.

Sarason, Irwin G., Glaser, Edward M., and Fargo, George A. *Reinforcing Productive Classroom Behavior.* New York: Behavioral Publications, 1972.

Sartore, Richard L. "Grading: A Searching Look," *Educational Leadership,* 32:4 January 1975.

Sciara, Frank J. and Jantz, Richard K. *Accountability in American Education.* Boston: Allyn and Bacon, 1972.

Scrimshaw, Nevin S. and Gordon, John E. *Malnutrition, Learning and Behavior.* Cambridge: Massachusetts Institute of Technology, 1968.

Sears, Pauline S. and Sherman, Vivian S. *In Pursuit of Self Esteem.* Belmont, California: Wadsworth, 1964.

Silberman, Charles E. *Crisis in the Classroom.* New York: Random House, 1970.

Silberman, Charles E. "Murder in the Schoolroom," *The Atlantic Monthly,* Vol. 225, June 1970: 82–97.

Sigel, E. E. and Hooper, F. H. *Logical Thinking in Children: Research Based on Piaget's Theory.* New York: Holt, Rinehart and Winston, 1968.

Smith, Robert L. and Troth, William A. "Achievement Motivation: A Rational Approach to Psychological Education," *Journal of Counseling Psychology,* Vol. 22, No. 6, 1975.

Solzhenitsyn, Aleksandr. *Gulag Archipelago.* New York: Harper & Row, 1974.

Stauffer, Russell. *The Language-Experience Approach to the Teaching of Reading.* New York: Harper & Row, 1970.

Stevens, John O. *Awareness: Exploring, Experimenting, Experience.* Lafayette, Calif.: Real People Press, 1971.

Swaim, James E. "Is Listening Really More Effective for Learning in the Early Grades?" *Elementary English,* November-December 1974: 1110–1113.

Taylor, Harold. *The World as Teacher.* Garden City, N.Y.: Doubleday, 1970.

Thatcher, David A. *Teaching, Loving and Self-Directed Learning.* Pacific Palisades, California: Goodyear, 1973.

Thomas, Susan B., *Malnutrition, Cognitive Development and Learning.* Illinois: ERIC Clearinghouse on Early Childhood Education, August 1972.

Tillich, Paul. *The Courage to Be.* New Haven, Conn: Yale University Press, 1952.

Today's Education. Special feature on "Motivation," September-October 1975. Washington, D.C: N.E.A.

Toynbee, Arnold J. "Why and How I Work," *Saturday Review,* April 5, 1969: 24.

Vandever, Thomas R. and Neville, Donald D. "Modality Aptitude and Word Recognition," *Journal of Reading Behavior,* July 1974: 195–201.

Wadsworth, Barry J., *Piaget's Theory of Cognitive Development.* New York: David McKay Company, 1974.

Wees, W. R. *Nobody Can Teach Anyone Anything.* Garden City, N.Y.: Doubleday, 1971.

White, Paul Dudley. In "Magic of the Bicycle," motion picture produced by Schwinn Bicycle Co., Chicago, 1966.

Willey, R. D. *Learning and Thinking.* Unpublished manuscript from the research papers of Roy DeVerl Willey. Reno, Nevada: University of Nevada, 1971.

Yauch, Wilbur A. "Keys to Understanding in School Relations." In *The Teachers Encyclopedia.* Englewood Cliffs, N.J.: Prentice-Hall, 1966, Chapter 35.

Zilboorg, Gregory. *Freud and Religion.* Westminster, Md.: The Paulist/Newman Press, 1964, p. 31.

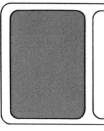

Index

Accommodation, 149, 150
Accountability, 252, 260, 261, 262, 263
Administrators, 241
Age-Grade Level, 61
Aggregate, 137
Aging, 290
Analysis, 137, 138
Aquinas, Thomas, 123, 124
Aristotle, 124, 189
Assimilation, 149, 150
Aston-Warner, Sylvia, 46, 62, 164
Authoritarian classroom, 35

Basic needs, 3, 24
Behavioral objectives, 212
Behavior conditioning, 207, 208
Behaviorists, 137, 139, 154
Benet, Alfred, 148, 149
Bigge, Morris L., 206
Boy, Angelo V., 111
Buddha, 77

Categorizing, 152
Challenging a grade, 259
"Children's Lib," 34
Churchill, Winston, 289
Classification, 152
Classroom atmosphere, 34, 35
Classrooms, 4
Cleanliness, 5
Closed classroom, 32, 233, 235
Closed school, 231, 232
Cognitive development, 151, 154
Color awareness, 172, 173

Commager, Henry Steele, 289
Commission on Reorganization of
    Secondary Education (1918), 294
Committee on Education (1960), 44
Community school, 232
Competition, 192, 193
Computer-Assisted Instruction, 210
Conant, James, 244
Concept development, 126, 127
Concepts, 126, 127, 128
Concrete operations, 151, 152
Conditioned response, 206, 207
Contingency, 124
Contingency Management, 213
Cooley, George Horton, 20, 21, 45, 140
Core curriculum, 140
Creativity, 290
Cultural universals, 140, 141, 142
Cunningham, Ruth, 94
Curriculum, 60, 61, 62, 63, 197
Curriculum builder, 60, 61

de Chardin, Theilhard, 136
Democratic classroom, 35
Descriptive objectives, 213
Developmental view, 237
Dewey, John, 154, 166, 234
Didactic materials, 166
Didactic material, 162, 166, 177
Diet, 166
Discipline, 34
Discrimination, 207
Doolittle, Liza, 44
Dressing frames, 167, 168

"Ease of control," 34
Edison, Thomas A., 128
Effectiveness, 262
Efficiency, 262
Elementists, 139, 154
Eliot, T. S., 123
Emotional needs, 5
Enthusiasm, 82
Environment, 163
Environmental nurture, 124
Equilibrium, 150
Essay tests, 256
Evaluation, 252, 253, 254, 257, 258, 260, 262
Existentialism, 33
Expanded self, 19, 22, 23, 24, 114
Experience, 123, 124, 125, 126, 127, 128, 129, 208
Extinction, 207

Faber, Daniel, 192
"Failure Complex," 45
Five-year Program, 82
Formal operation, 151, 153
Formal Schooling, 4
Formative evaluation, 257
Free discipline, 162
Freedom, 31, 35
Freud, Sigmund, 208
Frost, Robert, 31, 77
Furniture (classroom), 4

Gandhi, 77
Generalization, 207, 214
Generalizations, 128, 129
Gestalt, 208
Gestaltists, 148, 149, 163
Gestalt psychology, 136, 137, 138, 139, 140, 141, 142
Goal-setting, 191, 192
"Good," 33
Gordon, Edmund, 190
Grade inflation, 255
Grading, 46, 252, 255, 256, 259, 260
Graduate Record Exam, 82
Gross, Beatrice and Ronald, 240
Grouping, 235
Groupness, 22

Group performance rating, 275
Gussow, Joan D., 3

Hayakawa, S. I., 189
Head Start, 125
Heating, 4
Hereditary nature, 124
Hitler, Adolph, 94, 214
Holt, John, 256
Human Experience, 111, 112
Humanistic psychology, 208
Humanists, 137
Humility, 22
Hunt, Maurice P., 206
Hurok, Sol, 47
Hutchins, Robert, 243

Ideals, 108
Ideal teacher, 108, 109, 111
Illich, Ivan, 231
Incidental learning, 93
Innate ideas, 124
Integrated curriculum, 140
Integrity, 22
Intentional behavior, 151
Intentional instruction, 93

Jacobson, L. F., 45
Jencks, Christopher, 24, 125
Jesus, 77
Job Corps, 125
Joseph, Franz, 244

Kaiser, Henry, 260
Katona, George, 141

Laissez-faire classroom, 35
Language, 151, 152
Language development, 162, 164, 165, 166
Language experience, 62
Laswell, Harold, 3
Leacock, Eleanor B., 45, 47
Learner, 60, 61, 62, 63
Learning, 124, 126
Learning kits, 211
Learning style, 63
Letters, 173

Lighting, 4
Lindbergh, Ann Morrow, 114
Lippitt, R., 35
Locke, John, 124
Looking-glass self, 20, 21, 24, 45

Malpractice insurance, 79
Masks, 20
Maslow, Abraham, 23, 24, 35, 112, 208, 290
McLuhan, Marshall, 234
Mead, George, 20, 21, 24, 45, 140
Mental health, 79, 80, 81
Merton, Robert, 45
Michaelangelo, 78
Miss Dove, 78
Modalities of learning, 63, 64, 196
Moehlman, Arthur Henry, 137, 141
Montessori, Maria, 161, 162, 163, 164, 165, 166, 177, 178, 208
Montessori Method, 161, 174
Moses, Grandma, 289
Motivation, 188, 189, 190, 191, 192, 193, 194, 195, 196, 197
Motor development, 166
Motor education, 162, 163
Murdoch, Iris, 23

NEA Bicentennial Panel (1976), 294
Numbers, 173

Objective tests, 255, 256
O'Driscoll, Pat, 231
O.E.O., 125
Open classroom, 231, 235, 237, 238, 240, 242
Open evaluation, 269, 270
Open school, 231, 232, 238, 240, 241
Operant conditioning, 208
Orantes, Daisi, 19
Orwell, George, 207

Pass-fail system, 255
Pavlov, Ivan, 206, 207
Peer dependence, 22
Peer evaluation, 258, 264, 265, 271, 272, 273, 274
Permanent label, 46

Personal freedom, 5
Personality, 194, 195, 196
Personhood, 108, 242
Physical health, 79
Physical needs, 4
Physical self, 19
Piaget, Jean, 148, 149, 151, 153, 154, 163, 208, 237
Piatigorsky, Gregor, 292, 296
Pine, Gerald J., 111
Plato, 124, 244
Play, 239, 240
"Pod" design, 232, 233
Positivism, 33
Postman, Niel, 234
Pragmatism, 33
Praise, 196
Pre-operation, 151
Preparation, 81
Prepared environment, 177
Procrustes, 60
Programmed instruction, 208, 258
Prophetic counseling, 46
  curriculum, 48
  discipline, 47
  dollars, 47
Psychological self, 19
Puritan ethic, 78

Quantitative concepts, 152

Rating scale, 109, 111
Record card, 46
Recreational experience, 114
Reflected personality, 19, 20, 21, 24
  self, 22
Relativity, 33
Religious experience, 113
Respect, 6
Roe, 112
Rogers, Carl, 19, 114, 137, 208
Role, 93
  conflict, 94, 95
  modeling, 95
Role perception, 93
Roles, changing, 96
  traditional, 96

Rosenthal, R., 45
Rousseau, J. J., 166

Sandburg, Carl, 289
Schedule, 4
Schema, 149, 150, 153
Schulberg, Bud, 188
Schweitzer, Albert, 289
Self, 22, 34, 49
   actualization, 19, 23, 24, 292
   approval, 94
   awareness, 19, 21, 24
   concept, 19, 23, 24, 35, 46, 62, 82, 93,
      94, 95, 190
   control, 31, 33, 34, 35
   determination, 32
   directed, 33
   direction, 22, 32, 34, 35
   directedness, 31
   direction, 22, 32
   discipline, 31, 32, 33, 34, 35
   esteem, 19, 21, 22, 24
   evaluation, 94, 258
   fulfilling prophecy, 44, 45, 47, 112,
      154
   fulfillment, 35
   image, 19, 24, 35, 45
   worth, 32
Sensory apparatus, 170, 171
Sensory education, 162, 163, 164
Sensory motor intelligence, 151
Sensual experience, 124
Seriation, 152
Seven Cardinal Principles of Educa-
   tion, 294
Shakespeare, William, *Macbeth*, 252
Sheen, Fulton, 31
Sick leave, 80
Silberman, Charles, 4, 231, 234
Similarity and contrast, 124
Skinner, B. F., 208, 212
Social needs, 6
Socio-psychological, 19
Solitary confinement, 7
Solzhenitsyn, Aleksandr, 7
Sound, 176
   control, 4
Spatial development, 168

Spontaneous recovery, 207
S-R Psychology, 208
Statisticians, 154
Story, Frank, 289
Student's rating scale, 266, 267, 268
Summative evaluation, 257
Survival, 3
   training, 4
Synthesis, 137, 138

Tabula rasa, 124
Tagore, Rabindranath, 93
Teacher, 77, 78, 79, 80, 81, 82, 93, 94,
   95, 108, 109, 111, 112, 114, 256,
   257, 269, 271, 272, 273, 277
   (as Prophet), 45
   attitude, 49
   -learning process, 126, 127, 128,
     153, 214
   -pupil contact, 8
Teaching machines, 209
   team, 234
Teacher's role, 78
Tennyson, Alfred Lord, 295
Testing, 258, 259
Therapeutic experience, 111, 112, 113
Toffler, Alvin, 289
Token-Economy Programs, 214
Tracking, 48
TV Generation, 8

Ulysses, 295, 296
Unconditioned Response, 206
   stimulus, 206
Unit approach, 140
Utilitarianism, 33

Variety, 3
Ventiliation, 4
Vicarious experience, 128, 129
Vocational experience, 111, 112

Watson, John, 207, 208, 212
White, R. K., 35
Whitman, Walt, 60
Williams, Roger, 124
Wissler, Clark, 140
Wright, Frank Lloyd, 289
Wundt, Wilhelm, 137